INSIGHT GUIDES

The world's largest collection of visual travel guides

VIETNAM

Update Editors: Tim Larimer and Andrew Forbes
Executive Editor: Scott Rutherford

Editorial Director: Brian Bell

APA PUBLICATIONS

L

Part of the Langenscheidt Publishing Group

I t's taken over two decades, but the notion that Vietnam is a country, not a war, has taken root in the world's consciousness. And it's a fine thing, too, for Vietnam is of sufficient seductive power that it leaves all travelers awestruck, if not breathless. Equally pleasing is watching a nation awaken and redefine its future.

Over a decade ago, publisher and Apa founder **Hans Höfer** suggested the idea of a Vietnam guidebook to a Vietnamese friend. The first edition of *Insight Guide: Vietnam* came off the presses in 1991, which, at first, seems not so long ago.

But given the exponential rate of changes in Vietnam, both economically and socially, it was clear that, approaching the end of the 1990s, a thorough overhaul of the guide was essential. The Americans had lifted their trade embargo and opened an embassy. Vietnam became a full member of ASEAN. And less well known to the outside, but of significant importance for the average Vietnamese, was the banning of firecrackers.

But the Vietnamese are pragmatic and forward-looking. Their country has the potential to become another Asian success story. It has a ways to go, however. Vietnam is one of the world's poorest nations, with an infrastructure that is old and decaying. But its people are amongst the world's most literate (approaching 95 percent) and with considerable entrepreneurial zeal.

Vietnam's appeal is based not only upon the emotions that the name itself evokes, but also upon the many gaps in our knowledge of the country. Little is known about Vietnam's ancient and vigorous past, save for the past fifty years. So Apa Publications set out to produce a reference book, a landmark in the Insight Guide series.

West

T he original edition of *Insight Guide: Vietnam* was overseen by New Zealander **Helen West**. She had been studying Vietnamese history for years before she took on the post of project editor. West traveled extensively throughout Vietnam in search of its cultural heritage. She wrote several pieces for the book.

When it came time to revamp this guide, Apa's executive editor in Singapore, **Scott Rutherford**, began the search for fresh eyes to reinterpret the country. With a background as a newspaper and magazine writer and editor, plus several years as a photographer with *National Geographic,* Rutherford wanted someone with a solid journalism background to rediscover Vietnam and update the guide.

Rutherford

That someone was Hanoi-based **Tim Larimer**, who has lived in Vietnam for several years and is a frequent contributor to the *New York Times, Asian Wall Street Journal* and *The Economist.* As a result, Larimer has traveled nearly every backroad in Vietnam, and his narratives of the country and interpretations of the changes give *Insight*

Larimer

Guide: Vietnam an especially solid edge. (Too, he has an uncanny appreciation of deadlines.)

Assisting Larimer was *Asia Times* correspondent **Andy Soloman**, based in Hanoi since 1992. He contributed to sections on the northern provinces.

Dinh

Dac

From Vietnam's ancient capital of Hue comes one of the few scholars who has inherited the best of both Eastern and Western cultures. Author of several novels and many articles on his homeland, **Tran Van Dinh** – who now lives in the US – has a profound knowledge of the Vietnamese culture. His love of tradition provides an authentic Vietnamese flavor to this guide.

Prof. **Nguyen Tan Dac**, an ethnologist in Hanoi, is intimately acquainted with almost every corner of his native land. After the Vietnam War, he undertook extensive research on the hilltribe minorities of the northern and central regions. His first-hand expertise of the country's ethnographic roots has been a valuable contribution.

Writer **Diana Reid** traveled the length of the country on the Reunification Express, and her impressions of that journey constitute a special feature of this guide.

Not only have hairstyles and fashions changed in Vietnam, but, in fact, the visual contours and ambiance of the nation itself are radically different than even a few years ago. Of all Insight Guide destinations, Vietnam has changed the most visually.

Catherine Karnow has been a regular photographic contributor to Insight Guides, and to the famous *A Day in the Life* series of books, *Islands* and *National Geographic*. Based in San Francisco, Karnow returns home from her travels only long enough to change the paper in her fax machine. Her delightful photograph graces the new cover of this edition.

London-based **Jim Holmes** spent several months photographing Vietnam, traveling from one end to the other to capture the changes that have taken place. Numerous images from his effort fill this Insight Guide.

American **Joseph Lynch** is a relative newcomer to the region, having made Singapore his home base in 1991. Prior to his move, he made several photographic tours of the region. An intrepid traveler, Joe has traversed the length and breadth of the country in search of new and unique images.

Other frequent Apa contributors who put their considerable photographic talents to good use on *Insight Guide: Vietnam* included **Tim Page**, **Kim Naylor**, **Jean-Leo Dugast**, **Bill Wassman**, **Alain Evrard** and **Zdenek Thoma**.

Thanks are due to **Vietnam Tourism**, who provided several photographs and helped in making ground arrangements for Apa staff. Our appreciation also goes to **M. Rajaretnam**, Director of the Information and Resource Center in Singapore, who generously put its research material on Vietnam at our disposal.

— Apa Publications

CONTENTS

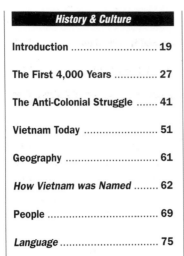

Preceding pages: violin student, Hanoi; market smile, Mekong Delta.

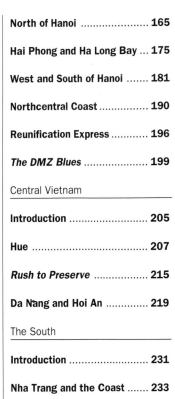

TRAVEL TIPS

INTRODUCTION

Five hundred years ago, in the early 1400s, the Chinese invaded Vietnam, one of many such invasions over the centuries. The Chinese were soundly defeated by the Vietnamese. Le Loi, emperor of Vietnam, might have had the Chinese prisoners killed. He chose otherwise. Le Loi apologized to the Chinese court for defeating its army, made peace with China, and provided the defeated Chinese troops with horses and ships for their return north.

Le Loi knew that, although momentarily defeated, China would never, never, disappear from Vietnam's future.

Indeed, the presence of its leviathan neighbor to the north has, perhaps more than anything else, sculpted the nature of the Vietnamese mind. Centuries of fending off China's invasions, while at the same time not making China *too* angry, has given Vietnamese a pragmatism, a patience, and a solid sense of national identity.

In fact, the Vietnamese have an uncanny and unusually deep feeling of national identity, and with it, of nation-building. Had the French and Americans seriously pondered Vietnamese history, the inevitable futility of their efforts would have been more self evident, and at an earlier stage.

Vietnamese like to recite a modern slogan: *Vietnam is a country, not a war.* But for much of the post-World War II years, until 1975, Vietnam was nearly synonymous with war, first with the French and later the Americans. Vestiges of the war remain in the bomb craters, old jeeps, and labyrinths of tunnels where entire villages endured the fighting. The craters have been converted to fish ponds, and the tunnels turned into tourist traps. Indeed, memories of the war are fading. Nearly sixty percent of Vietnamese today are less than 25 years old, born at or after the Vietnam War's end. They are the first generation in many not to know war in their homeland.

"All men are created equal. They are endowed by their creator with certain inalienable rights, among these are life, liberty and the pursuit of happiness." The meaning is familiar to every American as the foundation of the American constitution. But the words above are in the Declaration of the Democratic Republic of Vietnam, written in 1945 by Ho Chi Minh, a Communist revolutionary.

The Vietnamese government is unabashedly Communist. It is a Leninist regime that, nevertheless, sometimes transcends the Cold War stereotype of gray, oppressive, and anchored by a cult-of-personality leadership. While it has been oppressive, Vietnam's Communism is now also rather pragmatic, if not outright realistic.

"Vietnam's Communist Party... voiced a common yearning for equality and betterment", wrote a typically lucid *The Economist* in 1995. "Few communist parties so harnessed themselves to national ideals. Its cruelty might have been feared, but its daring and tenacity for a cause most Vietnamese supported – national independence – was admired."

Preceding pages: temple detail from Ha Tien; terraced rice paddies, northern Vietnam; sunrise on the Mekong River; flight attendant school. **Left**, on the Saigon River, Ho Chi Minh City.

When the Americans pulled out and the South was reunified ("liberated" has passed from pragmatic usage) with the North, the Hanoi government immediately turned the South into a Soviet-style economy. The result nearly left a carcass of a nation. By the mid 1980s, the country's economy was destitute. Inflation exceeded 800 percent. Large parts of the rural population were starving, or nearly so. Its neighbor to the north, China, had earlier trounced Hanoi by invading Vietnam's northern provinces. Moreover, Vietnam itself had been internationally ostracized by its own invasion of Cambodia. But unlike elsewhere in Asia, saving face is not an obsessive concern of the Vietnamese. Admitting that their socialization of the South was a fundamental error, the government shifted course towards a free-market economy with its *doi moi,* or new reform policy. The move was essential, and effective.

Vietnamese are highly educated and literate (over 90 percent), and they have an open desire to learn from others, and to admit mistakes. If they can define their future like they fought their wars, their future looks excellent as a nation.

But Vietnam remains one of the poorest countries in the world, with a per capita annual income of around US$250. Yet on the streets of Hanoi or Ho Chi Minh City, one does not sense a wretchedness or fatalism of poverty often encountered elsewhere in the Third World. Everywhere, there is the hum of activity, of a hard-working people anxious to build their country. There is a future to be made, and the Vietnamese intend to make it, corruption and the occasional reactionary knee-jerks of the government notwithstanding.

Photographs in the first edition of this book, published at the beginning of the 1990s, show bicycle traffic jams on urban streets. Nowadays, the occasional bicycle is lost amidst swarms of motorscooters. And the Vietnamese drive like they work: Looking only ahead, ignoring traffic to the sides, and stopping for nothing.

After fighting off foreign armies and colonial powers for centuries, Vietnam now must cope – by its own invitation, of course – with foreign capital, technology and ideas. For decades, Vietnamese were stuck in the economic doldrums, their intrinsic talents for commerce and entrepreneurship weighed down by a socialist system. Today, a leadership quick to acknowledge its past errors has turned to the outside, looking for advice, and money to build a modern society. But how much outside influence will it stand?

For even as the country repeats its mantra – *a country, not a war* – its long history of conflict has left the people with a natural tendency to be wary of foreigners, and to value self-reliance and to do things their own way. Years of battle have left Vietnamese with an innate pride, a national awareness that this impoverished land was able to defeat great powers and superior technology. And, too, throughout Vietnam's history is a thread of victimization – that it was foreigners who caused all of Vietnam's problems.

Yet, somehow, with the pragmatism of Emperor Le Loi half a millennium ago, the Vietnamese will define their future, and perhaps with resounding finesse.

Right: a mandarin in imperial finery.

The history of the land we now call Vietnam reads like a series of variations on the same theme: Invasion followed by occupation followed by rebellion followed by independence followed by internal squabbling followed by another invasion. Then the whole cycle begins again.

From the earliest records of civilization, what is now Vietnam faced repeated incursions from China to the north, even as late as 1979, when Chinese forces crossed the border in retaliation for Vietnam's earlier invasion into Cambodia.

This pattern has inculcated Vietnamese people with a suspicion of foreigners and with something of a victim complex. Even today, when discussing poverty in the Vietnamese countryside, many people are quick to lay blame at the feet of America and its military, or even the French colonialists, or even the centuries of fighting off the Chinese. Young men, steeped in this history that emphasizes the magnet Vietnam has been to outside forces, worry that one day they, too, will have to go off to war.

And the outside force most Vietnamese fear most today is the kingdom that threatened its existence repeatedly throughout history, China.

The Vietnamese were not without their own territorial ambitions, however. History books tend to ignore the country's own invasions of neighboring lands. But the country has had designs on what is now Cambodia and Laos, and there were early conflicts between the northern and southern parts of Vietnam. Long before Ho Chi Minh wanted to unify the country under the banner of Communism, the Viet people of what is now northern Vietnam had designs on, and eventually conquered, the Champa kingdom in the southern part of Vietnam.

Vietnam's ancient history reads like a book of legend, but with many of the pages torn or missing, due to a lack of early historical records. Like any ancient nation, Vietnam's

Preceding pages: Emperor's escorts, Hue; young Emperor Duy Tan and entourage. **Left,** dragon motif on Hue mausoleum. **Above,** traditional theme of simple pleasures.

earliest history has been generously embellished with legend and fairy tales. However, by combining Chinese and Vietnamese historical records, and Vietnamese folklore and recent archaeological discoveries, some of the missing pages have come to light. The first threads of Vietnam's history are inextricably intertwined with the history of the country that looms largest in the psyche of the Vietnamese people: China.

Source of the legend: The Han and the Viet cosmogony viewed the world through the

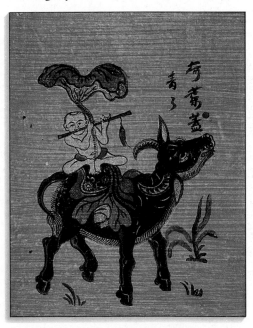

concept of the Five Elements: metal, wood, water, fire and earth, or sometimes Nghu Han, which represents Five Regions: the Center, South, North, East and West. The Center was represented by the earth and the color yellow, the South by fire and the color red, the North by water and the color black, the East by wood and the color green, the West by metal and the color white.

From ancient time, a kingdom controlled the heart of the Asian continent, its rulers basing their power on these concepts of the Five Elements and Five Regions. Known as the Middle Kingdom, or Chung Hoa, its power center was located in the Five Mounts

(Ngu Linh) Territory. It was peopled by many races, the two major ones being the Han and the Viet. While the Han were homogeneous, the Viets incorporated hundreds of tribes. The Viets settled south of the Yellow River and developed an agricultural culture, whereas the Han, in the northwest, became expert in hunting and battle skills.

The Viet chief ruled the Five Mounts Territory, and there were three consecutive rulers: Toai Nhan, who discovered fire; Phuc Hi, who discovered the I Ching and domesticated wild animals; and Shen Nong, who cultivated wild plants for domestic use and taught his people to grow rice. The Viets regarded themselves as descendants of these

named their territory Xich Qui, the territory of the Red Devils. This marked the first Viet exodus from the Middle Kingdom.

According to Vietnamese historical folklore, De Minh, a third-generation descendent of Shen Nong, fled to the southern territory of the Five Mounts and married Princess Vu Tien. Their son, Loc Tuc, became king of the South and called himself Kinh Duong Vuong, King of the Kinh and Duong Territory. He married one of the daughters of Dong Dinh Quang, a king from the lake of Dong Dinh territory.

Their son, Sung Lam, succeeded his father to become Lac Long Quan, Dragon Lord of the Mighty Seas. The Quasi-Legendary Ep-

first three chiefs of what is known as China's Three Yellows era, or Tam Hoang. The last, Shen Nong, is the direct link to the Viet.

By the end of Shen Nong's era, the Han had invaded the Five Mounts territory and occupied the highest mount, Thai Son. Their chief proclaimed himself Hwangdi, the Yellow Emperor of the Center, in accordance with the Five Elements concept.

This invasion ended the heritage of the Three Yellows era. Hwangdi referred to the Viets settled in the South as the southern barbarians, Nam Man. The Viets fled further south, where their chief proclaimed himself Viem De, the Red Emperor of the South, and

och and Hoa Binh Civilization Vietnam's National Annals tell of the marriage between King Lac Long Quan and the beautiful Princess Au Co, the daughter of King De Lai and descendant of the Immortals of the High Mountains. Their union gave birth to one hundred sons and the Kingdom of Bach Viet, whose one hundred principalities extended from the lower Yang Tse Kiang, to the north of Indochina. The kingdom prospered. But the Lord of the Dragon and the Princess of the Mountains, convinced that the difference in their origins would always deny them earthly happiness, decided to separate. Half of the children returned with their mother to the mountains, the others followed their father to the eastern sea.

The symbolism of Lac Long Quan's descendance from the Dragon Lord and Au Co from the Immortals holds significance for the Vietnamese, as the Dragon symbolizes the *yang* and Immortal the *yin*. Thus, the Vietnamese believe they are the descendants of Tien Rong, the Immortal and the Dragon, and these symbols constitute the Vietnamese people's earliest totems.

Civilized norms governed early relations between the Han court and the Viet kingdom. The Chinese historian Kim Ly Tuong recorded that, in the fifth year of Dao Duong, the emperor of the Yao Dynasty (2361 BC), the Viet Thuong kingdom sent a diplomatic delegation to the Han court and offered a "sacred turtle" (*linh qui*) as a friendship present. The turtle was thought to be a thousand years old, and its shell was covered with precious inscriptions in hieroglyphics. It was learnt later that Emperor Yao transcribed all these inscriptions, which he then called the "Calendar of the Sacred Turtle".

Expanding kingdom: The southern Viet kingdom of Xich Qui was divided into one hundred principalities, each governed by one of the 100 sons. In 2,879 BC, the eldest son was crowned as king of Lac Viet. He named himself King Hung Vuong, and Lac Viet was renamed Van Lang. His kingdom of Van Lang was the most powerful around, and it encompassed most of present-day northern and central Vietnam.

The kingdom of Van Lang prospered during the first millennium BC under the rule of eighteen successive Hung kings, who formed the dynasty of Hung Vuong. Founded in present-day Vinh Phu Province, the capital was divided into fifteen provinces. At this time, a certain King Thuc Phan governed the neighboring kingdom of Au Viet, another Viet tribe, to the north of Van Lang. His desire to bring about a marriage between his daughter and Hung Vuong's son was not shared by Hung Vuong, who scornfully rejected the proposal. The hereditary hatred this rebuff bred between the two Viet dynasties led to conflict and eventually, in 258 BC, during the rule of the rather weak 18th king, the destruction of Van Lang.

Left, an example of a Dong Son bronze drum.
Above, Chinese motif, 17th-century building.

Under the title of King An Duong Vuong, Thuc Phan established the new kingdom of Au Lac and installed his capital at Phuc An, where a spiral citadel was built. The remains of the citadel can still be seen to this day in the village of Co Loa, to the west of Hanoi in northern Vietnam.

Fifty years later, the kingdom fell into the hands of the northern hordes of an ambitious general, Trieu Da, from the south of the Middle Kingdom.

After vanquishing the other Chinese generals, Trieu Da founded the independent kingdom of Nam Viet, which included much of present-day southern China. He proclaimed himself king in 208 BC and founded the

Trieu Dynasty, which lasted until the 3rd century BC. His capital was located near present-day Guangzhou.

China's influence: Under the Trieu Dynasty, Nam Viet progressively entered the Chinese sphere of influence. In exchange for periodic tributes to the court of the Han emperor, Nam Viet received protection against foreign invasion. This period was marked by continual intrigues, including a Chinese emperor's plot to seize Nam Viet, a scheme that was exposed and denounced. Less than a century later, the Han emperor Wudi sent his mighty armies to conquer Nam Viet. Despite the defending army's fierce resistance – a quality that continued through the 20th century – Nam Viet yielded to the Han invaders.

It is generally believed that the decline of the Hung Vuong Dynasty created, over time, the fusion of legend with history upon which much of Vietnam's ancient history is based.

The first Chinese occupation lasted half a century, until AD 42. After Trieu Dau's defeat, the country became a Chinese protectorate under the new name of Giao Chi. Highly-qualified administrators were appointed as governors to rule the country, but their efforts to introduce Chinese literature, arts and agricultural techniques met with fierce resistance from the Viet people. Greatly frustrated by decades of Chinese influence and culture, the Vietnamese not only guarded their national identity, but fought fiercely to preserve it.

Sisters in revolt: Finally, in 39 AD, the oppressive rule and injustices of a cruel governor, To Dinh, provoked a victorious armed revolt against the Chinese authorities, led by two sisters, Trung Trac and Trung Nhi, heroines known as Hai Ba Trung. Their reign, however, was short-lived. Three years later, the superior strategies and arms of the Chinese armies overran them, and the country was again subjected to China's control.

The fall of the Trung sisters marked the second period of Chinese occupation. During this time, Nam Viet was administered as a Chinese province, and a campaign was launched against the Kingdom of Champa, in the south.

This period of Chinese occupation ended abruptly when a scholar named Ly Bon led an armed revolt and succeeded in chasing out the Chinese authorities. Ly Bon took control of the territory, naming the territory Van Xuan and founding the Ly Dynasty, which lasted until the Chinese once again regained supremacy in 545.

The particularly troubled era that followed was marked by frequent outbreaks of violent battles between the Chinese and the Vietnamese. It ended with the third period of Chinese occupation, which lasted from 603 until 938. During this time, the Chinese made concerted efforts to establish their culture and civilization in Nam Viet, which they renamed An Nam. However, numerous insurrections broke out despite the solid administrative structure imposed by the Chinese government of the Tang Dynasty.

Ngo Dynasty (939–967): Disorder accompanied the decline of the Chinese Tang Dynasty, giving the Vietnamese the chance for which they had long waited. In a protracted war that ended with the celebrated battle of Bach Dang, General Ngo Quyen vanquished the Chinese invaders and founded the first Vietnamese dynasty in 939. He named the country Dai Viet. Ngo Quyen then decided to transfer the capital to Co Loa, which had been the capital of the Au Lac kingdom, thus affirming continuity of the traditions of the Lac Viet people.

Ngo Quyen spent the six years of his reign fighting the continual revolts of the feudal lords. At his death in 967, the kingdom fell

THE COURT of the CHOVA or GENERAL of TONQUEEN.

into chaos and became known as *Thap Nhi Su Quan,* the land of twelve feudal principalities constantly at war. For more than twenty years, the country remained fragmented, and the external threat from China's Song Dynasty loomed large to the north on the border.

Dinh Dynasty (968–980): The most powerful of the twelve feudal lords, Dinh Bo Linh, rapidly elbowed out the others. He reunified the fragmented country under the name of Dai Co Viet and took the imperial title of Dinh Tien Hoang De (The First August Emperor Dinh). Well aware of the Chinese Song Dynasty's military might, Dinh Bo

Linh negotiated a non-aggression treaty in exchange for tributes payable to the Chinese every three years. This set the foundation of future relations with China that were to last for centuries.

On the domestic front, Dinh Tien Hoang established a royal court and a hierarchy of civil and military servants. He instated a rigorous justice system and introduced the death penalty to serve as a deterrent to all who threatened the new order in the kingdom. He organized a regular army divided into ten *dao*, or military corps. Security and order were progressively re-established, inaugurating a new era of *thai binh* (peace).

However, Tien Hoang's reign was not to

Le Dai Hanh. He retained the capital in Hoa Lu and succeeded in warding off several Chinese invasions by the Song court, but continued paying them tributes every three years in exchange for friendly relations.

With peace assured on the northern border, he decided to pacify the south. In 982, Le Dai Hanh launched a military expedition against the Champa kingdom, entered Indrapura (present-day Quang Nam) and burned the Champa citadel. The conquest of this northern part of the Champa kingdom brought about a marked Cham influence on Vietnamese culture, particularly in the fields of music and dance.

Le Dai Hanh's reign marked the first at-

last long. He was assassinated in 979 by a palace guard, who, according to the Annals, saw "a star falling into his mouth" – a celestial omen heralding promotion. The heir to the throne was only six years old and would not survive the mounting and pernicious intrigues of the court.

Tien Le Dynasty (980–1009): With the Queen Mother's blessing, Le Hoan dethroned Dinh Bo Linh's heir and proclaimed himself King

<u>Left</u>, the royal court at Tonkin (or "Tonqueen"). <u>Above</u>, woodblock-print depiction of the big cat (China) receiving tributes from servile mice (Vietnamese royal court).

tempt to consolidate the Viet nation. He devoted a great deal of energy to developing the road network in order to better administer the country's different regions. However, the local forces were still reluctant to yield to the central authority, and so mounted a succession of revolts. In 1005, after 24 years of difficult rule, Le Dai Hanh died.

In the ensuing period, the famous monk Khuong Viet managed to establish Buddhism as way of thought and as a long-overdue stabilizing pillar of the kingdom. Nevertheless, the Tien Le Dynasty eventually collapsed after the death of one of Le Dai Hanh's heirs, in 1009.

Ly Dynasty (1009–1225): The Ly, who reigned over the country for more than two centuries, were the first of the enduring national dynasties. Ly Cong Uan was a disciple of a famous monk, Van Hanh, who helped him rise to power in the Hoa Lu court. Assuming the name Ly Thai To, the new sovereign inaugurated his dynasty with a change of capital. The Annals mentioned that King Ly Thai To saw the apparition of an ascending dragon on the site of the future capital, and so decided to name it Thang Long (Ascending Dragon). In 1054, one of his successors, King Ly Thanh Ton, rechristened the country Dai Viet.

During the Ly Dynasty, Buddhism flourished as the national religion. Buddhist masters, who acted as *quoc su,* or supreme advisors, assisted the Ly kings in their rule. Several Ly kings – Thai Tong, Anh Tong and Cao Tong – led the Buddhist sects of Thao Duong and founded some 150 monasteries in the region of Thang Long, near what is present-day Hanoi.

Under the impulse of Confucian administrators, the Ly Dynasty consolidated the monarchy by setting up a centralized government and establishing a tax system, a judiciary system and a professional army. Important public works, including the building of dikes and canals, were undertaken in order to develop agriculture and settle the population.

The monarchist centralization endowed the king with three roles: absolute monarch and religious chief of the empire; mediator between the people and Heaven; and father of the nation. Meanwhile, the mandarin court became an institution composed of six departments: staff, finances, rites, justice, armed forces and public works.

In 1070, a national college was founded to educate future mandarins. The college, known as Van Mieu, has been restored and still stands in Hanoi. Knowledge of the Confucian classics, as well as the mastery of literary composition and poetry, were the main requirements of the rigorous three year course, which culminated in a very competitive diploma examination.

Tran Dynasty (1225–1400): An ambitious commoner, Tran Canh, married the Ly dynasty's last queen, Chieu Hoang. He shrewdly plotted and maneuvered his way to power and finally founded the Tran Dynasty. During this period, Buddhism, which had become predominant under the Ly Dynasty, continued to play an important role, but was subsequently weakened by its co-existence with Confucianism, Taoism and various other popular beliefs and customs. The century-old competitive examination system introduced during the first period of Chinese occupation underwent draconian revisions. An administration incorporating both the reigning king and the heir to the title of the previous reign was officially adopted to ensure its continuity, and to prevent any dispute between the two families.

The Tran Dynasty is renowned for its brilliant military victories, especially that on the Bach Dang River by the king's brother, Tran Hung Dao, against Kublai Khan's much larger Mongol armies.

During the reign, the country's territorial ambitions to the south continued. The king's sister, Princess Huyen Tran, married the King of Champa in 1307. The marriage extended the national territory southward with the peaceful annexation of the Hue region, and at the same time inaugurated the politics of diplomatic marriage.

Ho Dynasty (1400–1428): The king's marriage to the aunt of a minister, Le Qui Ly, was to prove a fatal move for the Tran Dynasty. Taking full advantage of his aunt's union, Le Qui Ly shrewdly maneuvered his way to power. He eventually assumed control of the kingdom and founded a dynasty under his ancestral name of Ho.

During his reign, the army was reorganized and reinforced. Taxes were revised and ports opened to trading ships, which were obliged to pay duties. Under a new fiscal system, coins were taken out of circulation and replaced with bank notes. Restrictions were imposed on land ownership. In the administrative domain, Ho introduced the extension of royal appointments to his loyal servants. The competitive examination system for administrators was modified to demand more practical knowledge of peasant life, mathematics, history, the Confucian classics and literature. Legal reforms were undertaken and a medical service established.

His reign prompted yet another attack from China. Well aware that Ho had usurped the throne, the Chinese Ming emperor sent 5,000 soldiers under the pretext of helping the movement faithful to the Tran Dynasty.

The Ming intervention led to the fall of the

Ho Dynasty in 1407. During the short period of Chinese occupation that followed, the Vietnamese suffered inhumane exploitation. The Chinese resolutely strove to destroy the Vietnamese national identity. Vietnamese literature, artistic and historical works were either burned or taken to China and replaced by the Chinese classics in all the schools. The Chinese dress and hair style were imposed on the Vietnamese women; local religious rites and costumes were replaced or banished; private fortunes were confiscated and taken to China.

Le Dynasty (1428–1776): The oppressed people found a new leader in the person of Le Loi, a man renowned for his courage and

Le Loi founded the Le Dynasty in 1428 and became king under the name of Le Thai To. He renamed the country Dai Viet and immediately began the task of its reconstruction after the devastation caused by the war. He reduced his army from 250,000 to 10,000 men and adopted a rotation system that enabled soldiers to return to the countryside to work and help boost food production.

The legal system was reorganized and the penal system revised. A new College of National Sons (Quoc Tu Giam) was founded to educate future administrators, with admission based entirely on merit and not on the prior prerequisite of social or family status.

Le Thai To died in 1443, leaving the throne

generosity. Under the title Prince of Pacification, he organized a resistance movement from his village and waged a guerrilla war against the enemy. By employing a strategy of surprise attacks targeting his adversary's weakest points, Le Loi managed to further weaken the enemy and at the same time avoid combat with the superior Chinese forces. His enforcement of strict military discipline ensured that no pillaging was carried out by his troops in the regions under his control, making him a very popular hero.

Above, print of traditional village, Hue, in the central part of Vietnam.

to his son, Le Thai Tong, whose sudden death not long after was followed by a decade of confusion and plots within the royal court. This troubled period ceased when Le Thanh Tong affirmed his power.

Under his thirty-six-year reign, the country prospered as never before. He revised the fiscal system, encouraged agriculture and placed great emphasis on customs and moral principles. A writer himself, he founded the Tao Dan Academy and wrote the first volume of national history.

Le Thanh Tong was by no means only a recorder of history, nor was the dynasty solely one of pacification. His reorganized army won an easy victory over the Champa army in 1471. His farmer-soldiers excelled not only on the battlefields, but also in the fields, where they established militarized agricultural communities wherever they went. In this way the national territory was gradually expanded southward, until finally the Champa Kingdom was completely absorbed and assimilated.

Secession wars: The increasing decadence of the Le Dynasty in the late 16th century led to the country's division into two rival principalities, as corrupt and useless kings succeeded Le Thanh Tong. Mac Dang Dung, a shrewd and scheming adviser at the court, seized control of the country, and founded

fying the north and re-establishing the Le authority in Hanoi, Lord Trinh returned to find Nguyen Hoang well entrenched in the southern court as lord and master of all, and liking where he was.

In 1672, after repeated tentative attempts failed to remove Nguyen Hoang, Lord Trinh finally consented to the partition of the country at the Linh River, which marked the 18th parallel. It was not, however, until after half a century of civil war that the Trinh and Nguyen lords eventually agreed to a period of co-existence. This respite lasted for more than a century, during which time the Le emperors played no more than a passive and ceremonial role.

the Mac Dynasty. During this time, descendants of the Le Dynasty rallied around Nguyen Kim and Trinh Kiem, looking for a way to overthrow Mac Dang Dung. After a series of fierce battles, they succeeded in occupying the country's southern capital, and in 1543, founded the southern court near Thanh Hoa. The war continued indecisively until the death of the Mac Dynasty's last king, Mac Mau Hop, in 1592.

In an effort to restore law and order to the territory controlled by the Macs, Lord Trinh left the southern court under the temporary control of Nguyen Kim's nephew, Nguyen Hoang, and set out for the north. After paci-

Tay Son Uprising (1776–1792): Frequent insurrections, provoked by the corruption rife within the disintegrating administration, broke out during the last years of the two royal courts. The seeds of a popular revolution were sowed as peasant insurrections grew into a force with which to be reckoned.

The Tay Son brothers – Nguyen Nhac, Nguyen Lu and Nguyen Hue – seized the day and staged an uprising against the leading Le lords, easily defeating them. However, Le Chieu Thong managed to flee to China, where he called for Chinese protection. In 1788, the Qing court decided to send an expeditionary corps to conquer the divided country.

To save the nation, Nguyen Hue proclaimed himself Emperor Quang Trung in Phu Xuan and overran the Chinese troops in a whirlwind campaign. He pacified the northern part of the country, from the Chinese border to the Hai Van Pass in the center, and devoted his energies to national rehabilitation, administrative reorganization and economic development.

Significantly, Quang Trung replaced the classic Chinese Han with the popular *nom* as the official written language. Unfortunately, his promising reign was cut short by his premature death not long after, in 1792.

Nguyen Dynasty (1792–1883): Nguyen's successor, Nguyen Anh, was supported by

suspected the Ming were Nguyen Anh's sympathizers, and this suspicion intensified after the leading Tay Son generals, Tap Dinh and Ly Tai, fled to Nguyen Anh's camp. After suffering defeat at the hands of their former generals in the Saigon region, the Tay Son army exacted their revenge and massacred thousands of the Chinese settlers.

The Bishop of Adran saw an opportunity to expand the church's influence and negotiated a promise of military aid for Nguyen Anh from the French government, in exchange for territorial and commercial rights. However, the French were busy with their own internal disputes and the promised aid never materialized. Undaunted, the bishop

Nguyen royalists, who saw him as the legitimate heir in the south. With their backing, Nguyen Anh took up the fight against the Tay Son brothers and after Quang Trung's death, extended control over the country with the aid of a French missionary, Monsignor Pigneau de Behaine, Bishop of Adran.

The Ming Chinese, who had fled the Ching invasion and settled in the Saigon region, regarded Nguyen Anh as the leader who could safeguard their settlement in the newly-annexed territory of Dai Viet. The Tay Son

Left, the earliest European residences in Saigon. **Above**, French officers in Da Nang, 1831.

organized funds and recruited troops himself. The training in modern military techniques proved invaluable to Nguyen Anh and his army, and it probably facilitated victory in 1801, when he subdued the Tay Son and proclaimed himself emperor.

A power struggle between French and Chinese factions began within the court. Although Nguyen Anh owed his accession to power to the French, he was nevertheless very suspicious of France's designs on his country, and under his reign, the court's Chinese faction took precedence. He came to rely more on the assistance of Confucian mandarins than the Catholic missionaries in the consolidation of his empire, not the last time national pride would win.

The reunified and newly renamed Viet Nam extended from the Chinese frontier to the Camau Peninsula in the south. Serious efforts were made to codify the law and develop the national administration along Confucian principles. Hue became the country's new administrative capital.

Gia Long replaced the Hong Duc Code by a new legislation, which bore his name and served to consolidate the monarchic power after thirty years of civil war.

The Nguyen Dynasty's monarchist absolutism was reflected in the extraordinary development of Hue as the most beautiful

city of Vietnam. Elaborate palaces, mausoleums, temples and pagodas were successively built here, all in keeping with the harmony of cosmic order.

The Nguyen kings also extended Vietnam's border into Laos and Cambodia, incorporating these two kingdoms as new vassal states of their empire. Conversely, they closed the country to Western penetration from the seas.

Fearing that the opening of the kingdom and the expansion of trade links would undermine the structure of the monarchy, they practiced a kind of isolationism with regards to the West.

Meanwhile, Prince Canh, Nguyen Anh's eldest son, had accompanied the Bishop of Adran to France during his negotiations with the French government. The prince was later educated at a missionary school in Malacca and converted to Catholicism. This made Canh the first Viet prince to be educated under Western ideas and teachers.

Military leaders within Nguyen Anh's army realized the superiority of modern Western military technology and so wished to utilize Prince Canh's knowledge to rebuild the country after the war. The prince was regarded by many as the one who could modernize Dai Viet and bring it into industrialization.

When the issue of Gia Long's successor was being discussed in court before his death, the power struggle between the French and Chinese factions resumed. The military generals, including Nguyen Thanh, the governor of Thang Long, and Le Van Duyet, the governor of Gia Dinh (Saigon), supported the French, wanting Prince Canh as the heir. However, most of the court ministers belonged to the Chinese faction and supported Canh's younger brother, Prince Mien Tong.

Again, it was the conservative Chinese faction that triumphed. Prince Canh reportedly died of measles at the age of 21. This prognosis was refuted by missionaries close to the court, who reported to the French mission that he had died of poisoning.

Once Prince Mien Tong was crowned Emperor Minh Mang, the French–Chinese divide officially ended. Most of Prince Canh's followers were either demoted or executed. General Nguyen Thanh was forcefully administered poison, and General Le Van Duyet's tomb was desecrated.

In the meantime, the Catholic missions had accelerated their proselytizing. This provoked Minh Mang's anti-Catholic policy, which ordered the persecution of Catholic missionaries from abroad, and also their Vietnamese converts.

An opportunity for peace, and with it, a chance to modernize and industrialize the country, was lost. It would not be the last time, either. For religious rivalries, political factions and foreign intervention, all recurring elements of Vietnam's history to date, would embroil it in tragic war once again.

Above, the young Prince Canh. **Right**, a map of Tonkin, from 1653.

37

Un nouveau fait d'armes vient d'être accompli au Tonkin par
héroïques soldats. — La place de Lang-Son est tombée entre leurs mai
et le 13 février à midi, le drapeau français flottait au-dessus de
citadelle.

Après la prise du camp retranché de Dong-Song, l'armée fit tr
jours de marche à travers des gorges presque impénétrables : le 11
brigade de Négrier attaquait et emportait le village de Vanoï; le
après de sérieux et sanglants combats livrés au milieu d'un épais bro
lard, la brigade Giovanelli prenait plusieurs forts d'assaut, repous
les Chinois de crêtes en crêtes et bivouaquait le soir à la sortie des gor
après avoir fait éprouver des pertes considérables à l'ennemi. — Le 13,

...rche rapide conduisait toute l'armée devant Lang-Son, et après une
...goureuse canonnade, les hordes chinoises étaient mises en déroute,
...ssant entre les mains de nos vaillants soldats des approvisionnements
...nsidérables et une grande quantité de munitions de guerre.

...Les troupes françaises ont été sublimes d'entrain et de vaillance, et ont
...pporté avec le plus grand courage la fatigue, le froid et l'humidité
...i régnaient pendant ces jours de lutte, du 9 au 13 février.

...Nos pertes sont de 99 tués et de 222 blessés; mais c'est par milliers
...e l'on a pu constater celles de l'ennemi, qui, au nombre de 20,000
...mmes, et malgré une vigoureuse résistance, a dû céder devant la valeur
...s soldats français.

Emperor Minh Mang's anti-Catholic policy gave the French a pretext to intervene in Vietnam. The cycle of invasion-and-occupation began anew.

The landing of a French party in the port of Tourane (present-day Da Nang) in August of 1858 heralded the beginning of colonial occupation that would last almost a century. The French government wanted to establish a strategic and religious sphere of influence in Indochina, but their demands to install a French consulate and commercial attache in Da Nang were rejected by the Imperial Court in Hue. The French responded to the slap by occupying Da Nang.

The later emperors, Thieu Tri and Tu Duc, became more and more entrenched in their Confucian doctrine, and court mandarins, increasingly blinded to the outside world, implemented a policy of isolation that forbade any contact with foreigners.

Seeing the danger of such a policy, the progressive mandarins in Emperor Tu Duc's court launched a movement to modernize the country. However, their proposals were rejected by the dogmatic mandarins. Consequently, the court of Hue was unequipped to defend the country against a modern and powerful enemy.

In 1861, the French took Saigon. Six years later the entire southern part of the country, rechristened Cochin China, was annexed as a French colony. The French extended control to the north in 1883. The center of Vietnam, renamed Annam, and the north, or Tonkin, became French protectorates.

Vietnamese were no happier living under French domination than they had been under the Chinese. In 1893, Emperor Ham Nghi and Phan Dinh Phung organized a royalist movement, Can Vuong, and staged an unsuccessful uprising at Ha Tinh. The Can Vuong movement survived until one of its leaders was killed by a Vietnamese traitor. Emperor Duy Tan's abortive attempt in 1916 to form a revolutionary movement saw to his

rapid replacement as sovereign of Vietnam by Khai Dinh.

By the beginning of the 20th century, various nationalist resistance movements had formed. One was composed almost entirely of aristocrats, intellectuals and young people, led by more radical Confucian scholars such as Phan Boi Chau, Phan Chau Trinh and Prince Cuong De, Prince Canh's great-grandson. In an effort to break from royalist thinking, they embraced the idea of democracy.

This resistance movement was greatly in-

fluenced by the Japanese victory over Russia in 1904, for it convinced the Vietnamese that Western power was no longer invincible. Phan Boi Chau and Cuong De established the Eastward Movement in 1907 and secretly sent students to study in Japan. French authorities, discovering the scheme, negotiated with Japan to extradite all Vietnamese students, but Japanese officials helped some of them escape to China.

When the exiled Vietnamese in China witnessed the 1911 Kuomingtang Revolution led by Sun Yat Sen, some were convinced Vietnam was ready for the same kind of coup. They formed the Vietnam Quoc Dan

Preceding pages: French troops overrun local positions at Lang Son. **Left,** colonial French troops entering Hung Hoa in 1884. **Above,** the young Duy Tan, emperor of Annam.

Dang Party, which later became the leading revolutionary party in the struggle against the French.

The revolutionaries were not yet united, however. A rift widened between the Westernized reformer Phan Chu Trinh and the nationalist Phan Boi Chau. Phan Chu Trinh opposed appealing for foreign help to unseat the French colonialists. He believed Vietnam could regain independence through the democratic process, and, in 1915, he went to Paris to rally Vietnamese exiles there and radical French politicians to support the Vietnamese struggle against colonial rule.

Nationalist sentiments intensified in Vietnam, especially after World War I, but tenta-

French intellectuals, who formed the French Communist Party in 1921. He went to Moscow to be trained as a *kominternshik,* an agent of the Communist International. He enjoyed the special privileges afforded him by his Soviet mentors and wholeheartedly espoused Stalin statesmanship.

In 1924, Nguyen Ai Quoc was sent to China as a delegate in Borodine's advisory team to the Communist Party of China. There, he contacted many young Vietnamese revolutionaries, and founded the Association of Vietnamese Youth, which competed with other organizations for the liberation of the country. For training purposes, some recruits were sent to Moscow and others be-

tive uprisings failed to obtain any concessions from the French. The Russian Revolution, while not provoking anything similar in Vietnam at the time, nonetheless had a tremendous impact on shaping Vietnamese history, primarily because of its influence on a young revolutionary, later to be known as Ho Chi Minh and the central figure of 20th-century Vietnam.

Nguyen That Thanh, under the alias Nguyen Ai Quoc, was working with Phan Chu Trinh on an anti-colonial petition put forward at the Versailles Conference, in 1919. Later taking the name of Ho Chi Minh, Nguyen Ai Quoc became involved with

came affiliated with the Chinese communist party. This situation fostered internal conflict within Vietnam's Communist party, between the pro-Chinese and pro-Soviet factions, for many decades.

In the same year, Emperor Khai Dinh died, and his son Bao Dai, then aged 12, ascended to the throne. Bao Dai was sent to France for his education and returned to Vietnam in 1932. The Vietnamese waited to see if the French would adopt more liberal politics, but it became clear they would make no real concessions.

In 1930, on the Komintern's instruction, Nguyen Ai Quoc successfully rallied several communist groups and founded the Indochinese Communist Party. For the first time in history, a revolutionary party was systematically formed with the unlimited financial and ideological support of an aspiring superpower.

Also in 1930, under the leadership of Nguyen Thai Hoc, the Quoc Dan Dang, inspired by the Chinese Kuomintang, launched a military revolt. Later, communist groups following the same path of armed revolt, known as the Nghe Tinh Soviets movement, staged a series of peasant uprisings. Unhappy with the instability, the French retaliated by taking severe measures against the fledgling movements.

continue administering Vietnam. In March 1945, realizing that allied victory was inevitable, Japan overthrew the French, imprisoned their civil servants and rendered Vietnam "independent" under Japanese "protection," with Bao Dai as chief of state.

The Japanese surrender some months later was the opening Nguyen Ai Quoc had hungrily anticipated. Earlier, the Central Committee of the Indochinese Communist Party had met in southern China and announced the formation of the Revolutionary League for the Independence of Vietnam, which later became known as the Viet Minh. Nguyen Ai Quoc used the Viet Minh as an instrument to apply his revolutionary strategy. In its

The apparent calm that reigned after the reprisals shattered with the first battles of World War II. In Asia, most coastal cities of China fell under the advancing Japanese forces, and in Vietnam, the Japanese rapidly occupied key regions in 1940.

World War II: For Vietnam, the explosion of World War II in September of 1939 was an event as significant as the French occupation of Da Nang in 1858. The pro-Nazi Vichy government of France accepted the Japanese occupation of Indochina, but was allowed to

creation he finally achieved "the union of diverse Vietnamese nationalist groups under communist direction," a goal that he had been working towards since announcing it as his immediate task to the Komintern in 1924.

At first, the Chinese Nationalist authorities supported the Viet Minh, but they later got wise to Nguyen Ai Quoc's new political affiliation. They imprisoned him and created a rival organization. However, they soon realized that Nguyen Ai Quoc's organization was needed, and so released him in 1943. They recognized Nguyen Ai Quoc as the chief of the Viet Minh, and he then adopted the name of Ho Chi Minh.

<u>Left</u>, Tonkin mandarin and his escorts. <u>Above</u>, Hang Bo Street, Hanoi, in 1938.

During this time, Ho's principal collaborator, Vo Nguyen Giap, set up guerilla units in several regions of northern Vietnam and created an intelligence network. Communist cells were organized throughout the country under the supervision of Truong Chinh, the young secretary general of the Indochinese Communist Party. These later became of inestimable value to Ho after Japan's sudden surrender in 1945. Here was the *thoi co* – the opportune moment – in which to launch the general insurrection.

Ho's resolute certainty of victory is reflected in the conclusion of one of his poems: "In 1945, the work will be accomplished." But, of course, in 1945, the work had really just begun.

At the end of World War II, Vietnam faced a political void, Bao Dai's government existing in name only. Apart from a handful of French civil servants and troops, whom the Japanese had imprisoned prior to France's removal, Bao Dai had no supporting troops – his own or those of outsiders – in Indochina.

Chinese Nationalist forces entered Vietnam as far as the 16th parallel to accept the Japanese surrender. The British assumed control of the south. By the middle of August, chaos and uncertainty reigned once again. Using the clandestine Indochinese Communist Party and the Viet Minh as intermediaries, Ho Chi Minh worked to become the dominant political force, occupying as much territory as possible.

The August Revolution began on 16 August 1945, when the Viet Minh announced the formation of a National Committee of Liberation for Vietnam. Three days later, Ho's guerrilla forces took Hanoi. Hue's turn came four days later, when Bao Dai's government was besieged and "asked" to hand over the royal seal. Bao Dai abdicated, believing that the Viet Minh was a national front supported by the allies. Ho's forces now controlled Saigon and practically all surrounding rural areas. Ho announced the formation of a provisional government in Hanoi, and in early September, he proclaimed himself president of the Democratic Republic of Vietnam.

However, Ho found himself in a strategically vulnerable position when the allied forces arrived. He camouflaged the existence of the communist elements within the Viet Minh and sought support from both the Chinese and the French. In an unprecedented move, the Indochinese Communist Party announced its dissolution in November, although, in reality, it continued to function.

Ho then prepared to negotiate Vietnam's future status with France. In the general elections, organized in January 1946, the Viet Minh won the majority of seats in the first National Assembly. Ho's government was approved at the assembly's first session in March, but at the second session in October, only 291 members, including 37 from the opposition, turned up. When asked to explain the poor turnout, one Viet Minh minister announced that the absentees had been arrested for criminal offenses. The coun-

try's first national constitution was approved by 240 votes to one.

The French finally recognized the Democratic Republic of Vietnam as a free state, within the French union. However, relations rapidly deteriorated. Hostilities mounted and reached a peak with the French bombing of Haiphong port. On 19 December 1946, Ho ordered a general offensive against the French in Hanoi, and at French garrisons in northern and central Vietnam. The decade-long war for independence had begun.

An enduring war of resistance: The war for national independence that began after the Japanese occupation constitutes a confused

44

period of contemporary Vietnamese history. Thousands of Vietnamese took up arms against the French, yet few knew the identity and allegiance of their new leader and his party. The population did not entirely understand the historical events happening in their country, nor could they imagine the consequences that were to follow. To them, at face value, Ho Chi Minh's new party appeared to consist of nationalists fighting for the common cause of national independence against the known enemy. And indeed, today, as the country adopts what it calls a market-oriented economy and dumps much of its communist system, the wars of resistance are stressed to have been fought by nationalists.

The emergence of Communist China towards the end of 1949 favored the communist-dominated struggle.

After Ho's guerrillas had wiped out several French posts on the Chinese border, the two regimes established direct contact for the first time. China, the old aggressor nation that had threatened Vietnam's independence, was now an ally. Beijing supplied the young republic with military equipment, substantial provisions and further aid to develop the Viet Minh army.

On his side, Ho attempted to increase his government's base of nationalist support. At the beginning of 1951, he merged the Viet Minh with the Lien Viet, or Patriotic Front,

On Ho's orders, Vo Nguyen Giap launched a general offensive against the French forces, but in the face of superior fire power, Ho's troops were forced to retreat to the countryside. They adopted Mao Zedong's guerrilla strategy of a "people's war and people's army," attacking and sabotaging isolated French units, rather than becoming embroiled in large-scale battles. It was a tactic reminiscent of Le Loi's against Chinese forces in the 15th century, and one that would be used again against the Americans.

Left, Ho Chi Minh, early 1950s. **Above**, Giap's forces take Dien Bien Phu from the French.

a new league for the National Union of Vietnam, and he announced the formation of the Workers Party (Lao Dong), a disguise for the Communist Party that officially had disbanded, but in reality was still active. The nationalists and non-communists were forced to choose between the new regime or the French colonialists.

Giap's guerrilla forces progressively extended their territory during 1952 and 1953. By the spring of 1953, several divisions were training in Laos and had joined forces with the pro-communist Pathet Lao.

In May of 1954, the French base at Dien Bien Phu suffered a humiliating defeat after a heavy artillery attack from Giap's forces, who used bicycles to carry supplies. The French forces in northern Vietnam evacuated to below the 16th parallel.

The war for independence officially ended on July 20, after long negotiations in Geneva. In finally gaining full national independence, Vietnam lost its unity. The Geneva agreement signed in August divided the country at the 17th parallel, pending general elections scheduled for the middle of 1956.

The northern part of the country became the Democratic Republic of Vietnam – North Vietnam – under the leadership of the Lao Dong party; the south became the Republic of South Vietnam. The last French troops left

The North-South divide: The elections stipulated by the Geneva Agreement never occurred. From 1954 to 1974, the two Vietnams had no diplomatic, cultural or commercial relations with each other. Immediately after the Geneva Agreement, a virtual state of war existed between the two parts of the country. North Vietnam's intensified armed and revolutionary activities made the prospect of reunification through free elections increasingly unlikely. Meanwhile, the United States had reinforced Diem's troops, turning South Vietnam into an American protectorate.

In December 1960, the National Liberation Front of South Vietnam (NLF) was formed and began launching revolutionary

Vietnam, and Indochina, in April 1956.

Bao Dai made a last appeal on behalf of the royalists. He asked Ngo Dinh Diem to become prime minister of what would become South Vietnam. Diem was a curious choice, a Catholic in a predominately Buddhist country who had been away from Vietnam for two decades, returning in the midst of a nationalist uprising.

In fraudulent elections, Bao Dai was deposed by Diem, marking the end of the Nguyen Dynasty and the beginning of the Republic of South Vietnam. But things would only get worse, setting the stage for Vietnam's next conflict.

activities against the unstable regime in the south. This southern communist movement, christened the Viet Cong, grew stronger in the early 1960s.

Facing mounting pressures, Diem ordered repressive measures against the Buddhist establishment. This move provoked a wave of suicides by Buddhist monks, who set fire to themselves in protest. In June 1963, the Venerable Thich Quang Duc, a 66-year-old monk, immolated himself on a street corner in Saigon. As his image blazed across the world's television screens and newspapers, the flames that consumed him were burned into the consciousness of Vietnamese, Americans and the international community. This signaled the beginning of the end for Diem's regime. Diem and his brother were murdered five months later by Diem's own officers following a coup d'etat, which was supported by the US government.

The following years witnessed a succession of coups d'etat. Several generals and civilians took turns presiding over the unstable and corrupt Saigon regime.

The beginning of 1965 marked the escalation of direct American involvement in Vietnam, when President Lyndon B. Johnson decided to send large numbers of troops to Vietnam. By the end of 1967, there were more than 500,000 American and 100,000

His successor, Richard Nixon, promised a secret plan to end the war, but this turned out to be nothing more than turning the bulk of fighting over to the South Vietnamese. In 1969, Ho Chi Minh died without seeing his work completed, and peace negotiations dragged on in Paris between 1968 and 1973.

The 1973 Paris Peace Agreement aimed to put an end to hostilities. The Americans pulled out their troops, but the two warring Vietnamese sides lost no time in violating the agreement. In 1975, as the Communist forces steadily moved south and the Saigon regime crumbled, the US Congress refused to offer additional military aid, in effect ending South Vietnam's ability to continue

allied troops in Vietnam. What many consider the war's turning point came in 1968, when the Viet Cong launched surprise attacks on Saigon and other cities throughout the south during the Lunar New Year, Tet. This Tet Offensive included a raid on the American embassy that stunned and embarrassed the United States, who began to see the war as futile. Johnson announced he would not run for re-election.

Left, Communist forces smashing through fence of the Presidential Palace, Saigon, 1975. **Above left**, Gen. Vo Nguyen Giap. **Right**, war residue lingered in both the north and south for years.

the war. The North's leadership launched its final offensive against South Vietnam.

On 30 April 1975, the northern army entered Saigon. The communist party's long struggle for power – under the banner of national liberation and reunification – finally ended in their complete victory.

Vietnam was now independent of foreign troops and control, and it could set its sights on national unification. But there would not be peace, nor freedom from foreign influence, for years to come. Indeed, Vietnam itself became militarily involved by occupying neighboring Cambodia, and in military battles with China itself.

A bright future seemed to stretch before socialist Vietnam after 1975, with the Vietnamese communist leadership making great plans for the rehabilitation of the country and the long years of war finally at an end. But a series of strategic blunders made – and later admitted – by the Hanoi leaders shattered all hope for a new era in Vietnam's history.

The party leadership, under the pressure of the northern conservative elements, dissolved the Revolutionary Provisional Government of South Vietnam and the National Liberation Front of South Vietnam.

In July 1976, Vietnam was officially reunified, thus breaking the fragile balance between the two parts of the country. A radical program of socialist construction was put forward at the Fourth Party Congress in December 1976. It called for the rapid socialization of the southern economy, with the forced collectivization of agriculture, small industry and commerce. This rapidly led to an unprecedented economic disaster, provoking new waves of refugees trying to flee the country. Further sapping the nation's resources was the internment of the south's intellectual and government leaders, and other highly-skilled, highly-educated people, in so-called re-education camps.

On the international front, in as early as 1977, Vietnam found itself in open conflict with neighboring Cambodia (then known as Democratic Kampuchea) and on a collision course with China – once again.

In 1978, Vietnam signed a friendship treaty – in fact, a security pact – with the former Soviet Union. Once again, Vietnam was entangled in the bloc politics of the communist powers and their proxies. The invasion of Cambodia by Vietnamese troops at the end of 1978 and the subsequent so-called "Chinese lesson" were to augur a new cycle of war, which was to absorb most of Vietnam's post-war energies. Vietnam's all-out alliance with the Soviet Union did nothing, in the long run, to help boost Vietnam's position on the international scene.

Preceding pages: traditional music for Ho. **Left,** Ho Chi Minh finally in Saigon. **Above,** young campaigner.

For the whole of the next decade, the presence of Vietnamese troops in Cambodia remained a central issue in the international arena, around which a coalition of nations – China, the United States and the members of ASEAN, the Association of South East Asian Nations – managed to enroll international support to isolate Vietnam.

Meanwhile, the Khmer resistance rendered Vietnam's control over Cambodia into a no-win dilemma. The Coalition Government of Democratic Kampuchea, established in 1982,

with Prince Norodom Sihanouk as President and with Khmer Rouge participation, received growing support from the international community. They occupied Cambodia's seat at the UN, while Vietnam lost most of its hard-earned international reputation.

The Cambodian war was becoming a costly stalemate. At the Fifth Party Congress in 1982, the old guard, under the guidance of party secretary general Le Duan, obstinately maintained Vietnam's course, hoping that, against all odds, it could consolidate its political and military edge in Cambodia, and at the same time stabilize the socio-economic situation in Vietnam.

Economic shifts: The new economic policies, introduced in 1979, managed to bring some respite on the domestic front, without improving the chronic weaknesses of Vietnam's economy.

The 1980s, however, saw the economy worsen on the home front. People were starving. There wasn't enough rice to go around. Meat was rationed. People stood in line for monthly and weekly allotments of food.

It was only at the Sixth Party Congress, in 1986, which followed the Soviet example of *glasnost* and *perestroika,* that the party decided to launch the country on an ambitious program of socio-economic renovation called *doi moi.* Under the new leadership of Nguyen

communist leaders, who feared the impact of these events upon their regime. While reaffirming the party's commitment to the reform agenda, Nguyen Van Linh repeatedly rejected any idea of political pluralism and a multi-party system for Vietnam.

Meanwhile, the demise of socialism in the Soviet Union and Eastern Europe contributed to the worsening economic crisis in Vietnam, as former members of the now-defunct Soviet bloc, besieged with domestic crises, were no longer in any position to continue their economic assistance to Vietnam and other client states, such as Cuba.

It was in this uncertain context that, in mid-1990, Vietnam adopted a new course in

Van Linh, the motto of the party was then "to change or to die." A new contract-system was implemented in 1988 to encourage Vietnamese farmers to cultivate their land, and rice production witnessed an immediate upsurge in 1989. Progress was also recorded in the sector of manufactured goods and commodities exports.

Until the end of 1988, socialist Vietnam followed the path of Soviet perestroika, but the Vietnamese leaders were soon to discover the bold and unchartered nature of Gorbachev's "new thinking."

The surge of turmoil in China and Eastern Europe in 1989 shocked the Vietnamese

foreign affairs. Vietnam's top leaders secretly visited China in order to mend fences with Beijing. Earlier, the withdrawal of Vietnamese troops from Cambodia, in September 1989, had cleared the way for the political settlement of the Cambodian conflict. The peace process was a difficult one involving the efforts of all the parties directly and indirectly involved: the Soviet Union, China, ASEAN, the United States, Japan, France and Australia.

In September 1990, a UN plan was finally endorsed calling for the setting up of a Supreme National Council, a cease fire and the cessation of foreign military assistance to the

Khmer factions under a UN control mechanism, pending the organization of free general elections in Cambodia.

With Vietnamese forces withdrawn from Cambodia, it seemed that the three-decade-old American embargo against Hanoi would finally be lifted. However, political pressure from US Senate hinged the end of the embargo on the full accounting of all missing American servicemen.

Meanwhile, European and Asian companies poured into Vietnam seeking investment opportunities in what many proclaimed as the last economic frontier. Hanoi and Ho Chi Minh City became boomtowns – hotels were renovated, international airline service

Clinton allowed the release of International Monetary Fund loans to Hanoi. Foreign investment in Vietnam increased. In early 1994, the United States lifted its trade embargo, and in the following year, President Clinton restored diplomatic ties, and an embassy was opened in Hanoi. In 1995, Vietnam became a full member of ASEAN.

Today, the leadership's challenge is to retain its firm grip on power as the country develops economically. The country's triumvirate of leaders are aging, yet there are no clear indications that anybody is ready – or being trained – to replace them.

Within the government and the Communist Party today, there are divisions of think-

to Vietnam increased, and telecommunications were upgraded.

In late 1992, the Americans working on the search for serviceman still listed as missing-in-action became convinced that Vietnamese authorities were cooperating and not withholding information. American businesses lobbied the administration of President George Bush to lift the embargo. Washington responded by allowing American companies to open representative offices in Vietnam. In 1993, the new administration of Bill

ing, some who want to continue liberalizing the economy and opening the door to foreigners, some who want to limit foreign investment to Asian countries, and some who want to slow down reform, fearing the party is losing control.

For now, the leadership appears to have little to fear in the way of opposition. This is primarily because the country's economy has been steadily moving up, and people throughout the country feel as if their lives are improving. The country's growth has been increasing at a pace of about eight percent a year. Income levels are still low – the average is about US$250 a year – yet

Left, peace at military cemetery, Cu Chi. **Above**, patriotism in the old quarter, Hanoi.

there are pockets of wealth developing in the urban centers. And because costs for basic needs – food, housing and schooling – are still relatively low, people have begun to enjoy a better lifestyle. Inflation, which had been spiraling out of control in the 1980s, is now at about 20 percent a year – still high, but not crippling. Vietnam is now the world's third-largest exporter of rice, and the country is pinning hopes of steady economic revival on a fledgling offshore oil-and-gas industry.

This is not to say there aren't problems. Much of the country – particularly in the countryside – is still mired in poverty.

Nearly 80 percent of the population lives outside the urban areas, and many live with-

out running water or electricity; most people don't have telephones. While Ho Chi Minh City and Hanoi appear to be humming with modern motorcycles and cars, in fact, a bicycle is still a luxury for most rural people.

Ahead is a widening gap between rich and poor as a wealthy class emerges. People from the countryside are flooding the cities looking for jobs; they find few places to live and little support from the government. As Vietnam begins to adopt a market economy, the socialist safety net is unraveling, meaning the elderly, veterans and uneducated are losing some benefits to which they have grown accustomed.

State agencies and state-owned companies – notoriously bloated and inefficient – are having to cull their work forces to compete in the blossoming market economy, adding to an increasing problem of unemployment. The population, too, is young – more than two-thirds of Vietnamese are under the age of 30. Many college graduates are unable to find jobs.

The government still controls the press, as well, and there are no free elections. Any criticism of the party or government is forbidden, and political dissidents are still thrown in jail. (Recently, Buddhist monks who belong to an outlawed organization were sentenced to several years in prison.)

That said, newspapers in Vietnam have become livelier, nonetheless, writing about crime, government corruption, police scandals and social issues like prostitution, drug abuse, AIDS, labor unrest and health care. Yet stories are strictly censored.

The atmosphere in Vietnam today is one of a country on the move with an authoritarian government looming in the background. Most people ignore it, hoping they will be left alone, yet realizing also that they must be careful not to offend the authorities.

Corruption is rampant in doing business – foreigners and Vietnamese alike complain they are nickel-and-dimed to death, with bureaucrats at all levels demanding "tokens" in order to get paperwork completed, licenses approved, offices opened.

Still, Vietnam, finally free of the military conflicts that for so long impoverished the people, has adopted a course of economic reform that may now be so far along that its leaders cannot control it. An infusion of capital has nurtured something of a consumer society, where young people, especially, have become materialistic.

Whether political reform will follow is yet to be seen. Right now, few people, other than overseas Vietnamese, seem to be clamoring for it. Most people will tell visitors that they want no more political conflicts, and certainly no more wars and military ventures. Yet as people begin demanding more things from a society becoming more open, conflicts between the old guard communists and the new age capitalists seem inevitable.

Above, war memories from commercial residue. **Right**, reviewing stand on veteran's day.

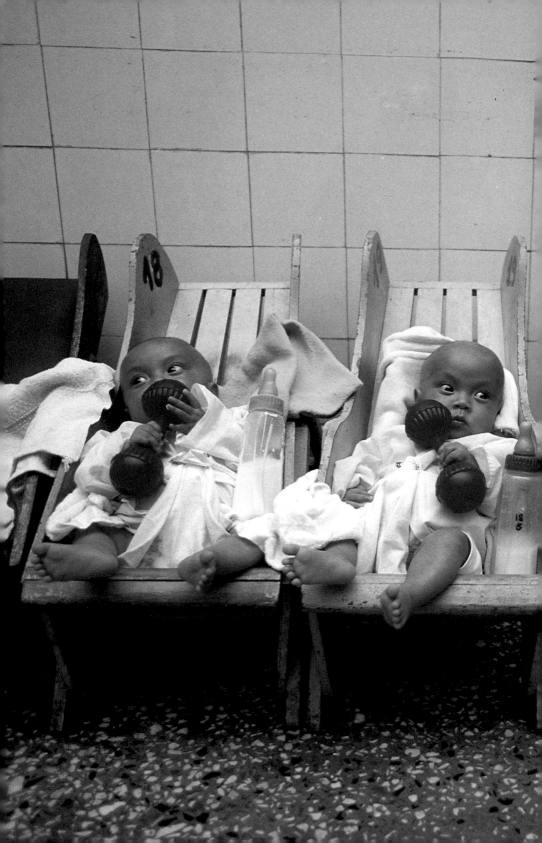

Designed like an immense, elongated letter S, Vietnam stretches the length of the Indochinese peninsula, bordering the South China Sea to the east. Its 3,730-kilometer (2,320 mi) frontier shares a 1,150-kilometer (715 mi) border with China in the north, and to the west, a border of 1,650 kilometers (1,000 mi) with Laos and 930 kilometers (600 mi) with Cambodia.

Mountains and forests make up more than three-quarters of Vietnam's total surface area. With a land area of 327,500 square kilometers (126,500 sq mi), Vietnam's territory also encompasses a vast sea area, including a large continental shelf and a string of thousands of islands stretching from the Tonkin Gulf to the Gulf of Thailand. These include the disputed Spratly (Truong Sa) and Paracel (Hoang Sa) islands, which China and other Southeast Asian nations also claim.

As the crow flies, Vietnam stretches 1,650 kilometers (1,000 mi) from Mong Cai, in the north, to Ha Tien in the south. At its widest point in the north, Vietnam is but 600 kilometers (370 mi) across; at its narrowest part, it is 50 kilometers (30 mi) across. The 2,500-kilometer (1,500 mi) coastline is dotted with beautiful beaches.

Situated between 8°33' and 23°20' latitude north and 102° and 109°27' longitude east, Vietnam is a land endowed with great physical beauty and diversity. The fertile imaginations of some geographers have likened the country, with its three regions – Bac Bo (north), Trung Bo (center) and Nam Bo (south) – to a set of scales, the north and south constituting two balancing baskets of rice supplied by rich deltas of the north's Red River and the south's Mekong.

Chains of mountains and profoundly carved valleys separate Vietnam from China, to the north. The most important valley is that of the Red River; the highest summit, Fan Si Pan, rises to 3,160 meters (10,370 ft) over the Hoang Lien Son mountain range, in the province of Lao Cai, near the Chinese border.

The plains of Cao Bang, Lang Son, Vinh

Yen, and the valleys watered by the Lo, Chay, Cau, Luc, Nam and Cung rivers, occupy the northern part of the region, extending over the immense Red River Delta, home to nine-tenths of northern Vietnam's population. The Red River flows from its source in the Yunnan region of China, across the north of Vietnam and heading southeastward to its coastal mouth.

Central Vietnam forms a long convex curve, within which are small plains wedged between the South China Sea and the high

plateaus of the Truong Son mountains. The terrain is characterized by dunes and lagoons in the east, towards the coast, and terraces of ancient alluvial deposits towards the mountains. The limestone peaks of Pu Sam Sao stretch along the border with Laos. The Central Highlands are rich in volcanic basalt soil and constitute one of Vietnam's most important forest areas, in addition to tea- and coffee-growing regions.

The Mekong River, known as Cuu Long Giang, or the River of Nine Dragons, is one of the longest rivers in Asia at 4,180 kilometers, or 2,600 miles. The Mekong flows from its source in the mountains of

Preceding pages: spunky eyes of youth, Saigon hospital; mourners at a funeral. Left, Ha Long Bay. Above, curves on Hai Van Pass.

How Vietnam was Named

The name Vietnam has become as synonymous with war as Agincourt, Waterloo, Gettysburg, Normandy and Bosnia. Yet few know the significance of the name, even though war, with its interminable sequels, has brought the country to the forefront of the world scene for more than half a century.

The country has been known as Vietnam (in the language, it is spelled in two words, Viet Nam) for only about 200 years.

The first national name of Van Lang was given to the country by the Hung, or Lac, ethnic group, inventors of the wet-rice cultivation technique and the bronze drums still used today by the

Muong minority. The Lac were followed by the Au, or Tay Au, who arrived from China. The two people integrated and formed the new kingdom of Au Lac.

Then came the Viet, or Yue, an ethnic group emigrating from the coast of China around 2,500 years ago. They came with other ethnic groups of the Bach Viet (the 100 Viet principalities of ancient China) on a long southward march towards the Indochinese peninsula, a migration of people from the north that would continue for more than 15 centuries.

The name Vietnam first appeared when Emperor Gia Long wanted to rename the country Nam Viet, in the early 19th century. Seeking the Chinese emperor's approval of the new national name, Gia Long sent his ambassador to China.

He pleaded for the reunification of the old land of An Nam and the new land of Viet Thuong, and for permission to change the ancient name of An Nam to Nam Viet.

After consulting his court, the Chinese emperor decided that the name Nam Viet would bring to mind the ancient kingdom of Nam Viet Dong, which had included the two Chinese provinces. The proposed name of Nam Viet might lead to misunderstandings or even conceal territorial ambitions.

The problem was solved by simply reversing the order of the two words to Viet Nam: the people (Viet) of the South (Nam).

Etymologists and anthropologists have defined the origins of the Viet people by separating the components of the calligraphy for Viet. On the left side of this ideogram is a character pronounced *tau* in Vietnamese, meaning to run. On the right is the complementary component pronounced *viet*, with the meaning and profile of an axe. This component carries with it the particle *qua*, which signifies a lance or javelin, the tools of a hunter.

This small ideographic analysis depicts the Viet as a race known since antiquity as a migratory, hunting people.

The word *viet* is the Vietnamese pronunciation of a Chinese character meaning beyond or far, and with the sense of crossing or going through. The character *nam,* meaning south, probably served to differentiate between the Viets in the north who remained in China and those who had left and headed south.

A long history of foreign invaders branded Vietnam with different names.

Marco Polo skirted the coast of Vietnam in 1292. In his writings appears the name Caugigu, which corresponds to Giao Chi Quan, Vietnam's name under the Han Dynasty, 111 BC–203 AD. This name was transformed to Kutchi by the Malays and later to Kotchi by the Japanese.

The Portuguese in turn named it Cauchi Chine, to distinguish it from Cauchi or Kutchi in India, also known as Cochin. This name was again summoned by French colonialists who called southern Vietnam Cochin China.

These names, when written or pronounced in the occidental manner, evoked a far more ancient name, Cattigara, which first appeared on one of 14 maps drawn by Ptolemy, the famous Greek mathematician and geographer.

Since the earliest antiquity, the Indochinese peninsula has played a major role in international trade relations and migrations, forming the link between India and China. This connection between the two ancient civilizations explains the name Indochina, first coined by the Danish geographer, Konrad Malte-Burn (1775–1826) in his *Universal Geographic* and still used today by some to refer to the region. ∎

Tibet, across China, through Burma into Laos and northern Thailand, and then across Cambodia before flowing through southern Vietnam into the South China Sea.

Over the centuries, the Mekong's deposits collected on a shallow, undersea shelf, forming an immense low-lying alluvial plain, the Mekong Delta, which extends over 75,000 square kilometers (29,000 sq mi). These alluvial deposits do not accumulate on the natural delta, but rather at the mouth of the Mekong, and around the Camau Peninsula, where they contribute to enlarging southern Vietnam by dozens of square meters annually.

Flora and fauna: The country's topographical diversity is matched only by the diverse

chemical defoliation, and an ever-increasing population growth have greatly accelerated this deforestation. Precious hardwoods are being felled in massive quantities for export. However, this wholesale depletion of forest could cost the country far more as flooding and erosion take their environmental toll.

Despite efforts to reverse this alarming trend, the government's reforestation program, which replants some 1,600 square kilometers (620 sq mi) annually, is not enough to cover the annual forest losses of 2,000 square kilometers (770 sq mi).

Vietnam's wildlife is, in general, identical to that of Bengal and the Malaysian peninsula. It includes species extinct in other parts

species of flora and fauna in its mountains, forests, plains and plateaus.

In prehistoric times, much of Vietnam was covered by dense forest. Tropical forests still cover around 40 percent of the country and contain more than 700 identified plant species, constituting a rich source of oils, resins, precious woods, industrial timber and medicinal plants. Exploitation of the environment over the millennia has greatly reduced Vietnam's forested regions, which have virtually been halved since 1945 alone. War,

of Asia among its 273 species of mammals, 180 species of reptiles, 273 species of birds and hundreds of species of fish and invertebrates. Among these are elephant, wild buffalo, rhinoceros, antelope, tapir, monkey, wild boar, tortoise, crocodiles, and hornbills.

Recently, evidence of two previously unknown species of mammals were found in Vietnam: a goat living in Nghe An Province, near Laos, and the horns of a bovine near the Cambodian border, in Dak Lak Province.

Environment: The country's development is putting new pressures on an already fragile environment. A growing population – now estimated to be approaching 80 million –

Left, foreigners brought their own names for Vietnam. Above, staying above water.

means that there are more demands on land. Recently, the government has wrestled with how much rice-growing land to convert for industrial use. The forests continue to be threatened by slash-and-burn farming techniques in the highlands regions, which in turn creates more erosion and flooding.

Much of the country was sprayed with chemical defoliants, such as Agent Orange, during the years of the American involvement in the war. The resulting contamination to the food chain was devastating. In the 20 years since the end of the war, however, the contamination of land has continued, as farmers have doused their crops with noxious chemicals – insecticides, herbicides, fertiliz-

ers – that have worked their way into the environment.

The cities are overcrowded, with garbage piling up and water sources polluted. Industrialization means there are more factories spewing out chemicals dirtying the air.

Climate: Vietnam's location in the Southeast Asian monsoon zone, between the Tropic of Cancer and the Equator, gives rise to a complex and humid climate that varies from region to region. The average temperature of 22°C (72°F) varies slightly from one season to another, but like anywhere, it is prone to sudden changes. A persistent dampness tends to make the temperature feel cooler.

Northern Vietnam's climate is influenced by the winds of central Asia, which give rise to a climate similar to that of China. Generally, two distinct seasons prevail. From November to April, the northern part of Vietnam experiences a relatively cold and humid winter. This is precipitated by invading polar air currents that sweep into Vietnam from Siberia and China, often bringing temperatures down to as low as 0°C (32°F) in the mountainous regions lying north and east of Hanoi, and a fine drizzle throughout most of the winter months.

Summer, from May to October, is characterized by higher temperatures, heavy rain and often typhoons. Both the north and center experience their hottest months during June, July and August.

The climate varies from north to south in the central part of the country. Towards the northern provinces, the climate is almost identical to that of the Red River Delta, whereas towards the south, the provinces have more in common climatically with the Mekong Delta area. In Hue, the cold season lasts from November to March, with almost continual drizzle falling, often for periods of up to a week.

Southern Vietnam's climate is characterized by a relatively constant temperature, sudden changes during the monsoon and a punctual rainy season, from May to October. There is a relatively dry season from November to February, and a dry season from February to April before the rains. The south experiences its hottest months in March, April and May, when temperatures may reach 35°C (95°F).

The rains, affected by the monsoon winds arriving across the ocean and the geographical position and relief of the various regions, are usually abundant. Between May and December, the warm and humid summer monsoon brings higher temperatures, a humidity of between 80 and 100 percent, and heavy rain to most of the country. During this season, violent typhoons often ravage the coastline betwenn Qui Nhon and Camau, causing considerable damage. The high plateau regions are usually much cooler than the coastal areas, and experience a marked nightly drop in temperature year-round.

Above, lightning strikes above Perfume River. **Right**, muddy monsoon water, Mekong Delta.

Who are the Vietnamese people? Although 90 percent of the population lists as its ethnicity *kinh,* the accepted term for the native race, in reality most Vietnamese have evolved from a mixture of races and ethnicities over thousands of years. That mixture is quite naturally the result of repeated invasions from outside Vietnam, particularly from China, and continual migrations within Vietnam, most commonly from north to south.

So in Vietnam today, there are the predominant kinh, but also dozens of distinct minority groups, including the Cham and Khmer of the south, two groups whose own kingdoms were long ago vanquished by invading Vietnamese from the north.

Minority groups have been among the last to share in the prosperity under Vietnam's recent economic renovation – with one exception. Ethnic Chinese, who as recently as the late 1970s were run out of the country because of tensions arising during a brief northern border clash with China, have not only benefitted, but, in many ways, have fueled an economic revival, particularly in Ho Chi Minh City.

Other groups, however, have not been so fortunate. Usually living in remote, undeveloped mountainous regions with little fertile ground, their existence is worlds removed from the hustle and bustle of Vietnam's urban centers.

The Vietnamese: Studies of folk songs from the hill region of northern Vietnam, and from the coastal area in the northern part of central Vietnam, affirm that the Vietnamese originated in the north's Red River Delta.

These agricultural, fishing and hunting people were probably totemist. Their costume, although unique in Indochina, is found in certain Oceanic islands. The nautical, dance and war scenes depicted on their ancient bronze drums reveal a marked similarity to the mystical traditions of the Dayaks of Borneo and the Batak of Sumatra.

Throughout monsoon Asia, which includes northern Vietnam, a shared culture existed

from a very early era, as evidenced by its tools, vocabulary and certain essential rites and traditions, such as the blackening of teeth, water festivals, bronze drums, kites, tattooing, betel nut and cajeput, pole houses, cockfighting and mulberry cultivation. Remains of five races have been found in Vietnam: Melanesians, Indonesians, Negritos, Australoids and Mongoloids. The most predominant of these were the Indonesians and Mongoloids. The times of the prehistoric Vietnamese are kept alive in the collective

memory of the Vietnamese people through numerous tales, legends, and popular songs, which recount at length the traditions, customs and manners of this people, including the making of bronze drums and their annual cruise up the Red River. The cruise evoked the homeric battles between the God of the Mountain and the God of the River in their pursuit of the same Vietnamese princess, which marked the end of a reign, the fall of the spiral citadel and the beginning of Chinese domination.

Recent studies on the origins of the Vietnamese people show that the people who settled on the Indochinese peninsula and its bordering regions came from China, the high plateaus of Central Asia, islands in the South Pacific and various other parts of the world. Thus, Vietnam can be considered a proverbial melting pot into which major Asiatic and Oceanic migrations converged.

It is most likely that the first natives of Vietnam originated from several ethnic groups. The most important of these were the Hung, or Lac, specialists in wet-rice cultivation and inventors of the bronze drums, and who inhabited the Red River Delta and central regions, and the Muong, from the high wooded plateaus and mountainous regions.

Two major Viet emigrations from the coastal and southern provinces of the Chi-

Malayo-Indonesian element to the fair-skinned contingent from the valleys of the Yang Tse Kiang, when they merged with the first native occupants of the Red River Delta around the third century BC, founding the Kingdom of Au Lac.

The many centuries of intermingling between these races has produced the Vietnamese people of today.

In their search for vital living space, this vigorous, tenacious and courageous people crossed the mountain ranges of central Indochina and more than 3,000 kilometers (1,800 mi) in their move to the south. They crossed into central Vietnam in 982, then reaching Hue in 1306, Quang Ngai in 1402,

nese empire added to this population. The first occurred during the 5th century BC, at the fall of the Viet kingdom of the low Yang Tse Kiang valley, and the second, during the 3rd century BC, when the Au, or Au Tay, from Kwang Si, invaded northern Vietnam.

They progressively established themselves in the coastal regions, gradually making their way inland via rivers until they eventually reached the high regions, inhabited by the native Lac people in the Red River Delta, and the Muong at Hoa Binh and Thanh Hoa.

The Vietnamese population's southward expansion from the Red River Delta of northern Vietnam brought an important native

Binh Dinh in 1470, Phu Yen in 1611, Ba Ria in 1623, Nha Trang in 1653, Bien Hoa in 1658, Saigon in 1674, Phan Rang in 1693, Phan Thiet in 1697 and finally Ha Tien in the southernmost province of the Mekong Delta in 1714. In this expansion, they overran the kingdoms of Champa and Cambodia. By 1714, the Viet empire extended from the Chinese frontier to the Gulf of Thailand.

Ethnic minorities: The Viet, or Kinh, form the majority, representing about 90 percent of the population. More than 50 ethnic minorities inhabit the mountainous regions that cover almost two-thirds of Vietnam. (Recently, a small tribe of fewer than 100 members was found in northern province, a tribe distinct from previously identified ethnic groups.) Vietnam's one million Chinese constitute another important minority group. Only 3,000 have kept their Chinese nationality, while the rest, referred to as Hoas, have adopted Vietnamese nationality.

On the whole, whether naturalized or not, many Chinese remain loyal to the costume and traditions of their country of origin. They settled in Cho Lon, which today flourishes as the Chinese community's commercial center in southern Vietnam and is but 10 kilometers from the center of Ho Chi Minh City. Mostly shopkeepers and traders, they habitually regroup in communities well or-

The Cham and Khmer number around 400,000. The Chams inhabit the Phan Rang and Phan Thiet regions, while Khmer are found in the Mekong Delta. The Chams possessed a brilliant culture that lasted for only a short duration, yet its vestiges can still be seen in the ruins of the Poh Nagar Temple and the shrines and Buddhist monasteries at Dong Duong, and in the large scale irrigation systems, temples and towers of central Vietnam. Most of their architectural and sculptural vestiges relate to their religious beliefs, linked with ancient legend and polytheist in cast. Its prevailing image was that of a woman regarded as the mother of the country who gave birth to the dynastic rulers.

ganized for trade and the researching of possible new markets.

The ethnic minorities living in the mountainous regions in central and southern Vietnam form another important group. Called Montagnards by the French, these tribes include Muong, Ra De, Jarai, Banhar and Sedang living in the high plateaus of the west. Totaling around 700,000 people, they have always opposed foreign influence and only recently have begun to integrate more into the national life.

<u>Left</u>, boys at a mid-autumn festival, Hoi An. <u>Above</u>, glances from Black Thai girls.

Large blocks of vertical-standing stones, or *menhir,* symbolizing the God of the Earth, represented another Cham cult. Later, Hinduism and Indian culture would influence the Chams, as can be seen in *linga* images; Mahayana Buddhism, too, became an influence. Today, the Cham people preserve their customs, language and script with a religion that is a modified form of Hinduism.

Northern Vietnam: The highlands and midland regions of northern Vietnam are home to many ethnic minorities and diverse tribes, including the Tay, who number just under a million and are found in village groups in the provinces of Cao Bang, Lang Son, Bac Thai,

Quang Ninh, Ha Giang, and Tuyen Quang, and in the Dien Bien Phu region.

Their villages, or *ban,* are located in valleys near flowing water, where they build their traditional houses, usually on stilts. They cultivate rice, soybeans, cinnamon, tea, tobacco, cotton, indigo, fruit trees and bamboo on the mountainsides above the village. The influence of Viet culture is evident in their dialect and customs, which distinguish them from the other Tay-Thai speaking groups.

The Nung, in many aspects similar to the Tay, share the same language, culture and customs, and often live together in the same villages, where they are referred to as Tay Nung. Numbering about 340,000, they live in Cao Bang and Lang Son provinces.

There are about 76,000 Thai living along the Red River, in the northwest of Vietnam, often together with other ethnic minorities. Their bamboo or wooden stilt houses are constructed in two distinctly different styles. The Black Thai build homes shaped like tortoise shells, while the White Thai construct rectangular dwellings.

The women wear long, black sarongs and short tops with silver buttons. They are very skilled weavers and produce beautiful embroidery using motifs of flowers, birds, animals and dragons.

The San Chi, numbering more than 77,000, live in village groups mainly in Ha Giang, Tuyen Quang and Bac Thai provinces, but they are also found in certain regions of Lao Cai, Yen Bai, Vinh Phu, Ha Bac and Quang Ninh provinces. They are of the Tay-Thai language group and arrived from China at the beginning of the 19th century.

San Chi ritual dances reflect the life of the community. Alternating groups of boys and young girls perform traditional love songs in a festivities that can last all night.

The Giai, also of the Tay-Thai language group, number about 30,000, and emigrated from China about 200 years ago. Their villages are often built very close to those of the Tay, Nung and Thai.

The Giai believe the universe has three levels, with man in the middle between the highest level, heaven, and the lowest, a vile place inhabited by sinners. An ancestral altar occupies the central position in a Giai home. Each vase of incense represents a divinity such as the sky, the earth, the ancestors, or the god of the home. The Giai have numerous proverbs and maxims that constitute a kind of moral code.

The Lao number about 7,000 and belong to the Tay-Thai language group. They are actually closer to the Thai minority then their Laotian namesakes across the border. They are found along the Vietnam-Laos border in the Song Ma district of Son La Province, and around Dien Bien Phu and Phong Tho in Lai Chad Province. Their homes are built on stilts in the form of a tortoise shell, like those of the Black Thai. Their traditional costume also resembles that of the Thai.

Their elaborate rice-growing techniques are similar to those of the Thai. They are also

skilled craftspeople, particularly in ceramics, weaving and embroidery.

The Lu belong to the Tay-Thai language group. They number around 3,000 and are found in the Phong Tho and Sin Ho districts of Lai Chad Province, in well-arranged villages of 40 to 60 dwellings. They arrived from China and occupied the Dien Bien Phu area as part of the Bach Y settlement in the first century AD. The Lu's famous Tam Van Citadel, dedicated to Buddha, was noted by the Black Thais on their arrival in the 11th and 12th centuries.

The Hmong, who number more than 400,000, are found in villages known as *giao* throughout the highlands of eleven provinces: Cao Bang, Lang Son, Bac Thai, Ha Giang, Tuyen Quang, Lao Cai, Yen Bai, Son La, Lai Chad, Hoa Binh and Thanh Hoa.

Due to their wars with the feudal Chinese, they emigrated to Vietnam from the southern Chinese kingdom of Bach Viet at the end of the 18th and beginning of the 19th centuries. Once in Vietnam, they settled in northwestern provinces.

Maize is their main staple, but rice is often grown on terraces irrigated with the aid of an irrigation system. Hemp is grown as the main textile material and cotton is also cultivated in some villages. Poppy and Job's tears are among the plants cultivated for medicinal purposes. Fruit such as plums, peaches and apples, produced by the Hmong, is highly valued throughout the country, although transportation problems make selling the produce difficult. They collect gentian, cardamom, honey, fungi, bamboo and many medicinal herbs from the forests, which constitute an important source of income.

As skilled artisans, the Hmong produce a variety of items, including handwoven indigo-dyed cloth, paper, silver jewelry, leather goods, baskets, baby carriers, kitchen utensils and embroidery. Many of these are increasingly sold to tourists.

The Hmong have no written language. Their legends, songs, folklore and proverbs have been passed down from one generation to the next through the spoken word. They have developed a varied culture, rich in popular knowledge concerning the nature of society – extolling liberty, justice, charity, the work ethic and virtue, and condemning laziness, meanness, hypocrisy and lying.

Totemism is still evident in Hmong culture where spirit worship, animist rites and exorcism are still practiced. Buddhism, Taoism and Confucianism have left their mark on some Hmong societies, introducing beliefs in reincarnation and the idea that men are superior to women.

Catholic missionaries attempted to convert the Hmong at the beginning of the century, and although some churches were built at Sa Pa and Nghia Lo, the evangelical efforts didn't succeed.

The Dao first arrived from China in the 18th century. Belonging to the Hmong-Dao language group, the Dao number about 35,000 and are found in the mid- and lower-regions of Thanh Hoa Province, living in large villages or small isolated hamlets, cultivating rice using the slash-and-burn method.

The Dao are very skilled artisans. They

Above left and **above**, sartorial differences between the Muong, Dao and Meo groups.

make their own paper, used primarily for writing family genealogies, official documents and religious books. For centuries, the Dao have used Chinese characters to record their genealogies, rhymes, folk tales, humorous tales, fables and popular songs. The women plant cotton, which they weave then dye with indigo. Their embroidery is worked directly onto the cloth from memory, the traditional designs firmly fixed in their minds.

Central Highlands: The Jarai, or Gia Rai, are located in the provinces of Gia Lai, Kon Tum, and Dak Lak, and in the north of Phu Khanh. They belong to the Malay-Polynesian language group and arrived in the Tay Nguyen Highlands from the coast a little less than

2,000 years ago. They live a sedentary lifestyle in villages known as *ploi,* or sometimes *bon.* Jarai villages, with at least 50 homes, are built around a central *nga rong,* a communal house.

The community is composed of small matriarchal families, with each family an economically-independent unit within the village. A council of elders, with a chief, directs village matters. The chief is responsible for all the village's communal activities.

Jarai cultivate fruit trees, rice, beans and other cereals, and raise buffalo, goats, chickens and pigs, primarily to offer as sacrifices to their various gods and spirits. Oxen, horses

and elephants are raised as working animals, and horses are also used to hunt wild boar.

Young girls take the incentive in choosing a marriage partner, making their approach through an intermediary. The promise of marriage is sealed with the exchange of bronze bracelets, with the ceremony proceeding in three steps.

First, the bracelet-exchanging rite is performed in front of the two families and the intermediary. Then the young couple's nightly dreams are interpreted, a ritual that predicts their future prospects. Finally, the actually wedding ceremony is held at home of the man's parents.

Jarai funerals are extremely complex affairs with endless rites, particularly in connection with the careful construction of the burial house. Inside it are placed carved wooden sculptures representing men, women and birds. Jarai believe the deceased is transformed into a spirit and joins ancestors in another world.

The Ra De, or E De, found mainly in Dak Lak Province, number more than 140,000. Like the Jarai, they belong to the Malay-Polynesian language group. They live in wooden longhouses, built on stilts, in villages known as *buon,* with as few as 20 and as many as 70 dwellings.

Each longhouse shelters a large matriarchal family under the authority of a *koa sang,* the most senior and respected woman. She directs community affairs, settles internal conflicts and is also responsible for the safekeeping of all the communal heirlooms, bronze gongs, ancient jars used for preparing rice beer, a large seat carved from a single tree trunk reserved for the khoa sang, and special stools reserved for hosts and musicians. The village's autonomous organization is run by the *po pin ea,* the chief, who is elected to take care of communal affairs.

The Ra De employ the slash-and-burn techniques to clear the land. Rice, the main crop, is cultivated along with sugar cane, melons, cotton, and tobacco.

Nearly every village has its own forge to produce and repair farming implements. Basketry, fairly rudimentary pottery and indigo cloth are produced by the Ra De for their own use.

Left, 19th-century Meo tribeswomen. **Right**, page of Latin–Annamese religious text.

LANGUAGE

In the Vietnamese language, the word for natural disaster is *thien tai,* from Chinese. The word for cheese is *pho mat,* from the French *fromage.* Too, there are sounds and words from English, and from Russian. Such is the linguistic melting pot of Vietnam.

Thousands of the words in the contemporary Vietnamese language – as much as 80 percent of the language – comes from Chinese, a reflection of the centuries of invasion–occupation–rebellion between Vietnam and its massive neighbor to the north, but also the influence of Chinese literature.

There is a touch of French, with words that entered the lexicon first during the colonial period of the 18th and 19th centuries, and well into the 20th century. A dab of English was left by the Americans during the Vietnam War, and subsequent years of Communist brotherhood with the former Soviet Union – and Soviet advisors – introduced Russian. In fact, expressions and nomenclature indicating 20th-century technology and ideas are often expressed with French, English and Russian words.

The newest foreign linguistic invasion – that of consumer marketers – is represented by Japanese. For example, the word most commonly used to refer to a two-wheeled motorized vehicle? *Honda.*

Variations: Distinct dialects within Vietnam reveal strong regional identities, as well. Often northerners and southerners confess they cannot understand each other. Foreigners might need two translators: One to translate the foreign language into Vietnamese, another to translate the translator's northern dialect into southern Vietnamese. Some letters of the alphabet are pronounced differently. The vocabularies of northerners and southerners contain distinct words, and even the syntax is different.

Yet the country does share one language. Its roots, while still debated, come from a similar mix of cultures and languages, a mixture of Mon-Khmer, Thai and Muong.

It is not a pure language, but rather a blend of several languages – ancient and modern – that has evolved through Vietnam's contact with other cultures. In addition to Vietnamese, the country's many ethnic minorities speak their own distinct languages and dialects. In the Mekong Delta, for example, so many people speak the Khmer of Cambodia that local television has a Khmer-language broadcast.

Written Vietnamese: Chinese influence during the first centuries of Vietnam's history led to the extensive use of characters known as *chu nho,* which replaced an ancient written script of Indian origin, preserved and used today only by the Muong minority.

Even after independence in the 10th century, all books and government documents were written in chu nho. Scholars continued to used it for some decades.

After independence, scholars realized the necessity and advantages of developing a separate written Vietnamese language. Several tentative attempts were made to modify the characters of Chinese, but it was a 13th-century poet, Nguyen Thuyen, who managed to incorporate the previous efforts into a distinct, but very complicated script known as *chu nom.*

Although standardized for popular literature, chu nom never received official recognition, and most Vietnamese writers continued using the Chinese calligraphy.

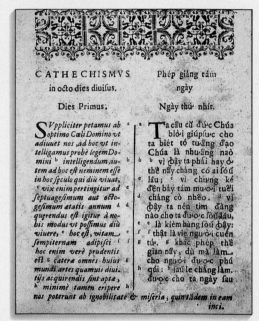

Today, Vietnam has a romanized alphabet, thanks to a French Jesuit missionary, Alexandre de Rhodes, who developed a script called *quoc ngu,* in 1651.

Quoc ngu was, at first, used only by Catholic church and the colonial administration, gaining widespread popularity only in the early part of this century. The study of quoc ngu became compulsory in secondary schools in 1906, and two years later, the royal court in Hue ordered a new curriculum, entirely in quoc ngu. It became the national written language in 1919.

Now, only scholars use the traditional calligraphic chu nom to decipher ancient carvings and writings. And during holidays, such as the lunar new year (Tet), people buy scrolls written in the Chinese Han for their homes. ∎

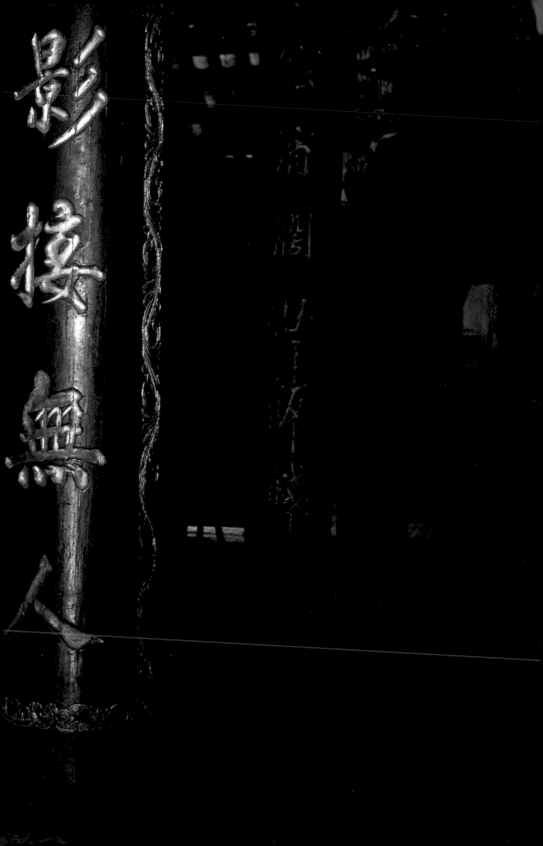

When men lack a sense of awe,
there will be disaster.
— *Tao Te Ching*
by Lao Tsu (6th century BC)

Our karma we must carry as our lot,
let's stop decrying Heaven's whims
and quirks.
Inside ourselves there lies the root of good:
the heart outweighs all talents on this earth.
— *The Tale of Kieu*
Nguyen Du (1765–1820)

Several thousands of years ago, the Viet tribes moved from China in the *nam* (south) direction towards the Song Hong (Red River) Delta. They settled in a beautiful land surrounded by high mountains, deep waters, thick forests and narrow plains. Inspired by the wonders of nature, the Viet soon realized that only with blood, sweat, tears and sharp eyes could they preserve their newly-acquired *dat* (earth) and *nuoc* (water).

To succeed, the Vietnamese have for centuries had to be conscious of the forces around them – the seen and the unseen, the favorable and the hostile – and to understand their nature and intentions, and to resist them if necessary and co-exist with them if possible, but never to provoke their anger.

To make sense of this immense web of influences and the matrix of powers, the Vietnamese have looked to what is in heaven, on earth, and amongst the people themselves. To penetrate the mysteries of heaven, to understand the workings and movements of the earth, and to establish relationships with people, Vietnamese traditionally have sought the highest form of knowledge: the way in which things emerge, exist, progress, disappear and re-emerge.

They seek the religions. In Vietnamese, they are *ton giao,* the highest and most elevated knowledge, or *dao giao,* the knowledge of the Way, or simply, Dao the Way.

These words, like much in Vietnamese culture, are actually borrowed from the Chi-

nese, who colonized Vietnam two thousand years ago. Among the colonialists were the usual tyrants and exploiters, but, too, compassionate administrators and dedicated teachers, who brought with them religions, philosophies, organizational skills and especially their written characters, the *chu han.*

This influence from the Chinese created both grave dangers and potential opportunities – the possibility of losing a Viet identity and independence, and the opportunity of assimilating and adapting the best of Chi-

nese civilization and culture. (In some ways, it is a process that continues today, as the proud Vietnamese now open the doors to foreigners, attempting to learn the best from other cultures while maintaining a hard-fought independence.)

The early attempts at making the best of Chinese domination were honed within the village, the *cha* (later called *xa*) that is the foundation of Vietnamese life. The traditional village is a group of individuals associated with one another in families, clans and extended families

The village's economic activities, in which all inhabitants participate, are concentrated

Preceding pages: monk at Giac Vien Pagoda, Ho Chi Minh City. **Left,** a patient Buddha. **Above,** shrine for highway travelers.

on growing food, especially rice, which requires constant observation of nature, the precise coordination of cultivation, and a bonding communal effort.

The experience gleaned collectively by the villagers, who struggled against the adverse forces of nature, over the centuries helped to create patterns of work and thought. Living together in growing communities, the peasants developed a code of public morality that involved participation and responsibility to ensure peace, order, group cohesion and loyalty – all the foundations of politics, the aim of which is social order.

However, as in most societies and cultures, social stability alone did not always provide an answer to the villagers' anxieties of threat from the unknown. It was unable to give meaning to their daily existence, or to provide them with a sense of connection to their human or natural environments. Through their polytheist or animistic religion, they respected and worshipped the forces that influenced, supported and threatened their welfare. Many of these belief systems are still held in Vietnam today.

Lofty answers: Foremost in their religious hierarchy is a heaven above, which the Vietnamese (with a tendency to humanize everything, in order to better deal with it) called Ong Troi, the honorable Heaven with a masculine cast. They approach him with food offerings, requests, complaints and prayers. In principle, Ong Troi is the keeper of human fate, and in charge of all the unseen powers and vague mysteries of the universe.

Together, the gods of the earth, water and mountains define and transform the geomantic structures that determine the orientation of houses, cities, graves and temples, and configure the good and bad luck of families, communities and nations.

Between heaven and earth, but never separate from them, is the human being, both male and female, the dead and the living, the ancestors and the descendants.

Each of the realms – heaven, earth, and human – has its own rules, regulations, modes of transformations, elements of good, bad, ugly and beautiful, and above all, its own deities. These deities are everywhere – in stones, trees, lakes and animals – and they are praised, fed, housed and revered with ritual offerings and appropriate behavior. The richness and variety of these worlds and

their manifestations has preoccupied, confused and dazzled the traditional Vietnamese, often leaving them little sense of space or privacy to eat, sleep, and make love, the basic human needs.

That perception results from their sense of awe for the visible and invisible forces of nature, their observation and interpretation of these forces and the ways and means they have found to compromise and co-exist with them, or resist them. Above all, the belief is grounded in their intimate relationship with the land on which they live, procreate and bury their dead, in their deep faith in the continuity of the Viet nation, and in their sacred mission to defend and build their land

and water (*dat* and *nuoc*). The secret wish of all Vietnamese is to attain *nhan* – a word borrowed from the Chinese meaning "contemplating the moon through a window," laughing off the glory and the burden of the day and immersing one's self in the serenity of a moonlit night.

In addition to the pagodas and communal houses found in traditional villages, there are smaller places of worship where both benevolent and malevolent divinities and spirits are worshipped. These include the *den,* used to commemorate a deified emperor who offered particular help to the village, or to a national hero; the *mieu,* usually situated on an elevated piece of land, reserved for the cult of both benevolent and malevolent gods and spirits; and the *ban,* where divinities not worshipped elsewhere are worshipped.

When the Chinese imposed their rule on Vietnam, they brought with them their agricultural know-how and their books on religion, philosophy and general wisdom, written in one of the most advanced (and complicated) scripts of all time, Han characters. The Vietnamese loved these characters, which visually and stylistically represented the meaning and feeling attached to each word.

Although the Vietnamese fought against Chinese political domination and economic exploitation, they selectively screened and

moved from one another in society. Under Communist rule, religious faithful have at times faced persecution. Churches and pagodas were shuttered. In recent years, however, the government has loosened its restrictions and there has been a resurgence of religious interest within the country. Pagodas are crowded with the faithful and curious on holidays, and on important dates of the lunar calendar; schools for training Buddhists monks have been allowed to open. Catholic churches are filled.

Yet, there are still signs of restraint. An example is the government preference of particular Buddhist organizations or sects over others. For example, some Buddhist

assimilated what they considered the best of Chinese culture. The Chinese teachers, some of whom were administrators, were accompanied by Confucian scholars, Buddhist masters, Taoist wanderers and I-Ching thinkers-diviners. All of these religious influences persist in Vietnam today, as well as the religions introduced in later generations, including Hinduism and Islam from India, and Christianity from Europe and America.

Church and state: As in other societies, religion and politics have never been far removed from one another in society.

Left, outside Thien Mu Pagoda, Hue. **Above**, Mac Cuu Temple, in the Mekong Delta's Ha Tien.

monks are loyal to a rival sect that existed in South Vietnam before the end of the war, but which was then outlawed by the Communists when they installed their own state church. Some monks and lay people associated with that outlawed sect were arrested and imprisoned, not for religious reasons, authorities say, but because they attempted to organize anti-government movements under the guise of helping flood victims.

There is little evidence that the outlawed Buddhist organization has much of a following in Vietnam. But the arrests give ammunition to human rights organizations, and to anti-communist Vietnamese living overseas.

Like the Emperor Minh Mang's anti-Catholic policies and the southern President Ngo Dinh Diem's jailing of Buddhists in earlier years, crackdowns today on dissident Buddhists would only call attention to them and turn them into symbols of repression.

Confucianism: As an ideology, Confucianism has endured longer than any other belief system, in both the East and West, and it has crossed many national borders into all parts of the world. It is based on the teachings of Confucius, born around 550 BC and who lived at a time of great political turmoil. As a teacher and unsolicited adviser to kings, he compiled sets of ideas on relationships between ruler and subject, parents and chil-

in theory open to anyone except actors and women. Many, however, learned Confucianism at home from their parents. The examinations, which also included knowledge of Buddhism, Taoism or Tan Giao, were extremely competitive. From 1075 to 1919 – more than 800 years – just slightly over 2,000 doctorate degrees were granted.

Those who earned their degrees received a hat and tunic from the emperor, and were welcomed home with great pomp and ceremony by the entire population. Those who failed went quietly home to their villages and earned their living as teachers. In this way, villagers were introduced to Confucianism.

For over 2,000 years, Confucianism has

dren, husband and wife, student and teacher.

Confucius was more of a moral and ethical guide than a spiritual leader. He refused to discuss life after death, the unseen or the mystical, and he was primarily interested in social order based upon compassion, etiquette, loyalty, knowledge and trust.

Confucianism reached Vietnam through the Chinese over 2,000 years ago. It became the official doctrine of the imperial government examinations, the first of which was held in 1706, and the last in 1919.

The Vietnamese monarchy recruited its high officials according to the results of these competitive examinations, which were

remained a pillar of the Vietnamese moral and spiritual establishment. By the time Vietnam regained its independence from China, it would possess a large number of Vietnamese scholars with almost a millennium of institutional Confucian studies behind them. The Vietnamese imperial dynasties adopted Confucianism because of its ability to sustain a system of social order, but without much repression, and for its code of social mobility based on merit.

Buddhism: Introduced across the sea from India and over land from China, Buddhism extended the question of knowledge from the social order to the general human condition, in an attempt to reach a rational analysis of the problems of life and the way to their solution. The Buddha (563–483 BC) perceived these realities or truths and announced the Four Noble Truths in his Sermon of Benares. Existence is unhappiness; unhappiness is caused by selfish cravings; unhappiness ends when selfish cravings end; selfish cravings can be destroyed. Attaining the last of the truths could be done by following the steps of the eight-fold path: right understanding, right purpose (aspiration), right speech, right conduct, right vocation, right effort, right alertness, right concentration.

"Right" means conforming to the Four Noble Truths. Central to Buddhism is the

namese Buddhist master was sent to the Japanese court to teach Buddhist music. From the 2nd century AD to the 10th century, two popular sects – the A-Ham (Agama) and the Thien (Dhyana in Sanskrit, Zen in Japanese) – peacefully competed for Vietnamese followers and believers.

Gradually Thien prevailed, despite its exacting practice, which requires continual training in self-discipline, and in mastering the "techniques" of breathing, meditation and right concentration.

Thien is one of the many sects of Mahayana Buddhism widely observed in China, Japan, Korea and Vietnam. Less dogmatic than others, it is receptive to the diverse cultural

concept of Brahman, the Absolute origin, the equivalent of the Chinese *tai chi*. Vietnamese have embraced Buddhism for more than 2,000 years; today, it is the predominant spiritual belief. To Vietnamese Buddhists, Brahman represents the unknown and unknowable, the source and embodiment of reality, knowledge and bliss. Vietnamese Buddhism is a fascinating blend of several branches of Buddhism.

More than one thousand years ago, a Viet-

Left, distinctive Tay An Pagoda, Chau Doc; Khmer monk, Mekong Delta. **Above**, religious retreat in the Marble Mountains; Hoi An temple interior.

and social conditions of different countries, and of different eras.

The other branch of Buddhism, the Hinayana or Theravada (found in Sri Lanka, Burma, Thailand, Laos, Cambodia and parts of southern Vietnam), is more orthodox, yet co-exists with Mahayana.

Village worship: In practically every Vietnamese village from north to south, one finds a *chua* (pagoda) and a *dinh* (communal house). The villagers worship Buddha in the chua, which is cared for by resident monks. On the first and fifteenth days of the lunar months, villagers visit the chua, bringing flowers, joss sticks and fruit to pay homage to the Buddha. They also attend services at the pagoda on the evenings of the 14th and 30th days of the month, to repent for wrongs committed and vow to act in the right way.

Buddhist practices at the village level are not exactly those of Zen, which requires guidance by a well-trained master, but rather are a mixture of Zen and Amitabha, commonly called Pure Land, a devotional faith.

It is believed that Amitabha achieved Buddhahood on the express condition that he receive all who sincerely call upon his name at death, and so carry them to the Western Paradise, where they may seek ultimate perfection (Nirvana) under happier auspices than on earth. The concept of the compas-

sionate Bodhisattvas (Bo Tat), who postpone their own entrance to Nirvana through loving concern for the salvation of others, is at the heart of Amitabha. Its practice consists essentially of concentrating the mind through self-absorption and chanting the name of Buddha. Those who practice Pure Land must abstain from killing, stealing, banditry, lying, adultery, wrong speech and intoxicants. Its adherents are expected to recite the name of Amitabha Buddha, the Amitabha Sutra and perform good deeds to gain merit for self and family. They believe that merits accumulated through good deeds will ensure a happy and joyful present life and a safe

delivery to the land of absolute bliss, the Pure Land, after death.

Taoism: *Tao Te Ching,* the Book of the Way and its Power, begins with: "The Tao that can be told is not the eternal Tao." Tao is the highest and most active level of a static consciousness, the general law of the motion of the universe, and of all things. It is both energy and matter, the moment when the contradictory forces of yin and yang fuse in temporary harmony to provide people and things with a sense of direction. In Chinese, it is represented by a character showing a head in a forward position.

An important book of reference for Taoists and Buddhists alike is the *I Ching,* or The Book of Changes. The book uses symbols – simplified and stylized in signs and codes – to integrate a number of separate communication systems into a seemingly "mysterious" whole. It contains 64 triangles and hexagons arranged in broken and unbroken lines, which, along with its basic text, represent "the process of vast and never-ending cosmic change. These endless chains of actions and interaction assemble and divide the myriad objects proceeding from and flowing into *tai chi,* the Still Reality underlying the worlds of form, desire and formlessness". In the Chinese characters for I Ching, the word "I" represents a lizard, perhaps a chameleon.

In villages where Buddhism, Confucianism, animism and other forms and places of worship coexisted, Taoist priests were also made welcome. In these villages, special places of worship known as *dien,* or *tinh,* are found. Introduced to Vietnam at about the same time as Confucianism, Vietnamese Taoism does not have the hierarchy of schools and systems as in China. On the philosophical level, it is expressed in the thoughts and poetry of Confucian and Buddhist intellectuals. However, Taoist priests and their places of worship are found in villages among the common people. At this level, Taoist practices become a maze of superstitions, magic manifestations and mystic healings.

Ancestor worship: Within many Vietnamese homes, and inside all pagodas, one can find an altar dedicated to ancestors. Although many traditional beliefs and superstitions have waned, ancestor worship remains of high moral and social significance within Vietnamese society. On anniversaries of deaths, and on traditional festival days, the relatives of the deceased gather together, with the eldest son of the deceased presiding over the ceremonial offerings of food and incense. Then the entire family visits the grave of the deceased. The ceremony ends with family members prostrating themselves before the altar and burning paper "money," which provides the dead with funds to make their life happier in the other world.

Failing to worship one's ancestors is considered an act of grave filial impiety that condemns the ancestors to a life of hellish wandering, subsisting on charity.

Christianity: To this universe with its rainbow of institutionalized religions, philosophies and animist beliefs came Catholicism.

ture: the romanization of the written language, and the introduction of modern scientific methods of Western logic.

Many Vietnamese, from all classes of society, converted to Catholicism. This development worried the mandarins and ruling classes, who saw the new religion as a threat to the traditional order of society and its rites, particularly the belief of heaven (*nam giao*) and ancestor worship.

Between 1712 and 1720, a decree forbidding Christianity was enforced in the north. In the south, foreign missionaries were sent packing in 1750 when Christianity was forbidden. Levels of tolerance toward Christianity varied among leaders. Under Emperor

The first Western missionaries set foot in Tonkin, in northern Vietnam, in 1533, followed later in central Vietnam, in 1596. But theirs was only a brief stay. It was not until 1615 that the first permanent Christian missions were founded – in Hoi An, Da Nang and Hanoi – by Portuguese Jesuits.

Unavoidably, the introduction of this organized and culturally foreign religion generated its share of misunderstanding and conflict. Yet Catholicism contributed two major transformations to Vietnamese cul-

Left, tower of Thien Mu Pagoda, Hue. Above, statuettes on an ancestral altar, Hanoi.

Minh Mang (1820–1840), who viewed Christianity as "the perverse religion of Europeans" that "corrupts the heart of men," a decree was enforced forbidding the entry of Christian missionaries to Vietnam. Thieu Tri, who reigned for a short time afterwards, was more tolerant, but his successor, Tu Duc (1848–1883), reinforced the prohibition of Christianity. This period of persecution lasted until the mid 1860s, when a treaty ceded territory and commercial rights to the French and granted freedom for Christians to practice their faith.

Between 1882 and 1884, another wave of persecution hit the Catholic church, and many followers paid with their lives for their faith. The persecution ended in 1885, with the French conquest of the entire country.

Many Catholic orders established themselves throughout the country, establishing convents, schools, colleges, hospitals and seminaries. This religious freedom, however, was checked by World War II and the Japanese occupation of the country. After the signing of the Geneva Agreement in 1954 and the division of the country, over half a million Catholics fled the North for the tolerance of the South.

Since the end of the Vietnam War in 1975 and the unification of Vietnam, the Catholic Church has lived under the written law of the

Socialist Republic of Vietnam, which guarantees the freedom of religion or non-religion under an official Marxist–Leninist ideology. All Catholic schools in the country have been nationalized.

Despite persecution, the church in Vietnam has continued to grow, and today there are an estimated five million practicing Catholics. Churches are crowded on Sundays and on religious holidays.

Recently, the Hanoi government has begun to loosen its restrictions on the Catholic Church. Seminarians have been allowed to be ordained and parishes have been allowed to teach children the faith. However, it still maintains the right to veto who the Vatican can name as a cardinal in Vietnam, in part because the Vatican had earlier attempted to nominate a relative of the former South Vietnam leader, Ngo Dinh Diem. In heavily Catholic areas, such as Dong Nai Province, just north of Ho Chi Minh City, the countryside is dotted with churches in the midst of a rebuilding frenzy.

American Protestant missionaries began work in the Mekong Delta area from the beginning of the 1900s. Their evangelistic efforts, however, were concentrated mainly with the ethnic minority groups living in the high plateaus of central Vietnam; in fact, today, minorities make up the majority of the Protestants in the country. Many Protestant church leaders were imprisoned after reunification. Yet despite restrictions, Protestantism continues to grow, although with a much smaller presence than its Roman Catholic counterpart.

Islam: Vietnam's small Muslim community consists mainly of ethnic Khmers and Chams. A 10th-century stele inscribed in Arabic, found near the central coastal town of Phan Rang, provides the earliest record of Islam's presence in Vietnam.

Although the Chams consider themselves Muslim, their religious practices are not fully Islamic. They do not make the pilgrimage to Mecca; although they do not eat pork, they do drink alcohol; they pray only on Fridays, celebrate Ramadan for only three days, and their rituals co-exist with animistic and Hindu-based worship.

Hinduism: Vietnam's Hindus make up a tiny percentage of the population. The Kingdom of Champa was greatly influenced by Hinduism, still practiced by the Cham community today. The ancient Hindu god-king Shiva, represented in the phallic form of linga, appears in early Cham religious sanctuaries, such as the first temple built at My Son in the 4th century. The influence of Indian art, with representations of the Hindu gods Brahma and Vishnu, is apparent in Cham architecture and sculpture.

The Hinduism practiced today in Vietnam, like Islam, is an adaptation of the original form that reached Vietnam from India at a very early date.

<u>Above</u>, Muslim men in the south. <u>Right</u>, interior of the Hue cathedral.

The Cao Dai sect began when Ngo Van Chieu, an obscure official in the French colonial administration, received a message from a "superior spirit" during a seance in 1919, telling him of his future religious vocation and urging him to look hard for the *dao,* or the Way. In 1921, a "superior spirit" revealed itself to him as Cao Dai, meaning literally, High Terrace, or Supreme Being.

A few years later, in 1926, Cao Daism was officially recognized by the French colonial administration.

Cao Daism attempted to bring all existing faiths in Vietnam under one single supreme creator, or Cao Dai, beginning first with three major religions – Buddhism, Taoism, Confucianism – and later Christianity, Islam, and other doctrines and beliefs.

Victor Hugo, Sun Yat Sen, Napoleon Bonaparte, Joan of Arc, Louis Pasteur and even Winston Churchill are among the host of figures revered by Cao Daism.

The followers fall into three groups: the religious order who observe strict rules of chastity, simplicity and vegetarianism; mediums, a group of twelve individuals who receive messages from the spirits; and the faithful, the followers who obey the directives of the religious order.

The sect's highest authority is a pope, and religious practices take the form of prayers four times daily in front of the altar of the supreme being. This can be an elevated table at one end of the main room in the home. In the temples, the altar consists of a paper globe painted with Cao Dai's symbol – an eye surrounded by sun rays. Statues of Buddha, Confucius, Lao Tsu, saints and deities are placed on the altar around a spherical glass symbolizing the Primordial Principle.

Cao Daism's pope, administration and holy see are found in the village of Long Than, in Tay Ninh Province, 85 kilometers (50 mi) northwest of Saigon.

Its ornate cathedral, described as the "Disney-like fantasia of the East" by Graham Greene, was built in 1927. Its exotic architecture reflects the influences of an assortment of faiths and cultures. Statues of Jesus, Confucius, Buddha, Brahma, Siva and Vishnu dominate the nave of the cathedral,

as do symbols of clairvoyance, human fraternity, and a little mysticism.

Cao Daism appealed to the peasants, with entire village communities becoming followers. In the early 1930s, its followers numbered somewhat over one million.

By the beginning of World War II, Cao Daism had become a "state within a state" and a target of French repression. The French tried to transform those who were enemies into allies during the first Indochina war, arming the Cao Dai with the hope of using

them against the Viet Minh. When President Ngo Dinh Diem came to power after 1954, he signed a *modus vivendi* with the Cao Dai forces. But it wasn't long before conflict arose between President Diem and the Cao Dai pope, who then fled to Cambodia, where he died in 1958.

Diem's efforts to build a national army and unify all the armed religious organizations under his command in South Vietnam met with resistance. But Gen. Trinh Minh The, the chief of staff at the time – and a member of the Cao Dai – was persuaded by the Americans to support President Diem in his fight against communism.

Trinh Minh The, who was loved and admired by his soldiers for his courage and austerity, fought together with Diem and defeated the other armed religious sects. During a military engagement, he was killed. Some believe he was assassinated on orders from Ngo Dinh Nhu, Diem's brother and political adviser, who viewed the Cao Dai general as a rival. The truth will never be known, as both Diem and his brother were murdered by Diem's rebellious officers during the 1963 coup d'etat.

lage, where one night during a violent storm, he went into a trance and emerged from it proclaiming himself founder of Phat Giao Hoa Hao – Buddhist Hoa Hao – meaning Peace and Kindness.

Unlike Cao Dai, Hoa Hao avoids glamorous and complicated ceremonies in favor of a return through prayer, meditation and fasting to early Buddhism's essential purity and simplicity. No temple was built, no religious hierarchy was set up. Yet the Hoa Hao, a variant of Buddhism, attracted about one

Today, there are no reliable statistics available, but the Cao Dai faith still has many followers in southern Vietnam.

Hoa Hao – return to purity: Like the Cao Dai, the Hoa Hao sect was created in the south of Vietnam. Its founder, Huynh Phu So, had suffered from a mysterious, incurable illness as a young man. Believed by his father to be possessed, he was sent to a mountain pagoda. Regaining his health, he returned to his vil-

Left, the ubiquitous eye above the altar, inside the Cao Dai cathedral, in the province of Tay Ninh. **Above**, the unique, and colorful, exterior of the cathedral.

million followers after only a few years.

They called their leader Phat Song, or Living Buddha. Phat Song was soon caught up in the political climate of the time, opposing both the communists and the French (while earlier, being aided by the Japanese secret police). By the late 1960s, many disillusioned nationalist intellectuals from urban areas had joined the Hoa Hao.

The rise and fall of the Hoa Hao followed a similar path to that of the Cao Dai, from revelation to evangelism, then into politics and armed struggle. After compromise, cooperation and confrontation, it was annihilated as a political and military force.

Tet is *the* occasion that unites the Vietnamese people, who devote their creative energy and resources preparing for it. Tet is, in fact, Vietnam's most important festival.

The word "tet" is a distortion of *tiet,* meaning festival. The full name, Tet Nguyen Dan, or Festival of the First Morning of the Year, refers to the beginning of the lunar year, which falls between the winter solstice and spring equinox. The lunar calendar is divided into twelve months of either 29 or 30 days, but every four years, in order to catch up with the solar calendar, there is a leap month. Due to this discrepancy between the two calendars, Tet does not fall on the same day every year in the solar calendar.

Of hearts and minds: Tet is the only time of the year when the usually discreet Vietnamese society truly opens its heart, mind and cooking skills for all to see. Embodied in both its ceremony and essence is the whole spectrum of Vietnamese mythology, and the entire notion of one's place within the family, with one's ancestors, and with the universe in general. It is a fascinating mixture of Buddhism, Taoism, and Confucianism, the three currents of religion that have blended with the original Vietnamese animistic beliefs and ancestor worship.

Under imperial Vietnam, Tet was observed by everyone – emperors and commoners alike. During the Ly Dynasty of the 11th to 13th centuries, the emperor would watch the annual boat race up the Red River as his imperial galleon glided southward to Hanoi. He would end the day by offering Buddhist rites at the seven-storied tower of the Doan Mon (Gate of Grandeur), followed by dinner with his court, counselors and the famous poets and scholars of the land.

The form changed somewhat during the Tran Dynasty (13th to 15th centuries), when the dawn of new year would find the emperor at the Vinh Tho Dien (Palace of Fame and Longevity) receiving greetings from the crown prince and mandarins.

On the eve of the new year, the emperor paid respects to his ancestors at the Truong Xuan Cung (Palace of Eternal Spring). These same rituals were observed by all Vietnamese monarchs until 1945, when the last emperor, Bao Dai of the Nguyen Dynasty (1802–1945), abdicated in favor of the presidency of Ho Chi Minh.

Tet rites begin a week before the lunar New Year's Day, but preparations actually start weeks before that. On the 23rd day of the 12th month, a ceremony is held in homes in honor of the Tao Quan (gods of the hearth), with fresh fruit, cooked food, paper models of a stork, a horse, a car, a pair of mandarin boots and a ceremonial dress (but no pants) offered to the Tao Quan. The Vietnamese,

with their inborn sense of humor and ridicule of the powerful, believe, or at least claim to, that the Tao Quan burnt their pants by staying too close to the kitchen. With or without pants, this is the time for the gods to return to the Kingdom of Heaven and present their annual report on the state of earthly matters and the individual family to the Emperor of Jade, before returning once again to earth on New Year's Eve.

The legend behind the Tao Quan originates from the tragic story of a woodcutter and his wife. They lived modestly but happily together, but lost their happiness as time went by and the marriage remained childless. The husband became unhappy; he began to drink too much and mistreated his wife. She, unable to stand it any longer, deserted him and married a hunter in the neighboring village.

Lonely and repentant, the woodcutter one day decided to pay her a visit and apologize, but soon after his arrival in the neighboring village, the hunter returned. To avoid any misunderstanding, the woman hid her former husband in a small thatched barn near the kitchen. The hunter was smoking his game in

long journey to Heaven, the Vietnamese believe their home has been left without protection and so look for ways to guard themselves against an invasion of bad spirits. They erect a *cay neu* (signal tree), a very high bamboo pole with a *khanh,* a sonorous clay tablet with a piece of yellow cloth attached to the top, in front of the home. The origins of this custom are revealed in a story that goes back to the birth of the Vietnamese nation, when the Vietnamese were constantly threatened by malevolent spirits. Lord Bud-

the kitchen when a spark from the fire set the small barn ablaze. The distraught woman raced to the barn to save her former husband; the hunter followed suit in an attempt to save his wife, and all three perished in the fire.

Deeply touched by such devotion, the Jade Emperor in Heaven made them gods. He assigned them the duty of watching over the welfare of people on earth from the vantage point of the kitchen, where, to this day, they are revered as the gods of the home's hearth.

When Tao Quan takes his annual week-

Cheerfully-masked roadside dancers in Can Tho, in the heart of the Mekong Delta.

dha took compassion on them and one day descended from Nirvana to visit them. He was immediately surrounded by all kinds of devils, with whom he struck up a deal for a small piece of land to be in exchange for precious stones, gold and silver, which he laid before them. When the devils asked him the size of the piece of land he had in mind, Buddha told them it would be as large as his gown. The devils agreed to this, thinking they had struck a very good deal, but when Lord Buddha dropped his gown it spread as far and wide as the territory of Vietnam. The devils were furious, but the deal had been made. Lord Buddha then advised the Vietnamese: "At the end of the year, when you invite your ancestors to your home for Tet, the devils may mingle with them. You must erect a high bamboo pole flying my emblem on a piece of cloth in front of your house to prevent the devils from coming to disturb you while you are enjoying Tet and your union with your ancestors." The custom of erecting a cay neu in front of the house during Tet is still observed in parts of the countryside, but has somewhat vanished from Vietnam's urban areas.

With the malevolent spirits frightened way by the cay neu, the Vietnamese set their minds to things of the material sort and prepare the *banh chung,* Tet's traditional

glutinous rice cakes stuffed with pork, fat, beans and dry onion.

Another indispensable feature, even for the poorest families, is a branch of peach tree blossom, the *cahn dao.* During Tet, branches of peach blossom can cost more than a day's average wages. In southern and central Vietnam, the peach blossom is replaced by *canh mai,* a branch of yellow apricot blossoms.

For maximum security against any possible intrusion by demons and bad spirits, the Vietnamese traditionally lit firecrackers to thwart the notorious devils Na A and his terrible wife, who cannot bear noise and light. In recent years, however, a profusion

of firecrackers had turned the cities and countryside into a battle zone. So the government, in 1995, outlawed firecrackers. Ingenious Vietnamese found a way to keep the demons away, however, with tape-recordings of firecracker noise.

After all these precautions have been taken, the Vietnamese calmly await the arrival of spring. The first day of Tet is always reserved for the worship of ancestors, who are ceremoniously welcomed back from heaven on New Year's Eve during the Giao Thua, the transition between the old and new year. Elaborately-prepared food offerings, together with the perfume of burning sandalwood, incense and *thai tien,* a type of fragrant white narcissus that blooms during Tet, await the ancestors at the altar. At midnight on the last day of the old year, all human problems, earthly worries, war, revolution, political intrigue and commercial transactions are left behind. A temporary general truce is declared between human beings and spirits. All acts performed, all events – whether favorable or unfavorable – that take place on the first day of Tet, are believed to effect the course of one's life for the year ahead.

The first sound heard in the new year is most important (disregarding the firecracker recordings). A cock crow signals hard work and bad harvest. The lowing of a buffalo heralds a year of sweat and toil, and a dog barking signifies a year of confidence and trust. Worst of all is the cry of an owl, a warning of coming epidemic and calamity, a woe for the entire community. The first visitor to the home has to be a man of virtue. This can be arranged before Tet in a discreet manner, but others will leave home at midnight and return a minute later.

One of the most important elements in celebrating Tet are *cau doi,* parallel sentences written in traditional black Chinese characters on red paper in Vietnamese *nom* characters, or romanized Vietnamese letters arranged to look like Chinese calligraphy. These are hung in the center of the home.

In many families, after gifts of money wrapped in red paper are exchanged, tradition requires that the father read his children's *tu vi,* or horoscope, hoping to assure that the new year is auspicious.

Left, firecrackers were banned in 1995. **Right**, an incense offering at a Buddhist altar.

According to the wise teacher Confucius, "Personal cultivation begins with poetry, is made firm by the rule of decorum and is perfected by music."

Before Western influences penetrated Asia, music had long played an integral part in religious ceremonies, but was not used for public entertainment.

The Dong Son drums, which depict dancers performing to the accompaniment of musical instruments, and the lithophone of Ndut Lien Krat, in the southern highlands of Vietnam, testify to the importance of musical and dance traditions in Vietnam since the Bronze Age. Along with the other arts, music received its share of Chinese influence over the years. It was also influenced by the music of the Hindu kingdom of Champa, in the south, which Vietnam gradually absorbed during its long southward march.

Court music had its beginnings during the Le Dynasty (1428–1788), when a Vietnamese mandarin was asked to establish a system of court music, following that of the Ming Dynasty in China.

He organized the following categories of music, each to be played at different religious and social occasions: *giao nhac,* played as an offering at the Esplanade of Heaven during the Emperor's triennial celebration of the Cult of Heaven; *mieu nhac,* played during ceremonies at the Court of Literature in honor of Confucius, and at anniversary commemorations for deceased emperors; *ngu tu nhac,* music of the Five Sacrifices; *cuu nhat giao trung nhac,* music for helping the sun and moon during an eclipse; *dai trieu nhac,* music for ordinary audiences; *dai yen cuu tau nhac,* music for large banquets; and, finally, *cung trung chi nhac,* palace music.

Throughout the 15th to 18th centuries, Vietnamese leaders took great interest in unifying the diverse orchestrations. These included complete orchestras, represented, for example, by the *phuong bat am,* a popular ensemble of eight timbrels, and various other theatrical orchestras.

Preceding pages: Khai Ninh's tomb, Hue; performers in traditional costumes. Left, backstage, Ho Chi Minh City. Above, dancer.

Ceremonial and religious music: In the coastal provinces of central Vietnam, songs known as *hat ba trao* – songs for worshipping the ocean spirits – are a popular tradition. One, called the *hat chau van,* is an incantation used in hypnotizing a person through musical tunes, rhythms and lyrics.

Buddhist music falls into two styles, the *tan* or melismatic chant, and the *tung,* or sutra prayers. The tan is accompanied by a string and percussion orchestra in syncopated rhythm, while the tung is a chant on

knowledge and enlightenment, and is recited by a monk and punctuated by strokes on a wooden slit drum.

Chamber music, performed by small instrumental ensembles for selected audiences of intellectuals, was confined to major cities. The most popular, known as *a dao,* takes its name from a historical story from the 15th century, at the time of the Ming invasion from China.

During the military struggle, all manner of weapons were used, including, on one occasion, a combination of female beauty and music. A country girl from Dao village in Hai Hung province, in northern Vietnam,

WATER PUPPETS

The Red River Delta of northern Vietnam is a low-lying plain that would be submerged in water during the rainy season every year if not for a vast series of dikes, the 7,000 kilometers (4,500 mi) of levees that criss-cross the rice paddies and villages.

"If not for the dikes," says one engineer, "all of northern Vietnam would disappear." Nature, it would seem, has long swamped the Delta. The dikes were first built out of soil 1,000 years ago. Prior to that time, during the Ly Dynasty of the 11th century, the Red River would swell each year like clockwork, spill over its banks and flood much of the region.

nal house. Their techniques were closely guarded secrets. Even now, some elderly water puppet masters are reluctant to pass on their secrets to younger generations. But the fear that the art will die out completely has persuaded some of the masters to teach apprentices.

Today, there are just a few troupes in Vietnam, with two in Hanoi. Many of the northern provinces have one troupe that tours villages.

A performance usually consists of about 12 acts, each of them telling a mythological story about Vietnam and its history. Traditional musicians provide background music. One story, for example, tells the story of the tortoise that lived in Hanoi's Hoan Kiem Lake and supposedly emerged from the depths to provide the good King Ly Thai Tho with the sword he needed to fight off Chinese invaders. Other stories detail

There is a point in this narrative of the Red River's history: the annual flooding of the lowlands inspired a form of entertainment to be found only in Vietnam, the water puppets.

"The farmers did not know what to do during the flood season, so they created this form of art," explained the artistic director of Hanoi's leading puppetry troupe, which travels the globe exporting this bit of Vietnamese culture.

Water puppetry combines Vietnamese love for mythology with the fierce nationalistic pride that is encouraged in the country.

The puppeteers stand behind a screen in water up to their waists, controlling the puppets movements with long bamboo poles. Centuries ago, every village would have a troupe that would perform in a pond in front of the *dinh,* or commu-

village life: planting and harvesting the rice crop, fishing, boat races.

The troupes tinker not at all with the traditional stories. Some have suggested they mechanize the puppets. For one thing, they are heavy, some weighing 20 kilograms and requiring four people to maneuver. For another, the puppets usually can perform just one movement at a time. Directors have toyed with the idea of adding more contemporary stories to the repertoire. But traditionalists have resisted such changes, so far.

And with increasingly-diverse entertainment available, especially to the young – television, video, karaoke, dancing – the future of the water puppets in none all too certain, given the wave of more contemporary amusements. ∎

used her charm, together with dance, song and music, to distract the Ming soldiers and so gain precious time to allow her countrymen to organize a guerilla attack. The Hat A Dao, the Song of the Lady from the Dao village, was composed by a group of mandarin scholars to commemorate the heroine's beauty, talent and patriotism.

Essentially, Hat A Dao is sung poetry performed at the home of a songstress. The audience takes famous poems and composes verses themselves, all sung to rhythmic accompaniment of the *phach,* a bamboo instrument beaten with two wooden sticks, and the *dan day,* a long-necked lute with three strings. The audience critiques by beating a drum.

the *dieu kach,* or northern tune, with its Chinese influence, and the *dieu nam,* or southern tune, with the slower tempo and sentimentality of the Cham culture.

Folk music takes the form of tunes sung and composed by villagers, illustrating their life in the countryside. This music falls into several broad categories: lullabies, known as *hat run* in the north, *ru em* in the center, and *au o* in the south; work songs, or *ho;* and the eternal love songs, *ly.*

There are ho and ly songs for each region, and for each season, every type of work and every leisure activity.

Ho refers to calling people to work in a rising and prolonged voice. A lead singer

By the beginning of the 20th century, the Hat A Dao had gradually became a refuge for pleasure rather than a center for song and poetry. Its counterparts, although lacking the same significance, include the *ca hue,* music-song of Hue, and the *dan tai tu,* music of the amateurs in southern Vietnam.

Indeed, each region of Vietnam has its own musical tradition, as do the country's 50-plus ethnic minorities. But generally, Vietnamese music falls into two basic groups:

Left, water-puppet performance, Hanoi. **Above**, traditional bamboo instruments at Hanoi Conservatory of Music.

begins the chant, which is then taken up by others in the working party. The most cherished of the ho is one called Ho Mia Nhi, usually sung by young boatwomen on the Perfume River, in Hue. Structured like a poem, this ho's four lines express deep thoughts and feelings, suitable for a river's transient moods.

Theater: In Vietnam, theater embraces all the major forms. The oldest recorded form of performance is the Tro He, a farce created by Lieu Thu Tam under the Tien Le Dynasty (980–1009).

During the Tran Dynasty (1225–1400), two new types of theater emerged, the *hat giau mat,* or masked performances, and the *hat coi tran,* or coat-less performances.

Today's theater, a blend of court theater, folk performances and foreign influence, includes three types of performances: *cheo, hat tuong* and *cai luong.*

Cheo is as old as the Vietnamese nation itself. The word cheo is a distortion of *tieu,* the Chinese word for laughter. Cheo's origins can be found in the religious and social activities depicted on the engravings of Bronze Age drums and urns. Developed from animistic customs, mime, dance, song, prayers and poetry, cheo reached its present form by the 10th century.

Performances usually are staged in front of

member of the audience to register approval; however, when the performance is poor, then the drum's wooden barrel is struck.

The length of a performance is determined by how much the audience has paid, and this is represented by a burning incense stick. When approval is marked by the drum, incense tapers are laid in a pile in honor of the player, lengthening, in turn, the performance – and the performer's fee.

The audience knows every detail of cheo, whose strict rules were set as early as 1500. Throughout a performance, the players explain events, stop to question the audience and take replies. Melodies familiar to everyone symbolize certain events: marriage, birth,

a village community house or Buddhist pagoda. The troupe's equipment is carried from village to village in a single box, which also serves as a unique part of the stage setting, representing whatever is required of it. Cheo plays provide a framework within which the players improvise. The troupe is judged according to its ability to vary and renew a familiar theme. The musicians sit to the right of the stage area with their drums, gongs, rattles, stringed instruments and a flute. These are not the only sounds to be heard.

To start the play, someone from the audience beats a large drum. When a performer sings well, this drum will be beaten by a

death. And all gestures, including movements of the eyes and mouth, have a specific meaning. A chorus and a clown express emotional highpoints. The clown, wearing black makeup, interrupts the players to comment on their lies and tricks, make fun of them and praise their good deeds. The audience often stops a player to demand a replay of an interesting or intriguing detail. Alert, critical and interested, audience members participate fully in this most democratic form of popular theater.

Essentially anti-establishment, it indirectly educates the peasants how to expose the injustices of those in power. Under some dynasties, cheo was forbidden and its performers prosecuted.

Unlike hat cheo, which is uniquely Vietnamese, hat tuong arrived from China in the 13th century, under the Tran Dynasty after the defeat of Mongol invaders. Among the war prisoners was a master of Chinese theater, Ly Nguyen Cat, who later became a Vietnamese citizen and taught Chinese drama to the Vietnamese court.

From the Chinese came red, rosy and black face makeup, ceremonial costumes, masks, stylized gestures and speeches, the majestic percussion and wind instrument music, and the emphasis on the heroic and the noble.

Hat tuong begins with a song introducing

tuong, although a copy of Chinese drama, was adapted to the Vietnamese character. Women replaced men in the female roles, and the orchestra was enlarged, incorporating Indian influences from the Cham culture. Today, hat tuong's orchestra includes cymbals, gongs, drums, tambourines, flutes and an arsenal of stringed instruments: the *dan nguyet,* a moon shaped lute; the *dan nhi,* a violin with a high register played by drawing two strings tight over a drum skin; the *thap luc,* a zither-like instrument with 16 strings plucked with the fingers; and the *dan bau,* whose single string, stretched over a long lacquered sound box, is both bowed and plucked to produce a variety of vibrato ef-

the drama's story line. Each player describes his character and role. The stage is nearly empty, except for special props representing the landscape: a branch for a forest, a painted wheel for a cart. The action, always dramatic, is guided by Confucian moral virtues and concepts, for example, loyalty to kings and devotion to parents. The orchestra sits at the side of the stage, accompanying not only the singing but also details of the activity and movement on stage.

In typical Vietnamese fashion, the hat

Left, smoking Dragon Dance Troupe. **Above**, stoned Cham dancers, Da Nang.

fects, and long resonances of great subtlety. The result is truly exquisite.

Hat tuong began as a theater for the elite. It allows criticism and flexibility, but in the end it is still very much a theater for the moral and social status quo.

Cai luong, or renovated theater, made its first appearance in the southern part of Vietnam in 1920. It interprets classical Chinese stories in a more accessible style. Influenced by the European stage, cai luong has evolved into its present spoken drama form, abandoning the cumbersome epic style in favor of shorter acts, emotional and psychological play and free dialogue.

Writers and poets have always occupied a place of high esteem in Vietnamese society. Well acquainted with struggle and hardship over the centuries, Vietnamese find their rich literary heritage – which reveals the spirit of the Vietnamese, as a nation and as individuals – a source of comfort, hope and inspiration.

A seemingly endless wealth of oral story-telling traditions, consisting of myths, songs, legends, folk and fairy tales, constitutes Vietnam's most ancient literature. Later, as the etnamese literature was soon enriched with new ideas of Western thought and culture. Indeed, Vietnamese literary prose and poetry was influenced by European literature, which introduced new ways of expressing ideas in novel ways – and, too, reflected the rising sentiment of nationalism.

During the 20th-century wars for Vietnamese independence from outside powers, northern writers limited themselves mostly to stories meant to unify the people and to inspire the population during difficult times.

society developed, scholars, Buddhist bonzes, kings and court ministers – many of whom were also talented writers and poets – wrote down their thoughts and epics using adopted Chinese characters (*chu nho*). This literature was greatly influenced by Confucian and Buddhist thought.

Even more poems and literary works were undertaken with the advent of *chu nom,* a complicated script based on chu nho. However, the Vietnamese found the romanized alphabet, introduced by foreign missionaries, to be a more accessible means of communicating, rather than the forboding need to use thousands of different ideograms. Vi- Communist Party cadres strictly controlled publishing after the end of the war, as well, and even today, government censors must approve writings before publication.

However, in recent years, control has been loosened somewhat. The publication in the early 1990s of *The Sorrow of War,* by a Vietnam War veteran from the North under the pseudonym of Bao Ninh, was the first war novel to confront the gruesome realities of war and the psychological effects upon surviving soldiers. Another writer, Duong Thu Huong, has had her works translated, and her writing includes thinly-veiled criticism of government and party officials. For a time, she was imprisoned for crimes against the socialist state.

Today, writers with reputations for writing critically are presumed to be under close surveillance. Despite the appearance of a new period of openness, Party leaders have warned at recent gatherings of writers that they must focus on ideas that are of a benefit to the nation. As one literary standard-bearer says: "We can write about problems, about negative things in society. But we must also finish with optimism." An improved econ-

time, whether it be a cyclo driver waiting for a customer, a laborer from the country taking a tea break or students at a cafe.

There are fewer writers now, but a professor of literature thinks this is a positive development in the long run. "We get rid of a lot of bad writers. Only the good ones can survive," he says. "Now people have other ways to use their creativity. Maybe instead of trying to write, they become good traders or businessmen. That is better for them and better for the country."

omy and increased contact with the outside world has meant that interest in literature, always intense in Vietnam, has declined somewhat. Today, there are television, translations of foreign works (American writer Sydney Sheldon is popular), and for children, comic books. (Kids are addicted to Japan's Doremon). Still, for such an impoverished country, the literacy rate is high, estimated to be above 90 percent, and it is not unusual to find people reading in their spare

Poetry: Above all else, poetry dominates the Vietnamese arts. The language of Vietnam is a natural tool for poetry, as each of its syllables can be pronounced in six tones to convey six meanings. By simply combining these tones and modulating certain words, a sentence turns into a verse and plain speech becomes a song. Another group of Vietnamese words made up of repeated syllables can cast a discreet shade on the meaning of words, conjuring up a particular color, movement, attitude or mood.

Vietnamese poetry falls into two major categories: *ca dao,* a popular folk song, oral in origin but collected and transcribed in

Left, author of *The Sorrow of War*. **Above**, those who passed the exams became men of letters and members of officialdom.

written form; and *tho van,* literary poetry written by kings, scholars, Buddhist monks, mandarins, Taoist recluses, dissidents, feminists, revolutionaries – even Marxists.

Poetry has become such an important medium of communication that even present-day political slogans must be written in verse to be effective.

Tale of Kieu: Nearly every Vietnamese reads and remembers a few chapters of a 3,254-verse story published 200 years ago called *The Tale of Kieu.* Pupils begin studying it in the sixth grade.

Kieu was written by one of Vietnam's most esteemed forefathers, Nguyen Du, and is now considered the cultural bible and

heart and mind of their nation. To them, its author, Nguyen Du, is the faithful interpreter of their hopes, and, too, the discreet confidant of their misfortunes.

Born in the village of Nghi Xuan, in northern Vietnam's Ha Tinh Province, Nguyen Du came from an old aristocratic family of mandarins and scholars. His father was prime minister in the Thang Long (now Hanoi) court of Emperor Le. He grew up in a country, under the nominal rule of the Le Dynasty, torn by civil war. When he was 24, the Le Dynasty, which his family had faithfully served for generations, was overthrown by the peasant-based Tay Son revolution.

After Gia Long, a descendant of the south-

window to the soul of the Vietnamese people. One may wonder how *Kieu* came to occupy its special position in Vietnamese literature. Why is the complex tale of a woman's personal misfortunes regarded by a whole people as the perfect expression of their essential nature, of their national soul? After all, the protagonist Kieu is a prostitute. "This shows," explains a Hanoi writer and critic, "how important the simple people are to Vietnamese. Our most important literary figure is not a king, not a warrior, not a hero, but a simple prostitute."

Regardless of age, gender, geography or ideology, to the Vietnamese the epic is the

ern Nguyen warlords, defeated the Tay Son brothers and was declared emperor, Nguyen Du became an official of several northern provinces, distinguishing himself as an honest and able administrator. In 1806, at the age of 41, he was summoned to the capital of Hue to serve as high chancellor.

Having reunited Vietnam, Gia Long faced the problem of national security, foremost of which meant establishing diplomatic relations with China. All Vietnamese envoys to China were chosen from the cream of Vietnamese *literati,* as it was by intellectual, rather than military, might that Vietnam sought to impress China. So Nguyen Du, already recognized as a great poet, was a natural choice to be emissary. After five years in China, he returned and devoted most of his time to literary pursuits until his 1820 death at the age of 53. A literary school founded in 1979 to train writers was named after Nguyen Du, over the objections of government officials who preferred to name the school after a war hero.

What makes *Kieu* as relevant today as it was two centuries ago is Nguyen Du's ability and courage to lay bare the whole spectrum of society. The vices and virtues, ugliness and beauty, nobility and trickery, all entangled in a seemingly hopeless tragic comedy, reflect the true face of Vietnam. The prosti-

time, they do not understand why this tai, which has helped them win their independence against formidable foreign invasions and enabled them to develop a respectable culture and civilization, has failed to bring them lasting peace and enduring prosperity.

Unable to solve this paradox, most believe they are *oan,* a word meaning wronged and which appears throughout *Kieu.*

The Vietnamese, like Kieu, see themselves as victims, punished for crimes they are not aware that they have committed. (One might speculate that when the United States bombed Vietnam under the guise of stopping the spread of communism, peasants probably wondered why they, and not Moscow, re-

tute Kieu also personifies the inherent contradiction faced by the Vietnamese.

"Within the span of a hundred years of human existence, what a bitter struggle is waged between talent and fate," lament the opening lines. And, in the conclusion, Nguyen Du writes, "When one is endowed with talent, do not rely upon it".

Deep in their hearts and behind their gracious modesty, the Vietnamese know they are not lacking in talent, *tai.* At the same

Left, gateway to the Temple of Literature, in Hanoi. **Above**, a calligrapher working on Chinese characters, Mekong Delta.

ceived the brunt of the firepower.)

Even Vietnamese who fled their country after the war ended in the 1970s turn to the tales of Kieu for comfort, especially in the cultural isolation of a new land and language. Huynh Sanh Thong, a Vietnamese scholar at Yale University who translated *Kieu* into English, wrote in his introduction that immigrants "know most of its lines by heart, and when they recite them out loud, they speak their mother tongue at its finest. To the extent that the poem implies something at the very core of the Vietnamese experience, it addresses them intimately as victims, as refugees, as survivors."

"Art" in Vietnamese is *my thuat,* which literally translated means "beauty skill." Vietnam's artists use traditional art to communicate their ideas through the mediums of music, poetry, dance, theater, painting, sculpture and even architecture.

Although Vietnam is a civilization some 4,000 years old, the country has no great monument like Cambodia's Angkor Wat. Many of Vietnam's ancient monuments have fallen prey to the ravages of war and the climate, as well as to neglect. However, despite the destructive forces of both nature and war, nothing has succeeded in destroying the vast legacy of art, crafts, architecture, theater and music.

Vietnamese folk art had gone into decline with French colonization at the end of the 19th century. In recent years, attempts have been made to revive it. Two thriving examples are woodcuts and lacquer ware.

Woodcuts: The best examples of this revival are the Tranh Lang Ho village paintings, which are mostly woodcuts. This art form – called Ho village paintings for short – existed from as early as the 11th century, during the Ly Dynasty. It was at first limited to black-and-white prints of the woodcuts, but after the 15th century, color was introduced. In accordance with the craft tradition, whole villages were given solely over to block printing. Many families in Ho village, located in Bach Ninh Province north of Hanoi, are collectively engaged in producing colored prints of traditional themes. The village craftsmen make their own paper and natural colors, and prepare the blocks in variations of classic models depicting good luck signs, historical figures, historical battles, spirits, popular allegories and social commentary.

Good fortune is symbolized by a corpulent pig decorated with garlands, often accompanied by a litter of suckling piglets. A hen surrounded by chicks symbolizes prosperity. The rooster, herald of the dawn, is the symbol of peace and courage. Social criticism is expressed by caricatures of mandarins, represented by croaking frogs and rats marching with drums and trumpets. Warriors are shown together with apes, tigers and other animal spirits, all in splendid colors. These blend humor, optimism and a canny ability to ridicule the corrupt and powerful.

Lacquer: Objects made of lacquered wood have been found in tombs dating from the 3rd and 4th centuries. Today, lacquer (*son mai*) goods, including paintings, screens, boxes, vases, trays and chessboards, are fast becoming a main export item.

Their quality is a result of the meticulous attention given to the preparation of the lacquer, and to the designs of a thousand-

year-old tradition. Two types of lacquer are used. Varnish lacquer is obtained by mixing lacquer resin with *mu* oil, while pumice lacquer, a higher quality and more durable lacquer, is produced by mixing lacquer resin with pine resin. Unlike varnish lacquer, pumice lacquer is rubbed and smoothed in water after painting to bring out a gloss finish.

Lacquer is prepared from the resin of the *cay son,* or lacquer tree, which is collected in the same way as latex. After being stored for a while, the resin is diluted with water, and then the dark brown surface layer known as oil lac is skimmed off. With the addition of various ingredients, this is used for the upper layer of lacquer paintings. This high-quality lacquer is poured into a bamboo or wooden vessel and stirred vigorously with a wooden pestle for eight to ten hours. (If stirred in a plastic or iron vessel, the lacquer turns black.) A small amount of colophony, a resin, is added to render it more elastic and suitable for polishing. Normal paint added to lacquer will also produce a black or grey color.

Special paints are needed for lacquer pictures: cinnabar, which produces various hues of red; pure gold or silver applied as thin

This is followed by a thin layer of cotton fabric or silk, followed by another layer of lacquer. The board is then left in a damp place for two or three days until dry, then coated with another layer of lacquer, a layer of lacquer putty, sawdust and kaolin, which render the board uniformly smooth.

The dried surface is rubbed with wet pumice before another two to four layers of lacquer are applied and left to dry for several days between coats, then painstakingly rubbed for hours. Only after all this prepara-

sheets or strips; blue goache; several kinds of aniline dyes that produce carmine red or green; and the yellow dye obtained from the seeds of hydrangeas. Eggshell fragments yield the purest white color, while fragments of mother-of-pearl, mollusk and snail shell produce a blue or violet sheen.

Lacquer artists painstakingly select and prepare the boards for their pictures. These must be smooth, dry and free of the smallest crack, scratch or imperfection before they are coated with several layers of lacquer.

Left, detail of temple carving. **Above**, the fine detail of inlaid lacquer work.

tion is the board ready for painting.

If the artist uses egg or mollusk shells, he cuts the shape in the upper layers of lacquer covering the fabric, smears the depression with black lacquer, which acts as a glue, and taps the shell into position with a tiny hammer. More lacquer is applied, then tinted with the desired dye.

When this is quite dry, the picture is rubbed down thoroughly to bring out the texture of the shell with its numerous tiny cracks. He will continue rubbing the picture with the palm of his hand until the contours become outlined and the lacquer acquires transparency and sheen.

The Vietnamese have always placed importance on the design and arrangement of buildings and burial sites. Not only are these based upon aesthetics, but architectural decisions must also conform to the advice of geomancers, the specialists still in practice today who consult the stars, lay of the land, and ancient Chinese *feng shui,* then determine the orientation, form and organization of any construction.

The idea is to harmonize building with nature, and this concept gives Vietnamese

The vestiges of Vietnam's oldest capital, Co Loa, with its unique spiraling ramparts, are still visible in Dong Anh district in the suburbs of Hanoi. Like much of ancient architecture, it was destroyed during the thousand years of Chinese colonization that lasted until the 10th century.

Once national independence was regained under the Ly Dynasty in the 11th through 13th centuries, architecture eventually blended Vietnamese art, Chinese influences and Buddhist inspiration. The Quynh Lam

architecture – in fact, most traditional Asian architecture – a unique visual appeal and sense of mystery.

Vietnam's most impressive architecture is seen in its palaces, imperial tombs, temples, pagodas and communal houses. Built of wood, stone and brick, these structures often are decorated beautifully with sculpture and woodcarvings.

Although the tropical climate has made it necessary to restore and rebuild some of these structures several times – very few buildings today remain standing in their original construction – they nonetheless represent ancient architectural styles.

pagoda, whose interior could shelter 1,000 statues of Buddha, and the Bao Thien tower, several dozen meters high, were landmarks of that era. Unfortunately, all that remains today are some stone and wood engravings, ceramics, stone sculptures, statues, pillar bases, bricks, bowls, plates and tea pots.

The dragon, a recurring element in carvings and sculpture, was depicted in this era as winding around in harmonious curves, its body progressively thinning to better reveal its inner energy. (Its later manifestations would reflect uneasiness about the state of the developing civilization.)

In the period that followed (13–15th centuries), artistic expression in architecture became more robust and self-confident. Emphasis was placed on stability and simplicity; greater attention was paid to equilibrium and balance. The Ho Dynasty's stone citadel in Thanh Hoa remains a testament to that period of design.

The dragon of this era no longer spreads out in endless convolutions – its body is now shorter, and its fearsome head has fewer fearsome details.

During the 16th, 17th and 18th centuries,

French Vauban fortified system and institutionalized knowledge acquired over thousands of years of war and defense.

The raw materials used in its construction came from all over the country: strong *lim* wood from Nghe An in the north and Gia Dinh in the south; stone from Thanh Hoa in the north; marble from Quang Nam in the center; bricks and tiles from Bat Trang in the north and from Hue itself. Skilled artisans, workers and decorators, numbering more than 80,000, were drafted from all corners of

the arts expressed a greater degree of creativity and originality. Serious attempts were made to use geomantic principles to harmonize construction with nature. These concepts, with their designs and decorations, were all successfully combined with foreign influences in the grand-scale construction of the Nguyen Dynasty's capital in Hue, from 1802 to 1945. The dynasty's founder, Gia Long, drew his inspiration from several sources – the Chinese capital Beijing, the

Left, the imperial city of Hue, from the south gate. **Above**, the multi-tiered tower at the Thien Mu Pagoda.

the country to participate in this massive and demanding effort.

The Vauban-style Imperial Citadel, which walls off half the town, comprises three concentric enclosures within a square plane: The Thanh Ngoai (External Enclosure), measuring 2,800 meters (9,100 ft) long on each side, is defended by a series of bastions with ten gates along its periphery. The structure is protected in the north, east and west by a large moat; in the south, the Hong Giang (Perfume River) itself serves as a natural defense barrier. Another fortress near the northeast corner is known as the Mang Ca (Fish Operculum) fortress.

The Thanh Noi (Inner Enclosure), measuring 600 meters (2,000 ft) on each side, has no defense installation but is nonetheless encircled by a large moat.

At the heart of the citadel is the T Cam Thanh (Forbidden Purple Enclosure), the private residence of the emperor and his immediate family.

The Citadel's site on the left bank of the Perfume River was chosen with great care. It is situated against the background of the Nui Ngu Binh (Imperial Screen Mountain), which protects it from the winds of the north.

Emperor Thieu Tri, a gifted poet and the third monarch of the Nguyen Dynasty who reigned from 1841 to 1849, explained the

choice of Hue as the nation's capital. He referred to both geomantic and strategic considerations. "It is protected by natural defenses. It stands at the convergence of the forces of allegiance of the cardinal points. In this enclosure of mountains and rivers, ten men can face one hundred and also the world." Scholars agree that Hue's location follows the configurations of the benevolent Thanh Long (Blue Dragon) and the aggressive Bac Ho (White Tiger), the two symbols of the conflicting and harmonizing forces of good and evil that move heaven and earth and regulate human destiny.

Hue's location also was considered to re-spect the free flow of Long Mach (Dragon Veins), which according to geomantic, or *feng shui,* concepts are the inner textures of the earth. Such considerations play a vital role when Vietnamese choose a site for a home or grave.

A geomantic evaluation of part of the Citadel's construction raises concerns, however. The moats, geomantically speaking, may have cut the Long Mach and in turn could bleed the Blue Dragon into white. Should such a geomantic hemorrhage occur, it would leave Vietnam and Hue powerless against the attacks of the angry White Tiger, characterized by floods, wars, revolutions, misery and bloodshed.

Hue is famous for its Imperial Tombs built on the pine-covered hills to the south of the city. Each tomb has its own form of landscaping, architectural style and particular charm, but all share the same general structure: a flagged wall zone in the middle of which stands the stone tomb, a main court, a pavilion housing the stone stele carved with the Emperor's deeds and virtues, a terrace decorated with statues of the Emperor's ministers, elephants and horses, and a high circular wall surrounding the Imperial tomb. Gia Long's mausoleum, considered the most majestic and dignified, exudes an aura of strength, stability and discipline.

The burial sites of Vietnam's kings, leaders, heroes and heroines remain for the most part intact despite the devastation of war.

Until recently, Vietnamese sculpture was mainly of a religious nature, as seen in the wood and stone sculptures decorated with symbolic religious motifs. They complement Vietnam's places of worship in a style that has changed little with time.

The best examples of traditional sculpture can be seen in the temples and pagodas, whose elaborately carved altars abound with wooden lacquered statues of man and animals, representing mythology and history. The village *dinh,* or communal house, in each village constitutes not only a meeting place for the people, but also a showcase for artisans. The carved wooden beams and pillars of the communal houses, pagodas and temples testify to the skills of anonymous craftsmen of a bygone era.

Above, temple courtyard, Ho Chi Minh City.
Right, an ancient Cham tower, near Cam Ranh.

For the sociable Vietnamese, a well-stocked dining table is an important symbol of hospitality, and visitors to any home, from Can Tho in the Mekong Delta to Hanoi in the north, will be overwhelmed with generosity from the kitchen pantry. In the poorest villages where people subsist mainly on rice, people will scrape together whatever they have to give to their guests.

The cuisine itself varies greatly by region. Even dishes that are staples throughout Vietnam are prepared differently in the north, center and south. Vietnam's cuisine is like much else in its culture, as it reflects the many contacts of the society with other cultures over the centuries – Chinese, Khmer and French the most notable.

Rice (*com* in Vietnamese) is the staple of the diet and the basis of the country's agriculture. In fact, the changing fortunes in rice production reflect quite a bit about Vietnam's economy. In the early 1980s, Vietnam relied on imports to feed its people; entire provinces of people were starving. Today, rid of its collectivized farms, Vietnam is now the third-largest rice exporter in the world – although persistent fears that the country will run out of rice cause the government to frequently halt exports and impose quotas. Any Vietnamese over the age of 20 remembers well standing in long lines for rations of meat, and then stretching a monthly rice allotment to its limit.

The years of Chinese influence and occupation are evident in the use of chopsticks and the tendency to eat plain white rice separately with other foods, rather than mixing them together.

On every table: Ubiquitous in Vietnamese cooking is the use of a fish sauce called *nuoc mam*. Set on every table like salt in Western countries or soy sauce in China, nuoc mam is used as an ingredient in many dishes, but also is combined with other ingredients as a condiment called *nuoc cham*. Every cook has his or her own formula, but usually the dipping sauce consists of chili, lime juice, garlic, sugar, and pepper. This is used as a dipping

sauce for a variety of snack-type foods. The fish sauce has something of a pungent aroma and flavor that can take some getting used to, but it is nonetheless a complement to the subtle flavors of the food. Manufactured in coastal cities, like Phan Thiet and Phu Quoc, the fish sauce is made by fermenting anchovies and salt in large wooden barrels for about six months.

Vietnamese cooks use many fresh herbs – lemon grass, basil, coriander, mint, parsley, laksa leaf – as well as garlic, lime and ginger.

These ingredients lend the cuisine a subtlety of flavor that sets it apart from other neighboring Asian cuisines.

Virtually every meal is accompanied by a delicious soup. Dessert is usually a simple fresh fruit, although ice cream is extremely popular, with or without the fruit.

French influence brought with it the baguettes and pate sold in the markets and roadside stalls today, and, too, an appreciation of French food, shared by visitors and locals alike in the country's numerous Vietnamese-run French restaurants.

Vietnam's 3,000 kilometers of coastline, innumerable rivers and waterways provide

Left, fresh local seafood, Ha Long Bay. **Above**, Vietnamese spring rolls feature raw vegetables.

an ample and varied supply of fresh fish and seafood year-round. Fresh- and saltwater fish, shellfish and crustaceans are eaten as the main source of protein in delicious dishes such as *cha ca,* a barbecued fish made in Hanoi, and in minced fishmeat cakes.

The Vietnamese have created very innovative dishes using pork, chicken and beef, sometimes combining meat together with fish and seafood. Whether it be boiled, barbecued, grilled, stewed or fried, the cuisines are a skillful and delicious blend of many flavors, textures and influences.

Regional cuisines: Variations are quite distinctive. Generally, food in the north tends to be more bland, using fewer spices and herbs

great amounts. In general, food of the south is not actually sweeter – just more flavorful.

Southerners, too, don't care for northern food, although fewer people in the south have traveled north to try it, as the traditional migration in Vietnam has been north to south.

The south has one essential advantage that diners cannot help but notice: better access to fresh fruits and vegetables. A wider variety of food is grown in the south, for one thing, and the growing seasons are longer. Many lush tropical fruits and vegetables – custard apple, sapodilla, durian, pineapple, star fruit, artichoke, rambutan and avocado – are hard to find in the north and, when found, are often of poor quality.

and heaps of MSG. In the central part of the country, the food is quite hot, but also boasts creative vegetarian cooking, particularly in Hue, where there are many Buddhists who follow a meatless diet. Southern cooking, familiar to Westerners who have eaten in Vietnamese restaurants in France, America or Australia, tends to be more flavorful and creative than that in the north. Often, the dishes themselves are the same, but they are prepared quite differently.

Many northerners complain they cannot eat Saigon's food; they claim the southern cooks dump sugar into everything. Sugar is used in some dishes, such as *pho,* but not in

Many southern delicacies are served with raw, leafy vegetables, bean sprouts and herbs and wrapped up in a do-it-yourself manner. This custom is probably indigenous to the area. The southerners, living in a tropical area, use more coconut milk in their cooking and create interesting dishes that combine sweet and sour flavors.

Here is a primer on some of the Vietnamese specialties visitors will likely encounter.

Cha gio (called *nem Saigon* in the north): small rolls of minced pork, prawn, crab meat, fragrant mushrooms and vegetables wrapped in thin rice paper and deep fried until crisp. Cha gio is rolled in a lettuce leaf with fresh herbs and dipped in nuoc cham. It makes a thoroughly satisfying meal.

Cha lua: Wrapped in banana leaves before cooking, this pork pate is served as a snack and on French bread for lunch.

Chao tom: A Hanoi specialty, this unusual appetizer is ground shrimp baked on sugar cane. The shrimp is removed from the sugar cane and rolled in rice paper with lettuce, cucumber, coriander (cilantro) and mint, and dipped in fish sauce.

Cuon diep: Shrimp, noodles, mint, coriander and pork wrapped in lettuce leaves.

Goi ga: Something like a chicken salad, it is shredded chicken marinated in onion, vinegar, mint and, sometimes, peanuts.

chicken, coriander, fish sauce and scallions.

Banh cuon: A steamed rice pancake rolled around minced pork.

Canh chua: A sour soup by which Vietnamese cooks are judged. Often served with shrimp or fish head, the soup is a fragrant blend of sweet and tangy flavors, using tomato, pineapple, star fruit, bean sprout, fried onion, bamboo shoots, coriander, cinnamon, and, of course, fish sauce.

Banh khoai: Called the Hue pancake, it is a specialty of that area and is something of an omelet. A batter of rice flour and cornstarch is fried with egg to make a pancake that is wrapped around pork or shrimp, onion, bean sprouts and mushrooms.

Ga xao sa ot: Sauteed chicken cooked with lemon grass, fish sauce, garlic, onion and chilis. Sometimes peanuts are added.

Bun bo: A Hue specialty, this is fried beef, served over noodles with coriander, onion, garlic, cucumber, chilis and tomato paste.

Hu tieu: Also called Saigon soup, hu tieu is chicken, beef, pork and shrimp served with a broth over rice noodles, with crab meat, peanuts, onion and garlic.

Mien ga: Another type of noodle dish, most popular in the south, this is a soup of

Left, southern cuisine, Hoi An. **Above**, *pho*, the traditional noodle soup, with chicken.

Pho, cuisine mistress: If there is a dish that defines Vietnam, it is a simple broth of rice noodles called *pho*, sometimes referred to as the mistress of Vietnamese cuisine.

Vietnamese usually eat rice with their meals at home, three times a day. But when they go out, they often eat pho. Vietnamese use foods as a euphemism for their relationships. When you tire of rice (your wife or husband), you take pho (a lover). This analogy suggests a racy – if not spicy – connotation to what is really a simple food.

Pronounced "fuh," the soup typically is eaten for breakfast or for a late-night snack, although many people take pho for lunch and dinner, as well. While the number and variety of restaurants in Vietnam has grown dramatically in recent years, the ubiquitous pho stall is still one of the most popular kinds of eateries. On nearly every street, someone is selling pho – a broth of rice noodles topped with chicken or beef, fresh herbs and onion. Sometimes, a raw egg yolk is added, and some pho aficionados like to add lime juice, hot peppers or vinegar. It is usually served with *quay* – a fried piece of flour dough.

There are indoor pho shops with tables and wooden benches, stalls with tiny stools on the sidewalk, and vendors who carry pho in pots strapped to bamboo poles. None of them have menus or tablecloths or serve anything

but pho. The floors are often dirty, the walls streaked with mildew. But the pho is always steaming hot and filling.

Pho is most popular in Hanoi, although it is widely eaten in Ho Chi Minh City and the other major cities, as well. It is not consumed as much in the countryside, however, for it is somewhat of a luxury.

In fact, before the country began reforming its economy in the mid 1980s, pho was considered contraband. Pho stalls were illegal, as the government, which rationed meat and rice to families, considered it wasteful to use meat in pho. Often vendors would hide their shops in the backs of their houses and sell pho only to knowing customers. Police often raided the joints and confiscated the pho pots, chopping blocks and soup bowls.

Today, the shops are everywhere, and the best places have customers queuing up in long lines for their morning pho.

Typically, a pho shop sells either chicken or beef – not both. Pho is one of several kinds of noodles Vietnamese eat. *Bun,* usually served with beef, is not a soup but dry noodles. *My,* more common in the south, is a wheat noodle eaten like pho. *Mien* is made similar to pho but eaten dry.

A life of pho: Pho, however, is the most common. The recipe is fairly standard, although cooks do add their own variations. One pho chef in Hanoi, a woman in her 60s who has a prosperous business selling 1,000 bowls of beef pho everyday, said she cooks the ingredients "until I feel they are ready." She oversees every aspect of the business, which means she has little time to sleep.

She cooks from midnight into the early morning, serves pho until early afternoon and then heads to the market to purchase ingredients for the next day's pho.

She begins her day at midnight, putting on a large pot of water to boil with beef bones and pork bones. She adds fish sauce (used in almost all Vietnamese cooking), ginger, onion and star anise, and then lets the pot simmer for about five hours. "The secret," she says, "is boiling lots of beef and bones."

To serve pho, she takes a bowl, drops in some rice noodles, tops them with beef – raw or cooked, depending on the customer's taste – and pours broth over it. Then she adds some chopped onions, mint, basil and pepper. Pho – like much of Vietnamese food, especially in the north – uses MSG, though customers wary of eating the additive can ask to have it left out by saying, "Khong mi chinh" – No MSG. Often cooks ladle on a large amount of fat, To have that omitted, customers request *khong beo*. Pho is best, the cook confesses, in the late afternoon or evening, after the broth has simmered the longest.

In a pho restaurant, wealthy entrepreneurs sit alongside policemen in uniform, cyclo drivers, laborers, office workers and students. "While eating pho, everyone is the same," says the pho seller.

Above, a busy streetside stall. **Right**, drying Chinese vermicelli, Mekong Delta.

Only recently has Vietnam emerged from years of international isolation, opening its doors to foreign investors. But after years of fending off foreign invaders and colonialists, the country's leaders – the top-ranking revolutionaries who played key roles in the country's drive for independence this century – aren't about to hand over the purse strings to slick businessmen in Armani suits.

In preparations for an important meeting of the ruling Communist Party, Do Muoi issued this statement: "Economics must be allied with politics. That is the rule of the Vietnamese Party." To translate: A booming economy and increased foreign influence must be controlled by the Communist Party.

Ironically, many Vietnamese and foreigners alike view this attitude as positive – at least for the business climate. Unlike other Communist nations – such as the Soviet Union – Vietnam has managed to remain politically stable amid economic reform. Exhausted by decades of war, few are eager to see any kind of volatile change in the government. Business investors, likewise, while edgy about how much control the government will assert over their enterprises, nonetheless like a politically-stable mood.

Reform and opportunity: Vietnam's economic reform program, called *doi moi* and first initiated a decade ago, is beginning to see results. In part, this is due to the influx of outside money – foreign aid and loans, and from direct investment. Outsiders see a huge and untapped consumer market: 75 million people, more than half of them under the age of 25, without established buying habits but with increasing disposable incomes. They see a well-educated, literate and trainable work force that requires jobs. They see tremendous needs to rebuild the nation's infrastructure: highways, telephone and power systems, and shipping ports.

The government administration, criticized for its inefficiency and redundant agencies, was reorganized in the mid 1990s, an apparent attempt to show that the government is serious about reforming not only the economy, but also itself. The reformers in the government now face criticism for the spread of what are considered social evils:

prostitution, drugs and pornography; an inability to control to the hidden economy, such as smuggling; and the growing influence of foreigners.

Yet they have a healthier economy on their side. The country's gross domestic product has been increasing at a heady 8 percent clip for the past several years, matching any of the region's economic tigers. Industrial output has expanded annually at an average rate of more than 13 percent for five years. Incomes are rising in urban areas – although

the average annual income is still a paltry US$250 a year. That figure is somewhat misleading, as the spending power of Vietnamese, particularly in the cities, is considerably higher, and because most Vietnamese deliberately hide just how much money they actually have. They refuse to use banks, for example, fearing the banks will collapse (as they have in the past), and fearing the government will know too much about their finances. Savings rates are sluggish; the government's inability to encourage people to use banks gives it less working capital .

The streets of the capital, Hanoi, and the largest city, Ho Chi Minh City (Saigon), bustle with enthusiasm and business energy. The shedding of a command economy and a lukewarm embrace of capitalism by the leadership (they prefer to call it a market-oriented socialist economy, and not capitalism) has been heartily endorsed by the populace. People everywhere are angling to make money, from the shoeshine boys who come in from the countryside to smugglers of consumer goods from China. The streets are filled with small private enterprises selling every imaginable consumer good.

the rice paddies where most people work. The state sector has been trimming jobs and eliminating whole sectors. The military has been down-sizing. And the population is young and growing. All of this means there is increased pressure on the labor market.

Workers are creative and learn quickly, but they are not highly skilled, meaning foreign firms must invest in training.

There are other worries on the horizon. Vietnam appears reluctant to privatize. In fact, its leaders don't even like to use that

But the country is still poor; some 40 percent of the population still suffers from malnourishment. Unemployment is on the rise. While almost everyone has some kind of job – more than three-quarters of the people work on farms in the countryside – an increasing number of people are underemployed. While nearly every household in the cities has a TV set, fewer than 10 percent do in the countryside. Motorcycles are the vehicle of choice in the cities, but are rare among

Left, both the *dong* and US dollar are currencies of commerce; the dollar is more convenient. Above, foreign companies seeking consumers.

word. Although the number of new private firms is on the rise, economists point out that the state sector is actually increasing its share of the country's industrial output.

Corruption and a frustrating tangle of red tape remain concerns. Everything from setting up an office to gaining a license can require paying off officials. It's a problem the government has attempted to address, but it seems unable to control middle-level bureaucrats, who are underpaid and see the opportunity to fleece foreign businesses as a natural adjunct to their meager salaries.

As one American businessman put it: "It is death by a thousand pin pricks."

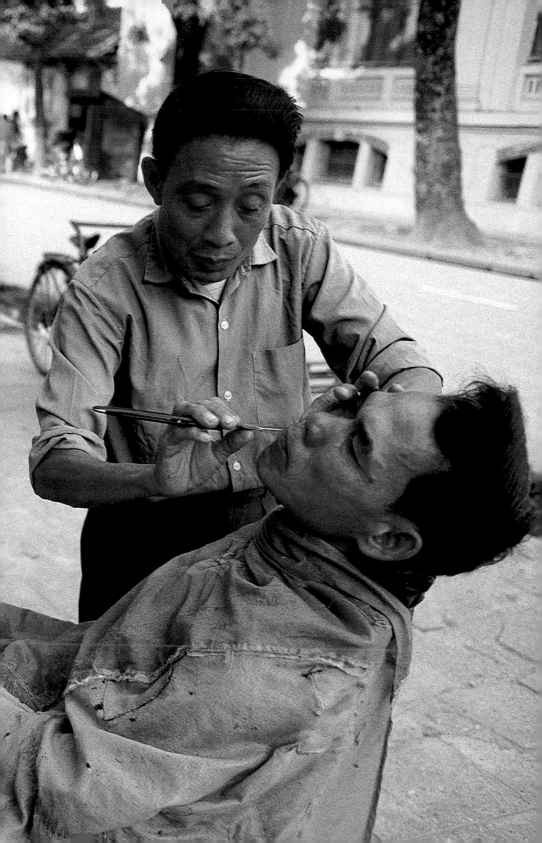

PLACES

Travel in Vietnam is anything but easy. After decades of war, and with an economy that was subsequently throttled, the country's infrastructure – or lack of it – can test the most hardened traveler's patience. But Vietnam is truly one of those destinations where the inconveniences pale beside the remarkable, and where the beauty of its people and culture seduce all.

One expects to find the remnants of a war-shattered country, even after two decades and more of peace, and indeed, one sometimes does. But the residue of war, in an odd irony, is now part of the country's tourism pull, whether for the tunnels beneath the 17th parallel – what was once the sadly-named DMZ, or demilitarized zone – or the rusting heaps at a war museum.

But the war is history, and beyond the memories of war, the bright tropical sun illuminates what seems to be a paradise... A coastline of serene, white sandy beaches and clear blue waters. Forested mountains with exotic animals. River deltas as expansive as the eye can see. But not all is tropical, of course. While the heat rarely lets up in the southern Mekong Delta, the winters of the northern Red River Delta can be cold and dismal.

Northern Vietnam is anchored by Hanoi, an ancient city established nearly 1,000 years ago. This political capital clings to the rhetoric of a socialist system, while at the same time embracing a government-controlled capitalism. The dilapidated villas and facades of the French colonial era give the city an ambience not found elsewhere in Asia.

Beyond Hanoi, the provinces of the vast Red River Delta reflect the traditional agricultural culture upon which the economy is based. And beyond the Delta's plains, the cooler mountain regions ascend towards the west and Laos, and northward towards China.

Southward, following the historical movement of the Viet people, the traveler finds a chain of coastal provinces washed by the South China Sea. In the old imperial city of Hue, an overwhelming sense of the past pervades its older streets. The antiquities don't end here. In the lands of the ancient kingdom of Champa are decaying sanctuaries, temples and towers that testify to the conquest by the Viet people from the north.

Then there is Ho Chi Minh City. Often still called Saigon, it is reviving its long-time image as a proverbial hustling and bustling city of people on the make and on the go. Where Hanoi is quiet, Ho Chi Minh City screams. Where Hue has a subtle and refined beauty, Ho Chi Minh City grabs by the lapels and shakes. If Hanoi is a city of earth tones, Ho Chi Minh City is neon, all lit up in gaudy lights.

Although the country is just now climbing out of a century of foreign domination and war, the traveler will find that Vietnam is a land of the ascending dragon, and a place finally at peace.

Preceding pages: morning traffic, Bac Thai Province; barbershop quartet; Lang Co peninsula; tea plantations, Central Highlands. **Left**, slow boat to northern Vietnam.

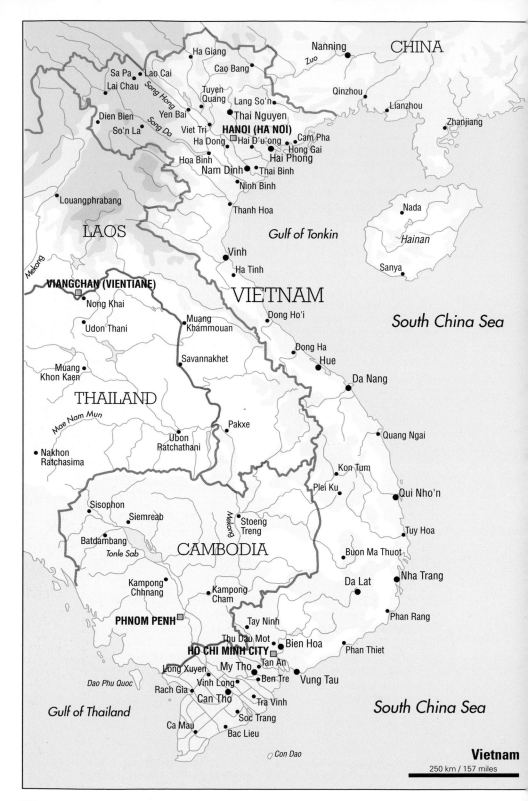

Vietnam

250 km / 157 miles

Central Vietnam

40 km / 25 miles

Ha Tinh
Cu'a Nhu'o'ng
HA TINH
Cu'a Khau
HON SON DUONG
Song Ngan Sau
Mui Doc
Ron
Gulf of Tonkin
Cha Noi
Phong Nha Cave
Cu'a Nhat Le
QUANG BINH
Dong Hoi
Ban Loboy
Dai Giang
Mui Lay
DAO CON CO
Vinh Linh
Vinh Moc Tunnels
Ban Muangsen
Ben Hai
Truong Son
National Cemetery
Cu'a Viet
Con Thien Firebase
Muang Xepon
Dong Ha
Quang Tri
Khe Sanh Firebase
QUANG TRI
Song Quang Tri
Song Bo
Cu'a Thuan An
Muang Phin
Xa Lanong
Imperial Citadel
Hue
South China Sea
Thien Mu Pagoda
Nguyen Emperor Tombs
THUA THIEN HUE
Mui Cho'n May Tay
Lang Co
Ban Top
A Luoi
Hai Van Pass
Mui Da Nang
LAOS
Atouat
Bach Ma National Park
Da Nang
Cham Museum
Ngu Hanh Son (Marble Mountains)
CU LAO CHAM
Hoi An
HON ONG
Plateau
Ho Chi Minh Trail
Singhapura (Tra Kieu)
Ban Phou Daotieng Noi
Saravan
Ben Giang
My So'n Cham Site
Chien Dang Cham Towers
Tam Ky
QUANG NAM DA NANG
Vung Dung Quat
CU LAO RE
Muang Khongxedon
Ban Phon
Khuong My Cham Tower
Mui Ba Lang An
Plateau des Bolovens
Nhan Hoa Hot Spring
My Lai Memorial
Pakxe
So'n Ha
Quang Ngai
Champasak
Attapu
Ngoc Linh 2598
QUANG NGAI
Duc Pho
Sa Huynh
Ban Khampho
KON TUM
Plei Can
Kon Plong
BINH DINH
Bong S'on
Muang Khong
Kon Tum
Phu My
CU LAO TRAU
Ban Xot
Virochey
Jrai Li Waterfalls
Duong Long Cham Towers
Cha Ban
Qui Nho'n
Stoeng Treng
Kon Tum Plateau
Plei Ku
An Khe
Quang Trung Museum
Thap Doi Cham Tower
CU LAO XANH
Tonle San
Ba Kev
GIA LAI
VIETNAM
Mui Ong Dien
Lumphat
Tonle Srepok
Phu Nhon
Song Cau
Tuy Hoa
CAMBODIA
A Yun Pa
PHU YEN
Mekong
DAK LAC
Cao Nguyen
Song Ba
Cung S'on
Song Da Rang
Ban Don
Dak Lac

Simao

Gejiu

Mengzi

Wenshan

Yuan Jiang

Jiangcheng

Phong Tho

Lao Cai

Song Chay

Bac Quang

Ha G

HA
GIAN

Song Da (Black River)

Muong
Nhe

Nam Na

6

Sa Pa

Fan Si Pan
3143

LAO
CAI

Song Hong (Red River)

Phu Den Din

LAI
CHAU

Lai Chau

Hoang Lien Son

VIE

YEN
BAI

Yen Ba

Phongsali

Tuan Giao

Song Da (Black River)

Mengla

**Dien
Bien Phu**

Dien
Bien

So'n La

SO'N
LA

Song Da
Reservoir

Louang
Namtha

Song Ma

SO'N
LA

Co Noi

6

Moc C

Phou Sam Sao

Nam Ou

Nam Tha

Muang
Xay

Xam Hua

Nam Sam

Nam Beng

L   A   O   S

M

Muang
Pakbeng

Menam Khong

Louangphrabang

Ban Ban

Nui

Tuong
Duong

NO

7

THAILAND

Muang
Xaignabouri

Xiangkhoang

Nui Tru

Muang
Phon-Hong

Muang Pakxan

Ban Pak-Leng

Viangchan
(Vientiane)

THAILAND

The

Nong Khai

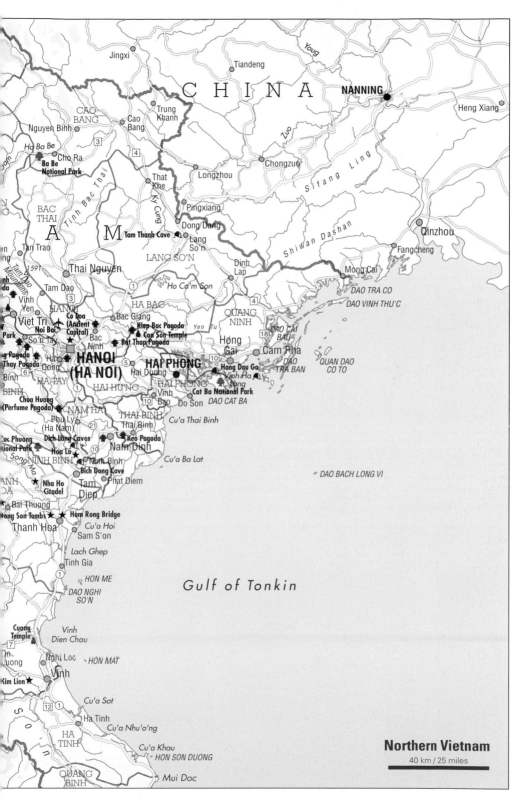

Jingxi
Tiandeng
Youg

C H I N A
NANNING
Heng Xiang

CAO
BANG
Nguyen Binh
Trung
Khanh
Cao
Bang
Qinzhou

Ho Ba Be
Cho Ra
Ba Be
National Park
That
Khe
Longzhou
Chongzuo
Zuo
Sifang Ling
Fangcheng

Tinh Bac Thai
Ky Cung
Pingxiang
Shiwan Dashan
Mong Cai

1591
Tan Trao
Tam Thanh Cave
Dong Dang
Lang
So'n
DAO TRA CO
DAO VINH THU'C

Thai Nguyen
LANG SO'N
Dinh
Lap

Tam Dao
Ho Ca'm Son
4
QUANG
NINH
DAO CAI
BAU

Vinh
Yen
HANOI
HA BAC
Yen Tu
18
Hong
Gai
DAO
TRA BAN
QUAN DAO
CO TO

Viet Tri
Co Loa
(Ancient
Capital)
Bac Giang
Kiep Bac Pagoda
Con Son Temple
Cam Pha
QUAN DAO
CO TO

Noi Bai
Son Tay
Bac
Ninh
Bat Thap Pagoda
HAI PHONG
10
Hang Dau Go
Long
Vinh Ha

y Pagoda
Thay Pagoda
Ha
Dong
HANOI
(HA NOI)
5
Hai Duong
Cat Ba National Park
DAO CAT BA

Binh
6
HA TAY
1
HAI HU'NG
Vinh
Bao
Do Son
DAO CAT BA

Chua Huong
(Perfume Pagoda)
NAM HA
10
Cu'a Thai Binh

Phu Ly
(Ha Nam)
21
THAI BINH
Thai Binh

uc Phuong
ional Park
Dich Long Caves
Hoa Lu
Keo Pagoda

Son
NINH BINH
10
Nam Dinh

Ma
Bich Dong Cave
Ninh Binh
Cu'a Ba Lat

ANH
OA
Nha Ho
Citadel
Tam
Diep
Phat Diem
DAO BACH LONG VI

Bai Thuong
ong Son Tombs
Ham Rong Bridge
Thanh Hoa
Cu'a Hoi
Sam S'on

Lach Ghep
Tinh Gia
Gulf of Tonkin

1
HON ME
DAO NGHI
SO'N

Cuong
Temple
Vinh
Dien Chau

7
HON MAT

On
uong
Nghi Loc
Vinh

Kim Lien
Cu'a Sot

12
1
Ha Tinh
Cu'a Nhu'o'ng

S
O
HA
TINH
Cu'a Khau
HON SON DUONG

QUANG
BINH
Mui Doc

Northern Vietnam
40 km / 25 miles

135

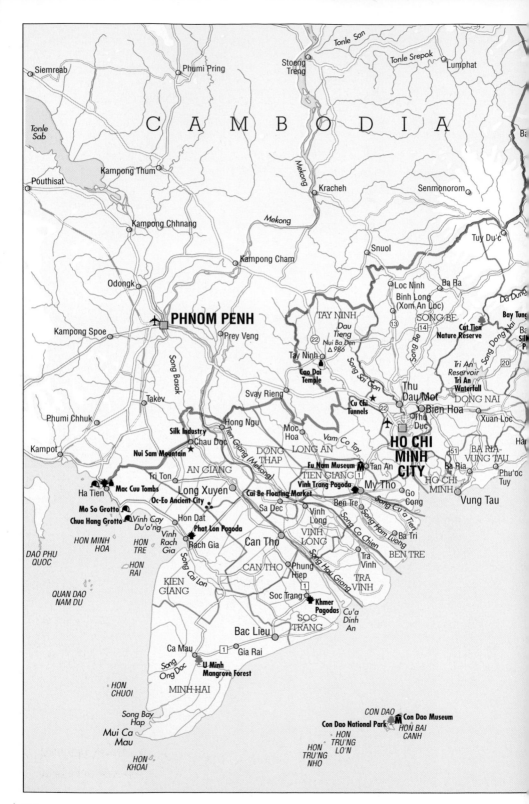

SIEMREAB · Phumi Pring · Stoeng Treng · Tonle San · Tonle Srepok · Lumphat

Tonle Sab

Pouthisat · Kampong Thum · Kracheh · Senmonorom

Kampong Chhnang · Kampong Cham · Mekong

C A M B O D I A

Odongk · Snuol · Tuy Du'c

PHNOM PENH · Prey Veng · Loc Ninh · Ba Ra · Da Dung · Bay Tung

Kampong Spoe · TAY NINH · Dau Tieng · Binh Long (Xom An Loc) · SONG BE · Cat Tien Nature Reserve · Sil P

Phumi Chhuk · Nui Ba Den Δ986 · Song Sai Gon · Tri An Reservoir · DONG NAI · Song Dong Nai · 20

Kampot · Tay Ninh · Cao Dai Temple · Thu Dau Mot · Tri An Waterfall

Svay Rieng · Cu Chi Tunnels · Bien Hoa · Xuan Loc

Silk Industry · Hong Ngu · Moc Hoa · LONG AN · HO CHI MINH CITY · Thu Duc

Chau Doc · DONG THAP · Vam Co Tay · Tan An · BA RIA-VUNG TAU · Har

Nui Sam Mountain · AN GIANG · Eu Nam Museum · TIEN GIANG · Ba Ria · 51 · Phu'oc Tuy

Tri Ton · Vinh Trang Pagoda · My Tho · HO CHI MINH

Ha Tien · Mac Cuu Tombs · Long Xuyen · Cai Be Floating Market · Ben Tre · Go Cong · Vung Tau

Mo So Grotto · Oc-Eo Ancient City · Sa Dec · Song Cu'a Tien

Chua Hang Grotto · Vinh Cay Du'o'ng · Hon Dat · Vinh Long · Ba Tri

HON MINH HOA · HON TRE · Vinh Rach Gia · Phat Lon Pagoda · VINH LONG · Song Co Chien · BEN TRE

DAO PHU QUOC · HON RAI · Rach Gia · Can Tho · Tra Vinh

QUAN DAO NAM DU · KIEN GIANG · CAN THO · Phung Hiep · Song Hau Giang · TRA VINH

Soc Trang · Khmer Pagodas · Cu'a Dinh An

SOC TRANG

Bac Lieu

Ca Mau · Gia Rai · U Minh Mangrove Forest

HON CHUOI · MINH HAI

Song Ong Doc

Mui Ca Mau · Song Bay Hap · CON DAO · Con Dao Museum

Con Dao National Park · HON BAI CANH

HON KHOAI · HON TRU'NG NHO · HON TRU'NG LO'N

136

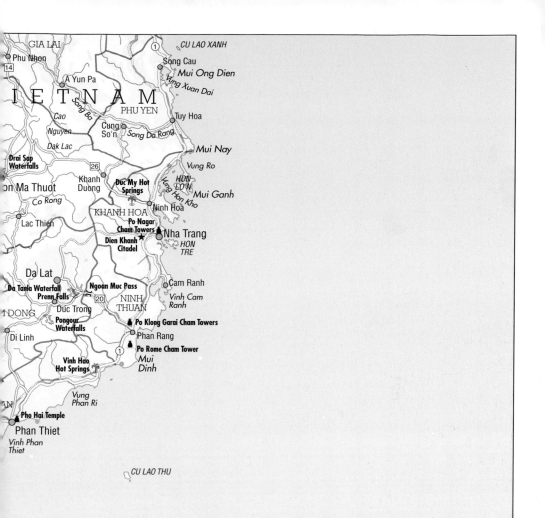

South China Sea

Southern Vietnam

40 km / 25 miles

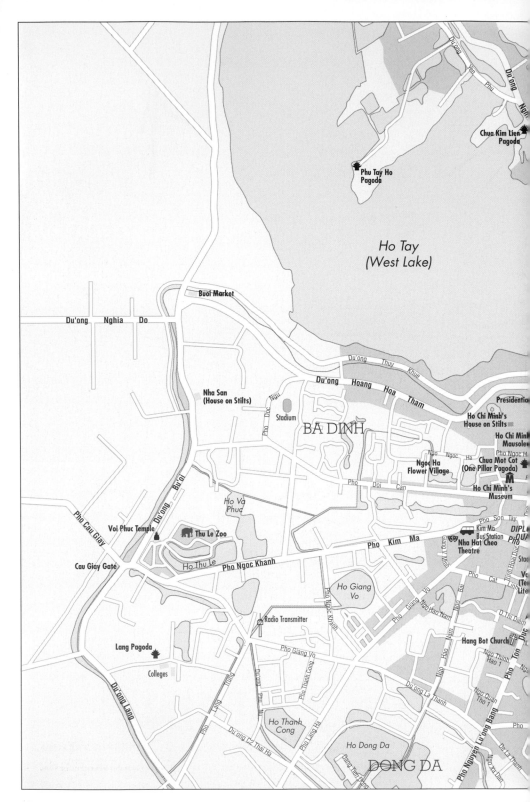

Ho Tay
(West Lake)

Chua Kim Lien
Pagoda

Phu Tay Ho
Pagoda

Buoi Market

Du'ong   Nghia   Do

Du'ong   Thuy   Khue

Du'ong   Hoang   Hoa   Tham

Nha San
(House on Stilts)

Presidentia

Ho Chi Minh's
House on Stilts

BA DINH

Ho Chi Minh
Mausole

Pho Ngoc H

Chua Mot Cot
(One Pillar Pagoda)

Ngoc Ha
Flower Village

Pho   Doi   Can

Ho Chi Minh's
Museum

Ho Va
Phuc

Pho Son Tay

Kim Ma
Bus Station

DIPL
QUA

Pho Cau Giay

Voi Phuc Temple

Thu Le Zoo

Pho Kim   Ma

Nha Hat Cheo
Theatre

Pho

Cau Giay Gate

Ho Thu Le   Pho Ngoc Khanh

Vo
(Te
Lite

Ho Giang
Vo

Hang Bot Church

Radio Transmitter

Pho Giang Vo

Ngo Thinh
Hao 1

Lang Pagoda

Colleges

Du'ong Lang

Ho Thanh
Cong

Ho Dong Da

DONG DA

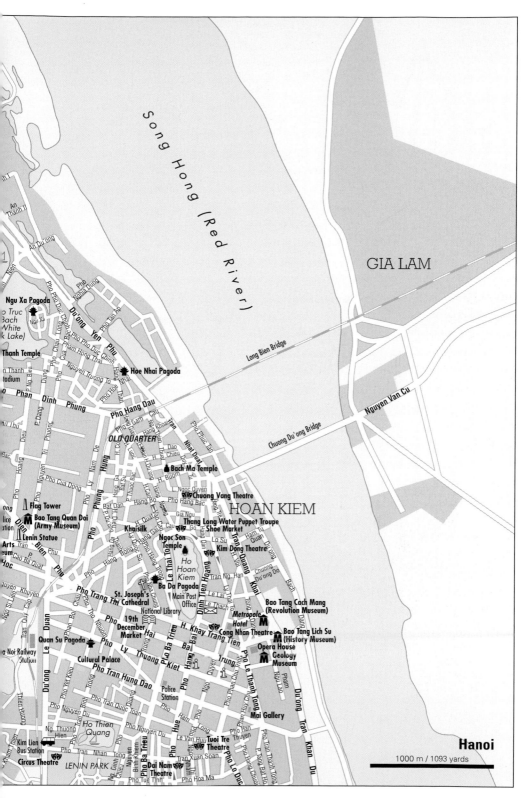

Song Hong (Red River)

GIA LAM

Long Bien Bridge

Nguyen Van Cu

Chuong Du'ong Bridge

Ngu Xa Pagoda

o Truc
Bach
White
k Lake)

Thanh Temple

n Thanh
tadium

o Phan Dinh Phung

Du'ong Yen Phu

Pho Nghia Dung

Pho Pho Duc Chinh

Pham Hong Thai

Nguyen Truong To

Hoe Nhai Pagoda

Pho Hang Dau

Cau

OLD QUARTER

Bach Ma Temple

Flag Tower

Bao Tang Quan Doi
(Army Museum)

Lenin Statue

Arts

eum

oc

lice
ation

Khaisilk

Chuong Vang Theatre

HOAN KIEM

Thang Long Water Puppet Troupe

Shoe Market

Ngoc Son
Temple

Kim Dong Theatre

Ho
Hoan
Kiem

Ba Da Pagoda

St. Joseph's
Cathedral

Main Post
Office

National Library

19th
December
Market

Bao Tang Cach Mang
(Revolution Museum)

Metropole
Hotel

Cong Nhan Theatre

Bao Tang Lich Su
(History Museum)

Opera House

Geology
Museum

Pho Trang Thi

H. Khay Trang Tien

Quan Su Pagoda

Pho Ly Thuong Kiet

Cultural Palace

Pho Tran Hung Dao

Police
Station

a Noi Railway
Station

Mai Gallery

Kim Lien
Bus Station

Ho Thien
Quang

Circus Theatre

LENIN PARK

Tuoi Tre
Theatre

Dai Nam
Theatre

Hanoi

1000 m / 1093 yards

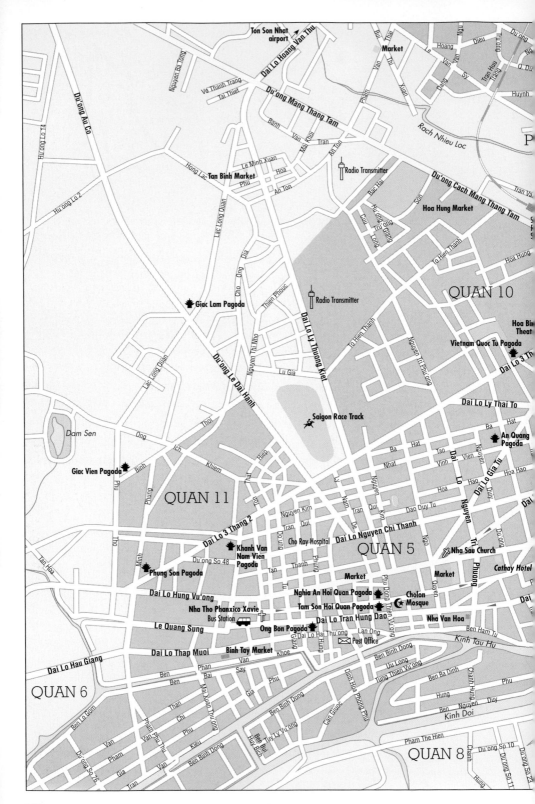

Ton Son Nhat airport

Market

Nguyen Ba Tong

Vo Thanh Trang

Tai Thiet

Du'ong Mang Thang Tam

Dai Lo Hoang Van Thu

Du'ong Au Co

Banh

Van Khoi

Tran

An Ton

Bui

Van

Thi

Xuan

Pham

Hoang

Le

Van

Sy

Dieu

Tru'ong

Du'ong

Ngu

Q. Du

Tran Hu'u Trang

Huynh

Hong Lac

Tan Binh Market

Le Minh Xuan

Phu

An Ton

Hoa

Radio Transmitter

Bac Hai

Son

Du'ong Cach Mang Thang Tam

Tran Va

Hu'ong Lo 2

Hu'ong Lo 14

Du'ong Tinh

Lac Long Quan

Cho

Ong

Thien Phuoc

Cu

Long

Cu

Lao

Hu'ong Giang

Hoa Hung Market

To Hien Thanh

Hoa Hung

Hoa Hung Market

QUAN 10

Giac Lam Pagoda

Nguyen Thi Nho

Lu Gia

Dai Lo Ly Thuong Kiet

To Hien Thanh

Radio Transmitter

Nguyen Tri Phu'ong

Hoa Binh Theat

Vietnam Quoc Tu Pagoda

Dai Lo 3 Th

Du'ong Le Dai Hanh

Dam Sen

Ong

Thoi

Ich

Khiem

Bin

Phu

Giac Vien Pagoda

Thoi

Hiep

Saigon Race Track

Ba

Hat

Nhat

Ba

Hat

Tao

Vinh

Dai

Lo

Vien

Nguyen

Dai Lo Ly Thai To

An Quang Pagoda

Dai Lo Gia Tu

Hoa Hao

QUAN 11

Nam

Tran

Qui

Hoa

Dao Duy Tu

Nguyen

Tan Hoa

Tho

Minh

Phung

Thai

Lu'u

Nguyen Kim

Tran

Qui

Du'ong

Thanh

Tan

Phung

Cho Ray Hospital

Dai Lo Nguyen Chi Thanh

QUAN 5

Tri

Dai

Dai Lo 3 Thang 2

Khanh Van Nam Vien Pagoda

Du'ong So 48

Phung Son Pagoda

Dai Lo Hung Vu'ong

Nha Tho Phanxico Xavie

Bus Station

Le Quang Sung

Market

Nghia An Hoi Quan Pagoda

Tam Son Hoi Quan Pagoda

Ong Bon Pagoda

Dai Lo Tran Hung Dao

Dai Lo Hai Thu'ong

Cholon Mosque

Market

Nha Sau Church

Cathay Hotel

Phu'ong

Quyen

Nguyen

Dai

Nha Van Hoa

Ben Ham Tu

Dai Lo Thap Muoi

Binh Tay Market

Giang

Lan Ong

Khoe

Post Office

Ben Binh Dong

Uu Long

Tung Thien Vu'ong

Kinh Tau Hu

Dai Lo Hau Giang

QUAN 6

Ben

Ben

Than

Phan

Bai

Mai Xuan Thu'ong

Chi

Phu

Say

Van

Gia

Phu

Dinh Hoa Phong Phu

Can Giuoc

Ben Binh Dong

Ben Ba Dinh

Chanh Hung

Phu

Hung

Nguyen

Duy

Ben Lo Gom

Du'ong So 26

Pham

Van

Gia

Tran

Van Phu The

Kieu

Ben Binh Dong

Ben Bui Huy Bich

Ben Tuy Ly Vu'ong

Pham The Hien

QUAN 8

Kinh Doi

Ben

Hung

Du'ong So 10

Du'ong So 11

Du'ong So 24

Rach Nhieu Loc

140

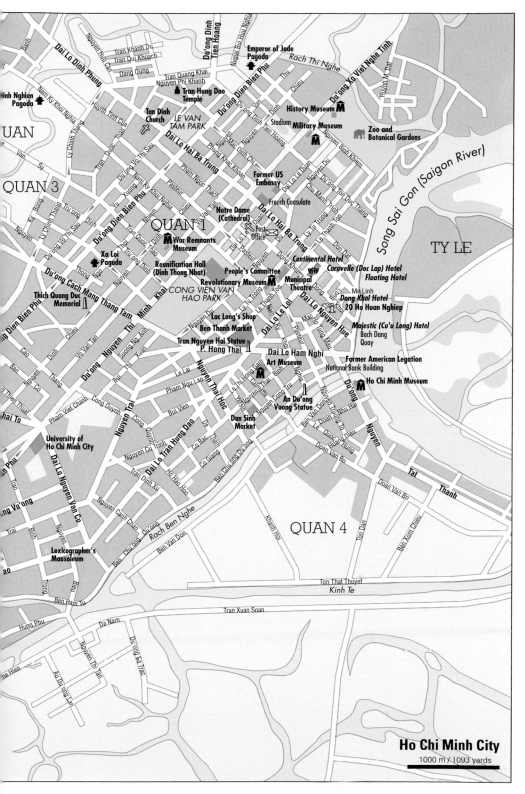

Ho Chi Minh City

1000 m / 1093 yards

THE NORTH

A journey through northern Vietnam begins in today's political capital, Hanoi, once the ancient capital of Thang Long. Visitors to Hanoi will encounter the cultures of both East and West, with the changing fortunes of history reflected in the architecture of its many traditional temples and pagodas, in the lingering presence of a French colonial past, and in the whirr of construction as the city's blossoming modern towers rise above it all.

Beyond Hanoi and its populous suburbs are the picturesque provincial regions, with their checkerboard-patterned paddy fields of rice, the nation's staple and export earner. Green belts of trees and bamboo enclose the villages, where traditional communal houses, pagodas and temples remain hidden from view.

Men, women, children and buffalo toil together in the fields, seven days a week, and in all weather. The scene is one of tranquil beauty, but the hardship and toll of this life is obvious.

On the coast to the east, touching the Gulf of Tonkin, the busy port of Hai Phong, the country's third-largest city, boasts Vietnam's only casino. Nearby, junks sail among the stunning scenery of Ha Long Bay, with its grottoes and caves and jutting rocks often shrouded in a mysterious, bewitching fog.

The northern territory, near the Chinese border, is home to ethnic tribes living in mountainous areas, and there is a booming border trade amidst isolated forest retreats.

Throughout the north, the pagodas come alive with festivals – both religious and nationalistic – that have honored spirits, gods and war heroes for centuries. This is a seductive countryside, the kind that leaves one with the desire of never leaving. There are waterfalls and more still, rainforests, mountain trails and village craftspeople making woodcarvings, pottery, embroidery and lacquered wood. Here in the north, contemporary Vietnam has the volume turned down a bit, as the traditional love of literature, art and music maintains a toehold against the modern diversions of television, karaoke and cellular phones.

Preceding pages: auspicious colors for a festival in Dong Ky; equally-auspicious colors for a merchant, Hanoi. **Left**, Ha Long Bay sunset.

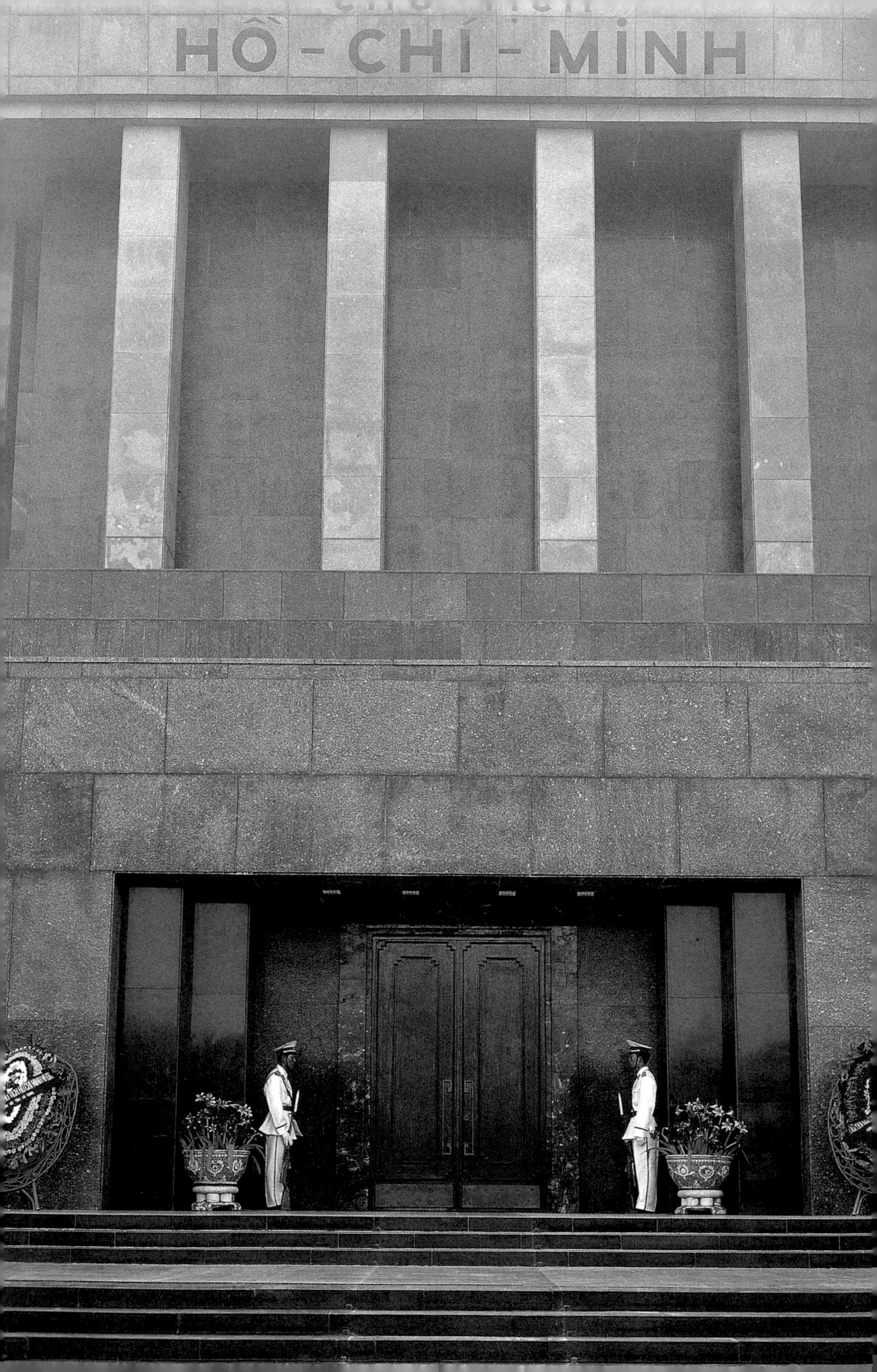
HỒ - CHÍ - MINH

HANOI

In Vietnamese, Hanoi is usually written as two words, *ha* meaning the river, in reference to Song Hong, or the Red River, and *noi*, meaning inside.

Hanoi's rich and complex history dates back to the Neolithic era, when the ancient Viet people settled in the Bach Hac and Viet Tri regions, in present-day Vinh Phu Province, at the confluence of the Red and Lo rivers.

In the third century, after a bloody, decade-long war against Chinese invaders, King Thuc Phan descended from the 100 Viet Principalities (a region of 100 separate states encompassing all of southern China, south of the Yang Tse Kiang River) and founded the state of Au Lac. He installed his capital at Ke Chu, the site of the vast spiral citadel of Co Loa (Old Conch).

After regaining independence, Vietnam's Ngo, Dinh and Le dynasties – of the middle of the 10th to the beginning of the 11th century – installed their capitals at Hoa Lu, 100 kilometers (60 mi) south of Hanoi. There it remained, until King Ly Thai To arrived in Dai La – an ancient city along the Song Hong, or Red River – in the early 11th century.

According to legend, Ly Thai To saw an enormous golden dragon emerge from the lake and soar into the sky above the site. On the strength of this omen, he moved the capital from Hoa Lu to Dai La, which he then renamed as Thang Long, or Ascending Dragon.

At the new site, he found the surrounding countryside too flat for defensive purposes, so he ordered that dikes and artificial hills be built. Even today, it is still possible to make out the contours of these ancient earthworks.

The royal capital grew from a small lakeside village built on stilts into a town. The area between the West Lake and the citadel became the administrative city (*kinh thanh*), where the mandarins, officers, soldiers and general public lived. In the heart of this was the royal city (*hoang thanh*), and behind its high walls was the forbidden city (*cam thanh*), where the king, queens and concubines lived in seclusion.

In 1010, the center of the royal city contained eight palaces and three pavilions. Eight new palaces were built during 1029, and further additions were made in 1203. The Temple of Literature, the One Pillar Pagoda and the Tran Quoc Pagoda were built during this time.

In 1400, the capital was transferred to Thanh Hoa by the usurper Regent Ho Qui Ly, who took over from the Tran Dynasty. His capital, Tay Kinh (Capital of the West), lasted until the Le Dynasty restored the capital to Hanoi in 1428.

From the 16th century onward, few new buildings were constructed in Hanoi. Gia Long built a smaller Vauban-style citadel, but its walls and gates were torn down during the colonial era, and all that remains of it today are traces of the flag tower.

The royal city was destroyed twice in less than 50 years, first in 1786, when King Le Chieu Thong ordered the destruction of the Trinh Palace, then in 1820, by Gia Long's son, Minh Mang,

in his fury at the Chinese emperor's recognition of Thang Long – and not Hue – as the capital. In 1848, Tu Duc had most of the remaining palace destroyed and its valuable contents moved to Hue, the 19th-century capital of the Nguyen emperors.

Foreigners' arrival: The beginning of the 17th century marked the arrival of Dutch, Portuguese, and French traders. Hot on their heels came Christian missionaries. The great influx of newcomers and diverse ideas from Europe brought many changes to the capital of Thang Long. The French presence and influence grew, eventually changing the course of Vietnamese history.

When Hanoi fell into the hands of the French in 1882, the city underwent transformation and modernization.

(Hanoi's later less-inspiring name, Dong Kinh, or Capital of the East, was transformed into Tunquin after Alexandre de Rhodes developed a romanized Vietnamese alphabet. Tunquin, in turn, beget Tonkin, which is what the French administration called the entire north of Vietnam during the colonial era.)

The face of Hanoi acquired an appearance reflecting a harmony between progress and tradition, although this harmony did not extend to the relations between the Vietnamese and their French overseers. In the wake of new roads and buildings, tradition suffered. The Ba Tien Pagoda was knocked down to make way for the cathedral, and the Bao An Pagoda was replaced by the post office. Today, all that remains of that pagoda is a small shrine beside Hoan Kiem Lake.

Hanoi's architectural legacy left behind by the French includes the Long Bien Bridge, the cathedral, Dong Xuan market (gutted by a fire in 1994), the French School d'Extreme Orient (now the history museum), Hanoi University, several hotels, many beautiful colonial villas and an opera house.

This architecture, and an abundance of trees and lakes around the city, give Hanoi a romantic air unusual among Asia capitals. What is ironic is that the capital city of fiercely-independent people, who have battled for generations against foreign colonialists, possesses a decidedly European air. While people in Hanoi love to brag about their beautiful city, what they don't often admit is that much of what makes it beautiful is the French influence.

Over the decades, the combined effects of war, climate, financial shortcomings and a lack of quality building materials had taken their toll on Hanoi's historical buildings. Apart from the colonial buildings used by the government or foreign missions, most were in a dilapidated state.

Recently, however, most of the finer older buildings in the city center have been spruced up by foreign companies using them as offices. Recently, city leaders have realized that the colonial architecture gives Hanoi a look unique among Asian capitals, a look that makes it attractive to tourists. Thus, the preservation of old Hanoi is now seen as having economic benefit.

As a revived economy boosts the fortunes of people in Hanoi, the challenge is to protect the charm and grace of the city against the forces of progress. While foreign visitors rhapsodize about the lovely old buildings and lament their demise, the people in Hanoi have a more immediate concern: suitable housing. Behind the facades of the colonial elegance, people live in crowded conditions, with several families sharing small houses, often with communal toilets and water for bathing. For them, preservation is a luxury that seems impractical. Indeed, the city suffers from a severe housing shortage, as many people from the outlying villages have made their way to Hanoi seeking better paying jobs or an education.

Today, with a population of about 3 million, Hanoi extends over 2,000 square kilometers (800 sq mi). The city center comprises four districts: Hoan Kiem (Restored Sword), Hai Ba Trung (Two Trung Sisters), Dong Da (where King Quang Trung defeated the Manchu invasion in 1789) and Ba Dinh. It also incorporates eleven recently-integrated suburban districts (*quan*): Thanh Tri, Tu Liem, Dong Anh, Gia Lam, Ba Vich,

Thach That, Phuc Tho, Hoai Duc, Dan Phuong, Me Linh and Soc Son.

The city center has evolved little since 1955, leaving Hanoi's original character very much intact, preserved in its traditional pagodas and temples, colonial architecture, tree-lined streets, and lakes. The soul of the old Thang Long city rests in the ancient town center, which dates from the 15th century.

But there is construction everywhere nowadays. The skyline is dotted with cranes and newer, taller towers. Older, crumbling buildings are getting knocked down or, in some cases, new facades. The new facades, unfortunately, aren't usually all that charming, but rather a standard glass-and-chrome front with large, brightly-lit signs.

West of Hanoi, hills extend up to the 1,200-meter (4,000 ft) summit of Mt Ba, 65 kilometers from the city. The city is bordered by Ho Tay, or West Lake, in the northwest.

Hanoi is accessible from the north by three bridges: Long Bien, Chuong Duong, and the newest, Thang Long, a modern span changing into a four-lane highway to Noi Bai Airport.

The 1,682-meter-long (5,520-ft) **Long Bien Bridge** was built by the French and opened in 1902 by Governor-General Doumer, after whom it was originally named. It suffered some damage from American bombing, but was continually repaired, and until 1983, all northbound road and rail traffic passed over it. These days, it is reserved for cyclists, pedestrians and trains.

Discovering Hanoi: In the very heart of the old town of Hanoi lies **Ho Hoan Kiem**, or Lake of the Restored Sword. If up early enough, visitors can catch locals seriously engrossed in their morning exercises – *tai chi kuan*, callisthenics, badminton, running – before going off to work. In the evening, especially on holidays, the lake is ringed by a carnival atmosphere, with vendors selling balloons and toys, and children dressed up in frilly dresses and music blaring from loudspeakers. Several outdoor cafes selling ice cream, coffee and beer look out on the water.

ang Tien
reet, near
pera House,
305.

A legend that sounds like a Vietnamese version of Excalibur tells of how King Le Thai To received a magic sword that he used during his 10-year resistance against the Ming domination (1418–1428). After liberating the country, the king took a boat to the center of the lake to return the magic sword given to him by the Divine Tortoise. The tortoise is said to have snatched the sword from his hand and disappeared into the lake. That, apparently, is how the lake acquired its name.

Near the middle of the lake stands the small, 18th-century tower, Thap Rua, or Tortoise Tower. A large tortoise is said to still live in the lake, and on certain days of the year – usually when the seasons change – people claim to see the tortoise emerge from the water.

Perched on a tiny islet (Jade Island) in the lake not far from the tower is the **Ngoc Son Temple** (Temple of the Jade Mound). The temple is reached from the shore via the brightly-painted red, arched bridge known as **The Huc**, or Sunbeam Bridge. On the small hillock at the end of the bridge stands a stone column in the form of a brush next to an ink well, and inscribed with three Chinese characters, *ta tien qing*, meaning "written on the blue sky." Also on the islet are the remains of a small communal house known as Tran Ba Dinh.

There is a nightly showing of **water puppets** on the northeast side of the lake, in a theater on Dinh Tien Hoang Street. The city's **main post office** is also on Dinh Tien Hoang, on the southeast side of the lake. To the north of the post office, there is a small park where sweethearts hold late-night trysts and where, during the day, young men and boys play soccer.

Across from the park is the **Government Guest House**, a compound with a hotel in the back and an ornate French colonial building, painted yellow with green trim, in front. It was once the palace of the French governor of Tonkin. Today, Vietnamese officials meet visiting foreign dignitaries here. It faces Ngo Quyen Street, across which is another small plaza with a fountain, and

Government Guest House

where young men play badminton. Next to the plaza is the unofficial hub for foreign business people, the Sofitel Hotel, more commonly known as The Metropole. Here, there is a sense of urgency in the hotel bar, as the talk is serious and whispered.

Not far from The Metropole is one of Hanoi's landmarks, the **Municipal Theater**, commonly called the Opera House. This grand building has recently been beautifully renovated.

Behind the Municipal Theater, the **Bao Tang Lich Su (History Museum)** occupies the old archaeological research institution of l' Ecole Francaise d'Extreme Orient. The museum opened in 1910, was rebuilt in 1926, and reopened in 1932.

Exhibits displayed here cover every era of Vietnam's fascinating and complex history. It houses an excellent archaeological collection dating from the Paleolithic and Neolithic eras, including relics from the era of the Hung kings, Neolithic graves, Bronze Age implements, the beautiful bronze drums of Ngoc Lu and Mieu Mon, Cham relics, stelae, statues, ceramics, and an eerie sculpture of the goddess Quan Am with her one thousand eyes and arms. One room features an ornate throne, clothes, and artifacts belonging to the thirteen kings of the Nguyen Dynasty.

Near the History Museum, the **Bao Tang Cach Mang (Revolutionary Museum)** on Tong Dan Street documents the struggles of the Vietnamese people from ancient times up until 1975. Among the exhibits are some of the long, wooden stakes used to cripple the Mongol fleet during the battle of Bach Dang, in Ha Long Bay, and an enormous bronze war drum from 2,400 BC.

From the north side of Hoan Kiem Lake, many streets lead to Hanoi's Old Quarter and, on Nha Chung Street, the oldest church in the city, **St Joseph's Cathedral** (the Vietnamese call it the "big church"), consecrated on Christmas night in 1886. It was built on the site of the Bao Thien Pagoda, which was razed to build the cathedral. (Two other Catholic churches in Hanoi can be found

Interior of the Opera House, now the Municipal Theater.

at the corner of Nguyen Bieu and Phan Dinh Phung streets, in a neighborhood dominated by the ministry offices, and near the corner of Ngo Quyen and Le Van Huu streets.)

A narrow passageway next to 5 Nha Tho, the street facing the cathedral, leads to the **Ba Da Pagoda**. This charming pagoda was built in the 15th century after the discovery of a stone statue of a woman during the construction of the Thang Long citadel. The statue, which was thought to have magic powers, disappeared and has since been replaced by a wooden replica. The pagoda's modest exterior belies its exquisite interior and atmosphere. An impressive line-up of gilt Buddha statues forms the central altar.

On Ly Quoc Su Street, to the right of the cathedral, is the small **Ly Trieu Quoc Su Pagoda**, also known as Chua Kong, the Pagoda of Confucius. It was founded under the Ly Dynasty in the 11th century and later restored in 1855. The pagoda contains some attractive wooden statues and an old bonze, who is

said to have lived there for over 60 years without ever leaving the building.

Part of Hanoi's charm lies in the pagodas, temples and *dinh* (community houses) that are encountered quite by chance. Some are still used for worship, although most have been transformed into schools, government offices or private businesses. The Hoa Loc Dinh, at 90 Hang Dao Street, was once a communal house for people from the village of Hai Duong. It is now a shop selling blue jeans. According to records discovered on a stele, these villagers settled here towards the end of the Tang Dynasty era and founded the artisan district of Thai Cuc, which became Hang Dao (Silk) Street.

The **Bach Ma Temple** (White Horse Temple) on Hang Buom Street is dedicated to the deity Bach Ma. Originally built during the 9th century, it was reconstructed in the 18th and 19th centuries. In regular use, it remains in a good state of repair.

A small house at 48 Hang Ngang Street houses the **Independence Museum**. Here, Ho Chi Minh wrote Vietnam's declaration of independence, which borrows considerably from America's own declaration of independence, and it was where communist revolutionaries met in secret.

The area around the **Dong Xuan market**, at the end of Hang Dao in the northern part of the Ancient Quarter, is an interesting place to explore. The market itself was gutted in a huge fire in 1994, but renovations have mostly restored its old ambience.

Merchants sell a variety of goods here, including baskets, wicker, small carpets, soup, vermicelli and rice. In the streets around the market, farmers squat on the pavement selling their produce directly to passers-by. Keep an eye out for caviar, French wine, champagne and Russian vodka, as they are surprisingly cheap in Hanoi, and definitely the genuine article, no less.

Florists add a welcome splash of color with their fragrant blooms. Nearby, a traditional medicine shop sells all manner of cures, including snake wine and lizards preserved in alcohol. Do not be

Shop of art articles, just like the sign says.

put off by appearances – the gecko elixir is excellent. Other vendors sell live snakes, birds and monkeys.

Southwest of Hoan Kiem Lake, several blocks away, the **Quan Su (Ambassadors' Pagoda)** is located on Quan Su Street. In the 17th century, the site was a house used to accommodate visiting foreign ambassadors and envoys from other Buddhist countries.

Two blocks away was the site of the infamous **Hoa Lo prison**, called the Hanoi Hilton by American POWs incarcerated here. It is of importance to Vietnamese communists for another reason: French colonialists imprisoned many Vietnamese revolutionaries in the building. Although the prison has been largely demolished to make way for a hotel and office tower, the main gate and front portion have been preserved as a museum. Across the street from the prison is the **Hanoi People's Court**. To the south of the prison and the Quan Su pagoda, there is a small lovely lake, **Ho Thien Quang**, where visitors can rent paddle boats. Across the street is an entrance to **Lenin Park** (and to the right, Hanoi's circus). Facing Tran Nhan Tong Street, the park is said to have been built by local voluntary workers on marshy land once used as a rubbish tip. This attractive park is designed around a large central lake. A small train for children runs through the park; there is an American fighter jet on display.

Heading west from the center of town is the **old French quarter**, or what is now the diplomatic area of Hanoi. Here, the old villas house foreign embassies and government offices on quiet, tree-lined streets.

The **Bao Tang My Thuat (Fine Arts Museum)**, on Nguyen Thai Hoc Street, features an expensive collection of artifacts. Exhibits cover some of Vietnam's ethnic minorities and history, and on display are beautiful wooden statues of Buddha dating from the 17th century, the Dong Son bronze drums, and other Vietnamese art, both that of ancient and contemporary times.

Nearby, across the street, is the **Van Mieu (Temple of Literature)**. Built in

Slow moment at the Fine Art Museum.

1070 under the reign of King Ly Thai Tong, the temple is dedicated to Confucius. In 1076, the temple was adjoined by the Quoc Tu Giam, School of the Elite of the Nation, Vietnam's first national university. Under the Tran Dynasty, the school was renamed the Quoc Hoc Vien, or the National College, in 1235. The Van Mieu became known as the Temple of Literature when the capital was transferred to Hue at the beginning of the 18th century.

Above the main entrance gate is an inscription requesting visitors to dismount from horses before entering.

The large temple enclosure is divided into five walled courtyards. After passing through the Van Mieu Gate and the first two courtyards, one arrives at the **Khue Van Cac (Pleiade Pavilion)**, where the men of letters used to recite their poems. Through the **Dai Thanh Mon (Great Wall Gate)**, an open courtyard surrounds a large central pool known as the Thien Quang Tinh (Heavenly Light Well). Here, under the trees on either side, 82 stone stelae, survivors of the original 117, rest on the backs of stone tortoises. The stelae are inscribed with the names, works and academic records of the laureates who succeeded in the three-year doctorate courses between 1442 and 1779.

The Dai Thanh (Great Success Gate) leads to the temple itself. Facing it is the Bai Duong (House of Ceremonies), where sacrifices were offered in honor of Confucius. Today, musicians perform traditional music during the day – a small fee is charged for those who chose to sit and listen.

Behind it are the Eastern Gate and the Great Success Sanctuary, which have been renovated. The last part of the temple, the Khai Thanh Sanctuary, on Nguyen Thai Hoc Street, is in ruins.

To the north nearby, on Dien Bien Phu Street, is one of the symbols of Hanoi, the **flag tower, Cot Co**. Built in 1812 under the Nguyen Dynasty as part of the Hanoi citadel, the hexagonal 60-meter (200-ft) tower is more or less all that remains of the citadel, which was destroyed at the end of the 19th century.

War relics at the Army Museum.

156

Next to it, **Bao Tang Quan Doi (Army Museum)**, was recently renovated and chronicles Vietnam's battles for independence and unification against the French and American patrons of South Vietnam. The crumpled wreckage of a B-52 bomber sits in an outside courtyard. Inside, there are uniforms of captured American pilots, photographs of war heroes, and items belonging to the fallen leaders of what was South Vietnam. In a small theater, grainy black-and-white footage of the last days of the Vietnam War is shown in front of a map that lights up to show the communist troops advancing into the south.

Across the street, there is a small, triangular-shaped park with a **statue of Lenin**. Children play soccer on the plaza in front of the statue, and in the park behind it, villagers from the countryside congregate with goods to sell. Few people pay much attention to Lenin himself, who seems something of an anachronism in a country that has cast aside much of communism for capitalism.

Further down Dien Bien Phu looms the imposing and impressive structure of **Lang Chu Tich Ho Chi Minh (Ho Chi Minh's mausoleum)**, in Ba Dinh Square. His embalmed corpse lies in a glass casket within this monumental tomb – contrary to his wish to be cremated. The place is usually closed for three months in the fall. Some say his body is packed off to Russia for an overhaul; others say he is repaired in the basement of the mausoleum.

The construction on the mausoleum began in 1973 and finished in 1975. Ho Chi Minh's embalmed body lies on top of a platform in a cold room, where visitors are ushered through quickly. No cameras or handbags can be taken inside. Foreigners are whisked to the front of the lines, which are usually long, especially on weekends. The strictly-guarded mausoleum is built of marble, granite and precious wood gathered from all over the country.

It was from this square that Ho Chi Minh read his declaration of independence speech on 2 September 1945. The same date, 2 September, is also the day of Ho's death. (Although it was offi-cially reported as 3 September for years, because officials did not want to dampen National Day celebrations that took place the day before.)

Behind the mausoleum, there is a quiet and shaded park with a pond, and a house built on stilts where Ho Chi Minh is said to have lived much of the time during the war. Nearby is the unique **Chua Mot Cot (One Pillar Pagoda)**. Built in 1049 under the Ly Dynasty, this beautiful wooden pagoda rests on a single stone pillar rising out of a lotus pool. The banyan tree behind the pagoda was planted by President Nehru of India in 1958 during an official visit to the young Vietnamese republic.

Legend has it that in a dream, King Ly Thai To saw the goddess Quan Am seated on a lotus leaf offering him a male child in her outstretched arms. Shortly after his dream, he married a young peasant girl who bore him the male heir of which he had dreamed. The king is said to have built the pagoda as a sign of his gratitude. The small **Dien Huu Pagoda** shares this lovely setting.

Behind the park with the pagodas is the modern **Bao Tang Ho Chi Minh (Ho Chi Minh Museum)**. A massive concrete structure, the museum has some rather bizarre exhibits, including giant bowls of fruit and an Edsel, but it also presents a thorough history of Ho Chi Minh's revolutionary life.

From Ba Dinh Square, where the National Assembly building is located across from the mausoleum, and where there is a war memorial, head north toward **Ho Tay** (West Lake), formerly known as the Lake of Mists. This lake, the largest in Hanoi, lies in an ancient bed of the Red River. Royal and warlord palaces once graced its banks; these were destroyed in feudal battles.

Today, the lake is the site of considerable building activity. Large villas, hotels and restaurants have sprung up in the area, which now houses the many foreigners living in Hanoi.

During an uprising against the occupying Chinese in 545, the national hero Ly Bon built a wooden-and-bamboo citadel at the mouth of the To Lich River, at the same time building the Khai Quoc (Foundation of the Country) Pagoda beside the Red River. In the 17th century, the pagoda was transferred to its present site on the tiny peninsula of the Ho Tay and renamed **Tran Quoc Pagoda** (Defense of the Country). The Tran Quoc is one of Vietnam's most ancient pagodas; its stele, dating from 1639, recounts the pagoda's long history. Visitors walk down a long path into a walled compound.

Legend says the lake was previously the site of a huge forest, the lair of a wicked fox with nine tails. The creature terrorized the neighborhood until it was drowned by the Dragon King, who in the process of unleashing the waters to get rid of the beast, created the lake.

No less fantastic is another legend that tells the story of an 11th-century bonze and a golden buffalo. The bonze, Khong Lo, had an enormous bronze bell made. When its sound first reached the ears of the golden buffalo, the confused creature, believing that he had heard his mother's voice, rushed immediately to-

Shoe stall, and plenty of shoes, and pottery works near Long Bien Bridge.

wards the south and in his stampede transformed the site into a lake.

Separated from the lake by Thanh Nien Street is **Truc Bach** (White Silk Lake). This was the ancient site of Lord Trinh's summer palace, which later became a harem where he detained his wayward concubines. The lake derives its name from the beautiful white silk these concubines were forced to weave for the princesses.

Just south of the Tran Quoc Pagoda, and on the opposite side of Truc Bach, is a small stone tablet commemorating the downing of an American bomber flown by Navy pilot (the sign incorrectly identifies him as an Air Force pilot) John McCain, who was one of the American POWs incarcerated at the infamous "Hanoi Hilton" prison, and who is now a U.S. Senator. He has visited Vietnam a number of times since the war, and was a vocal proponent of the eventual normalization of American relations with Vietnam.

Nearby, the ornate **Quan Thanh Pagoda** beside the lake was originally built during the Ly Dynasty (1010–1225). It houses a huge bronze bell and an enormous, four-ton bronze statue of Tran Vu, guardian deity of the north, to whom the temple is dedicated. It was Tran Vu who helped King An Duong dispose of the devils and ghosts that harassed and plagued the building of Vietnam's ancient capital at Co Loa.

In the middle of the lake, on a small peninsula, is a popular pagoda, **Phu Tay Ho**. Reached by following Yen Phu Street, and then walking down a long path, the pagoda is crowded on holidays and every month on the 15th day of the lunar calendar. Thousands of people make a pilgrimage here, and the walk is lined with restaurants, shops and karaoke bars. This pagoda is particularly popular with young Vietnamese, and it is said people go here to pray for a good husband or wife.

Outside the city center: In the south of the city on Pho To Lao is **Den Hai Ba Trung** (Temple of the Two Sisters), also known as the Dong Nhan temple after the village that surrounded the site

The flowers are always available.

at the time of its construction, in 1142. The temple is dedicated to the two Trung sisters who organized an uprising against the Chinese Han invaders in AD 40 – the first uprising against foreign invaders in Vietnamese history.

The temple has since been restored and contains some of the sisters' belongings. Two unusually-formed stone statues, said to represent the two sisters kneeling, are kept in a small room and brought out once a year, during February, for a procession that evokes their battle against the Chinese. Outside the central court are several small temples dedicated to the first Buddhists who constructed the temple.

A little further south on Bach Mai Street, the **Lien Phai Pagoda** and the Buddhist monastery, **Lien Phai Tu**, or Lieu Khai, is sheltered in an attractive garden. The temple was built under the Le Dynasty and reconstructed by one of the Trinh lords in 1732. The temple was restored in 1884 and again more recently. Three statues, two representing good and evil, occupy the main room.

The **Tay Dang communal house** in Hanoi's Bay Vi suburb is worth visiting for its beautiful architectural structure and carving.

It is not known exactly when the communal house was built, but inscriptions on one of its beams reveal that it was extensively restored in the 16th century, and that further repairs were again carried out in 1808, 1926 and 1942. Built entirely of hardwood, it comprises five partitions and four roofs, whose curling tops are decorated with *tu linh* – dragons, unicorns, tortoises and the phoenix – the four animals, according to folklore, that bring happiness. Many valuable woodcarvings grace the interior. Bas reliefs in this beautiful old wooden building depict detailed scenes from everyday life.

Behind Thu Le Park in Thu Le village, in the northwest of the city, is the 11th-century **Voi Phuc** (Temple of the Kneeling Elephants). It was built by King Ly Thai To in honor of his son, Prince Linh Lang, who distinguished himself during the resistance against the Sung invaders by charging the enemy with his squadron of elephants. The simple lakeside temple houses statues of the prince and his generals. In front of the temple are stone statues of kneeling elephants, from which the temple derives its name.

Nearby is the **Lang Pagoda**, located down a small street (too narrow for cars), off of Duong Lang. A large gate marks the street to the pagoda. The pagoda is dedicated to King Ly Thanh Ton and was later reconstructed sometime in the 17th century.

Southwest of the city, in Dong Da district, is the **Go Dong Da** (Mound of the Multitudes) on Tay Son Street, next to number 356.

Legend says that Go Dong Da was formed by the bodies of Chinese soldiers killed after Quang Trung's victory. Very little remains of the temple that was constructed on the site, but dozens of steps lead to the top of the mound. Beyond the mound is a large statue of Quang Trung, built in the social realist style that long dominated public art in Vietnam.

In the old part of the city, spices for sale.

Co Loa

I n the Dong Anh district of Hanoi's western suburbs lie the remains of the citadel fortress of **Co Loa**. Excavations in the area have uncovered quantities of ancient arms and many bronze arrowheads. Co Loa dates from 257 BC, when it served as the capital of the Thuc Dynasty, under King An Duong Vuong. Of the nine ramparts that covered an area of more than five square kilometers (2 sq mi), three are still visible. Architectural and sculptural works remain in the citadel's center.

Within the citadel's gateway, an historical banyan tree shades the shrine dedicated to Princess My Chau. Inside is a rough stone statue of a headless woman thought to be the princess. Further on is the upper temple dedicated to King An Duong Vuong. People gather here on January 6 every year to celebrate the king's efforts against foreign invaders.

The Vietnamese, with their irrepressible talent for blending history and legend, will tell you that King An Duong Vuong, of Tay Au, invaded Lac Viet after his request to marry the king of Vietnam's daughter was unceremoniously refused. He managed to annex the country of his coveted princess without too much difficulty and amalgamated the territories of Tay Au and Lac Viet to form the kingdom of Au Lac.

Well aware that this expansion would antagonize his great northern neighbor, China, An Duong Vuong wasted no time in building the walls of his new capital. But for some mysterious reason his efforts were frustrated and the walls repeatedly collapsed. The mystery was finally revealed when the golden tortoise, Kim Quy, appeared to the king in a dream and disclosed that occult forces were responsible. Aided by the tortoise, the king was able to defeat the evil forces and complete his indestructible fortress. China, however, wanted the fortress destroyed. General Trieu Da was picked for the task. However, the repeated attempts of his powerful forces proved futile. The golden tortoise again appeared to the king, and this time provided him with a magic crossbow.

The following day the Chinese forces suffered heavy losses from the arrows of the crossbow. Seeing this, Trieu Da realized that all was not as it appeared and so called for peace. He asked for, and was granted, the hand of the king's daughter, Princess My Chau, for his son, Trong Thuy.

During the honeymoon, Trong Thuy asked his young wife to show him her father's crossbow. The unsuspecting My Chau obediently did so, but Trong Thuy took the magic crossbow and substituted another in its place. The king was so furious when he discovered this that he beheaded the princess. Her inconsolable husband is said to have drowned himself in the well in front of the temple dedicated to An Duong Vuong.

Co Loa was not only Vietnam's very first capital, but also something of an architectural marvel. Three earth walls, 4 to 5 meters (13 to 16 ft) high, and at certain strategic points, 8 to 12 meters (26 to 39 ft) high, enclosed the capital. The eight-kilometer-long (5-mi) outer wall was reinforced with thorny bamboo hedges and surrounded by a deep moat that allowed troops and boats to circulate.

Watchmen scrutinized the horizon from watch towers built at the eight cardinal points of the citadel's ramparts. They continued their vigil throughout the night, kept awake by gongs that resounded every half hour until dawn. A marine conch shell was used to sound the alert. Due to the citadel's spiral form, sound from within it was amplified and carried as far as the surrounding villages. ■

NORTH OF HANOI

The rugged country to the northwest of Hanoi boasts, among other things, Vietnam's tallest mountain, an unusual marketplace where love is for sale, and the roots of Ho Chi Minh's communist revolution against occupying foreigners.

The province neighboring Hanoi to the northwest, **Vinh Phu**, is the cradle of the pre-Vietnamese Hung Lac people, and of the ancestral land of the Viet people, who first settled here before moving into the Red River Delta. Bronze relics 4,000 years old have been discovered in the region.

The area still bears the mark of the early settlers' presence in the remains of the **Hung temples**. These were built by the rulers of the Van Lang Kingdom between the 7th and 3rd centuries BC, when a line of 18 successive Hung kings graced the throne of Vang Lang.

In all, there are three Hung temples on Mount Nghia Linh, in Phong Chau district. The lowest temple, Den Ha, is reached by climbing 225 steps. Below the temple at the foot of the hill is an arched portal, flanked by two huge stone columns engraved with two parallel sentences glorifying the origins of the Vietnamese people.

A further 168 steps lead up to the middle temple, Den Hung. An additional 102 steps must be climbed to reach the superior temple, Den Thuong. The temple is dedicated to the deities of heaven, earth and rice, and to Than Giong, the infant hero, who in the third century BC is said to have chased out the Chinese Han invaders, assisted by a genie in the form of an iron horse. It was here that the last of the Hung kings transferred his power to the Thuc king, at the end of the third century. People from all parts of the country congregate here every March 10th, the anniversary of their ancestor's death, for the Hung temple festival.

Vinh Phu's diverse scenic beauty is enhanced by a range of flora, extensive green tea plantations, and in winter, the beautiful white blooms of *sasanca*.

To escape the heat and humidity prevalent through much of the year, many people flock to the mountain retreats and cooler temperatures at the **Tam Dao resort**, at an altitude of 880 meters (2,850 ft) and established in 1902. It sits on a large plateau within a valley about 90 kilometers (50 mi) northwest of Hanoi, in the Tam Dao mountain range. These mountains stretch from the northwest to the southeast, separating Vinh Phu from Bac Thai Province in the north.

The name Tam Dao, meaning three islands, derives from the three mountains, Thien Thi, Thach Ban and Phu Nghia, all at about 1,400 meters (4,500 ft) and which dominate the landscape, appearing from a distance like three islands jutting above a sea of clouds. Rare trees and plants cover the mountain sides, and the forests harbor many species of wild animals, butterflies and flowers. The resort's calm atmosphere is complemented by an average temperature much cooler than that of Hanoi. A stream known as Suoi Bac (Silvery Stream) meanders its way past the

foot of Mt Thien Thi, creating languid pools perfect for swimming. A waterfall cascades in three stages to form a lake; nearby are several pagodas.

In Lap Thach district in the northwest, the Binh Son Tower of the **Vinh Khanh Pagoda** rises 16 meters (50 ft) into the sky. Built under the Tran Dynasty in the 13th century, the 11-tiered, baked-clay tower is adorned with varied sculpture.

Nearby is the **Vinh Son snake farm**, in Vinh Lac district. Established over 10 years ago, it breeds snakes and produces snake wine, and an ointment containing snake venom that is used to relieve muscle and joint inflammation.

In early 1945, Ho Chi Minh arrived in **Tan Trao**, located high in the mountains east of **Tuyen Quang** town, north of Vinh Phu. Here, he set up the Communist Party headquarters, and later the provincial government of the Republic of Vietnam. The 1945 August Revolution began in Tan Trao, when Gen. Vo Nguyen Giap led the Viet Minh troops eastward to attack the occupying Japanese garrison at Thai Nguyen, in Bac Thai province. Simultaneous uprisings took place throughout the country. In Tan Trao today, there is a museum dedicated to Ho Chi Minh. Surviving here, too, is a giant banyan tree (there used to be two, but one fell in a storm in 1994) where Giap rallied his troops. Also located here are the Na Lua (Ho Chi Minh's simple jungle hut) and the Tay minority *dinh* (communal house), where the first national congress met.

Further north, the highland region of **Ha Giang Province** shares a common border with China in the north. This northernmost province is also one of Vietnam's poorest. The rocky, inhospitable mountains leave little room for rice cultivation. The people, mostly ethnic minorities, scrape a meager existence from growing maize. They grow some fruit, mainly oranges, and the production of honey is also on the rise. The Dong Van district, bordering China, has the highest illiteracy rate in the country at 98 percent.

Three large rivers – the Lo, Gam and Pho Day – flow through this province,

Spectacular and wild scenery of the north.

where primal forests provide a valuable source of timber, and of more than 1,000 species of medicinal plants. Heavy mists shroud the mountains during the winter months, when snow sometimes falls on the peaks in the higher regions.

West along the border, **Lao Cai** is the terminus for the second northern rail route to China. Here, too, the town is benefitting from cross-border trade. Vietnam's highest mountain, **Fan Si Pan**, which peaks at 3,143 meters (10,311 ft), rises above Lao Cai province.

Sa Pa, in the northeast corner, was a hill station created by the French in 1922 as a means to escape the oppressive Red River Delta summer heat. This has now become a favorite weekend destination of expatriates living in Hanoi, and for backpackers. Organized treks through the surrounding countryside can be arranged.

A main draw for foreign visitors remains the so-called "love market" on Saturday nights and Sunday mornings. Ethnic minority people in colorful traditional costumes meet to sing, dance and drink. Most importantly, it is an opportunity for all to have one-night affairs. Husbands and wives arrive, eat and drink, and then go off to find a lover for the night before meeting again in the morning, drinking some more and then tottering home.

The less amorously-inclined can hire a horse-drawn cart to visit Hmong and White Tay villages, the Bac Falls, the May Bridge and other scenic spots.

South of Lao Cai, **Yen Bai Province** is famous for its rubies. The area is dominated by Thac Ba Lake, which is dotted with islands. Visitors can hire boats to tour the lake and islands.

Northeast to China: The northern circuit from Hanoi to the Chinese border begins in Ha Bac Province and its key region of Bac Ninh, then crosses the rice paddies of the Red River Delta before entering the mountainous regions near the Chinese border, the site of several skirmishes between the Chinese and Vietnamese military in past years.

Ha Bac Province is full of historical, cultural and religious vestiges, and the

thnic
ninorities
ear Sa Pa.

area around **Bac Ninh**, the largest city, is home to more cultural and religious festivals than any other area in Vietnam.

Among the architectural remains are the ancient **Luy Lau Citadel**, and the temple and mausoleum of Si Nhiep, the governor of ancient Giao Chi.

The **Phat Tich Pagoda** (Relic of Buddha) on Mt Lan Kha, in Phuong Hoang village, was built in the 11th century under the Ly Dynasty. It has been badly damaged by the ravages of time and war, but a 40-meter (120 ft) stone statue of Amitabha Buddha dating from the 11th century remains intact within the pagoda.

A typical example of Buddhist architecture, the **But Thap Pagoda**, built under the Tran Dynasty in the 13th century and renovated in 1647, is found on the bank of the Duong River, in Dinh To village, Tien Son district. It incorporates a collection of both everyday and religious buildings, including Bao Nghiem, a stone tower 13 meters (40 ft) high that stands in front of the pagoda. The pagoda houses more than 50 Buddhist statues, including one of the goddess of mercy, Quan Yin, the Asiatic metamorphosis of ancient India's Bodisattva Avalokitecvara, with her thousand eyes and arms. Those who worship her believe that her many eyes and arms have supernatural power – the eyes to see and the hands to help those in need. The pagoda also contains statues of the two Trinh princesses, and of Thi Kinh, yet another goddess of mercy.

The village of **Lim**, also in Tien Son district, is the site of the popular Lim Festival, held every year shortly after Tet. For three days, from the 13th to the 15th of the first lunar month, people from all over the region converge on the village for the competitions of popular Quan Ho folk songs, sung alternately by groups of young men and women.

The traditional theater at the **Dinh Bang communal house** in Dinh Bang is something of an architectural marvel on stilts. Built of ironwood in 1736, the building is one of the largest of its kind in Vietnam.

Dong Ho village, in Bach Ninh, is

Field work near Sa Pa.

famous for its communal production of woodcut prints. The prints depict traditional themes, and their preparation is as historic in nature as the prints themselves. The various stages of production – carving the wood block, preparing the paper, obtaining natural colors from plants and minerals – are tasks mastered and shared by family members.

Cam Son Lake in Luc Ngan district is surrounded by limestone mountains. This tranquil and picturesque setting offers accommodation, with rest houses on some of the small islands in the lake.

The road north begins to climb into the higher elevations as it leaves Ha Bac Province and enters Lang Son. The ascent into the mountains presents stunning scenery.

Lang Son Province shares a common border with China's Guangxi Province. Mountains and forests cover 80 percent of the province's land area. Tigers, panthers, bears, deer, pangolin, chamois and monitor lizards are among the animals found here. Provincial specialties include forest products such as fragrant mushrooms anise, and a fine-flavored tobacco. Tay, Nung, Hmong, Zao, Hoa and Nghia are among the ethnic minorities living in the province. The Ky Cung River that flows through the province is unique in that it flows northward to China. The other rivers in the region all flow south.

Shortly before the town of Lang Son, near the Chinese border, is a waterfall known locally as the **Pissing Cow Falls**, so named because it flows over a cliff edge and then fans out. It is reached through a private garden and is a favorite spot for local children to play.

The narrow **Chi Lang Gorge**, a series of passes connected by tortuous tracks forged between high mountains south of the Chinese-Vietnamese border, is a battleground where the Vietnamese have fought many major battles against Chinese invaders throughout history. In 1076, the Vietnamese defeated 300,000 Song troops here, and in 1427, nearly 100,000 Ming troops received the same treatment. The gorge's northern entrance is known as Quy Quan Mon (Barbarian

order trade
s becoming
etter
rganized...

Invaders Gate) and the southern exit is called Ngo The (Swearing Path). The almost incessant fighting on this northern border has forged the temperament and galvanized the resilient character of the northern Vietnamese people.

The provincial capital, **Lang Son**, lies about 150 kilometers (100 mi) from Hanoi. The Ky Lua market, held in the mountainous region nearby, is a popular gathering place for members of the region's many minority groups.

Lang Son was destroyed by retreating Chinese troops in 1979, but it is now booming through new trade opportunities with the former enemy. The town is also the transit point for trains from Hanoi. In early 1996, the line reopened to cross the border.

Nearby is **Nhi Tam Thanh**, an area that includes numerous caves and grottoes, many of which are used for worship of spirits. Overlooking the site is **Waiting Woman Mountain**. Legend says an outcrop of rock is a woman who waited so long for her husband that she turned into stone. In the area are also

ruins of forts and walls built to keep the Chinese at bay.

Half an hour's drive north is **Dong Dang**, a town right on the border. The crossing here is known as the Friendship Gate, optimistically named, given the sporadic exchanges of gunfire between Vietnam and China up until 1992.

Lang Son is joined to **Cao Bang**, 120 kilometers (75 mi) away, by Highway 4. This road, which runs almost parallel to the Chinese border from the coast to the west, was the site of numerous skirmishes in the late 1940s between French colonial troops and the Viet Minh guerrillas. The Viet Minh's main base was in these mountains, and the French tried to maintain garrisons at Lang Son and Cao Bang. The Vietnamese ousted them from these areas by 1950, however.

Cao Bang shares a long border with China. Forest covers 90 percent of the province, and the climate is cool, particularly in winter when snow caps the high peaks. The picturesque **An Giac Falls**, in Trung Khanh district, are formed by a stretch of the Quy Xuan River falling from a height of 30 meters (100 ft). Many wild orchids grow in the region. Limestone mountains and forests surround another of the province's beauty spots, Lake Thang Hen, in Quang Hoa district.

South of Cao Bang, toward Hanoi, lies **Bac Thai Province**, a region intimately linked with anti-colonial resistance, particularly useful as its mountainous terrain rendered the region virtually inaccessible to French troops. The climate here is both tropical and subtropical, with an average temperature of 28°C (82°F) during the hottest month and 14°C (56°F) during the coldest. Palms with wonderful fan-shaped leaves and varieties of bamboo abound in the province.

Located on a modest mountain top, **Lake Ba Be**, in Cho Ra district, is the largest lake in the country. This impressive lake, over a kilometer wide and nine kilometers long, reaches a depth of 30 meters (100 ft) and offers an opportunity for a spot of sailing. The surrounding lush forests harbor numerous birds and animals.

Left, festival crowd. **Right**, market talk a Sa Pa.

HAI PHONG AND HA LONG BAY

Heading east from Hanoi eventually leads to white sand beaches washed by the **South China Sea**, or **Bien Dong**, which remains a constant source of contention between Vietnam and China – both claim rights to the sea and to the archipelago offshore, rich in oil reserves.

Before reaching the coast, the road passes through the relatively flat **province of Hai Hung**, famous for its beautiful orchards. Fruit from Hai Hung, especially longan and lychee, is reputedly the best in northern Vietnam, supplying the royal court in earlier times. Today, Hai Hung is known for its porcelain; the largest factory in northern Vietnam, built with the assistance of China, is located here. A food known as *banh cuon,* a rice pancake wrapped around minced pork, originates from Hai Hung.

In Hung Dao commune, the **Kiep Bac Pagoda**, 60 kilometers (40 mi) from Hanoi, dates from the 13th century. It is dedicated to the national hero Tran Hung Dao, who vanquished the Mongols in the 13th century and was made a saint by the people. His army encamped here in the Kiep Bac Valley. His statue – plus those of his two daughters, General Pham Ngu Lao, and the genies of the Northern Star and Southern Cross – are venerated in this temple. The temple festival falls on the 20th day of the eighth lunar month. This site is shared by an old garden of medicinal plants, formerly used in the army's medical service.

Nearby, **Con Son** is the home of another national hero, Nguyen Trai (1380–1442), who helped King Le Loi chase out the Ming invaders and free the country from Chinese domination at the beginning of the 15th century. At the foot of the hill, the well-maintained **Hung Pagoda** contains statues of Nguyen Trai, his maternal grandfather and the three superior bonzes, who founded the Truc Lam Buddhist sect. Some 600 stone steps lead up to the summit, where there is a superb view of the mountain ranges.

The road between Hanoi and **Hai Phong**, Vietnam's third-largest city and the north's most important port, is jammed with the clutter of an economic boom – trucks carrying goods to and from the port blare their horns and crowd out the bicycles and motorbikes laden down with chickens, bags of rice and pigs on their way to market. The country plans to build an industrial zone along this route, but plans have been delayed because of concerns that too many rice fields are being paved over to make room for factories.

Hai Phong itself occupies the right bank of the busy **Cam River**, 120 kilometers (75 mi) from Hanoi in the northeast of the Bac Bo delta. The city, built in 1888, is crossed by 16 rivers. The most famous of these is the **Bach Dang River**, where, in 938, the national hero Ngo Quyen defeated the large southern Han fleet. The Sung invaders suffered a bitter defeat here in 981 and the Mongols suffered the same fate in 1288. The first of the French warships arrived in Hai Phong in 1872 and the last units of the French expeditionary forces

left the same way in 1955. The port of Hai Phong, inland from the eastern sea, constitutes an important gateway for Vietnam's foreign trade.

Today, many industrial plants, engineering factories, glass, brick and cement works, and lime kilns are evident from the main road into Hai Phong. The city's industrial area sprung up after the French left, and more recently, local industry has grown to meet the demands of the construction in the area. Hai Phong was badly damaged by American bombing during the Vietnam War, but thousands of new residences have been built, and today the city is thriving.

More a busy port than a tourist attraction, a brief stop is long enough to take in the sights. The architecture surrounding the market, city center and the river betrays the former colonial presence. The fish market is worth a visit early in the morning, when the fishermen are arriving with their catches, often with some rather unusual sea products.

In the shops opposite the **Dien Bien Phu Street Theater Square**, a variety of handicrafts – including mats, brass and cast iron figures, and tortoise-shell, horn, lacquer and mother of pearl inlay articles – are sold at reasonable prices.

Like every city in Vietnam, Hai Phong has its temples. The **Du Hang Pagoda** in the south of the city was built three centuries ago. The **Nghe Temple**, built in 1919 in the city center, is dedicated to Le Chan, the valiant woman warrior who aided the Trung sisters in the uprising against the Chinese in 39 AD. The **Hang Kenh Pavilion**, on Nguyen Cong Tru, houses a surprising 500 wooden sculptures representing the themes of everyday life.

The **Cung Chuc communal house** in Cung Chuc village, Vinh Bao district, is worth visiting for its unique architecture, and clay statues. The traditional entertainment staged here during local traditional festivals includes water puppetry and water buffalo fights.

The **Elephant Mount**, near Hai Phong, offers the **Long Hoa Pagoda** and vestiges of a citadel fortress dating from the Mac era of the 16th century.

Backwaters of Hai Phong

Halfway up the mountain, the Chi Lai communal house has been converted into a museum, where neolithic bronze artifacts are displayed. Caves within the mountain served as guerrilla base camps against the French.

From Hai Phong, travelers can also visit the **Bao Ha woodcarving village**, which has earned a reputation for its high-quality woodcarving ever since it was founded by the master craftsman Nguyen Cong Hue, in the late 17th century. After his death, his students carved his likeness and built a temple in his honor. One of his most famous statues can be seen in the **Ba Xa Temple** at Bao Ha. Most of the work produced by the village craftsmen is of a religious nature; however, they also turn out a variety of carved animals. The fragrant jackwood is the wood most preferred by the craftsmen, who value its beauty, lightness, and softness.

From Hai Phong, ferries travel to Ha Long Bay, stopping along the way at the **Cat Ba archipelago**, 80 kilometers (50 mi) from the coast. Its 366 islets and islands cover some 20,000 hectares (50,000 acres). The area is known for its beautiful beaches and interesting grottoes. The largest island, **Cat Ba**, occupies 190 square kilometers (75 sq mi). Its beautiful landscape features forested hills, coastal mangrove and freshwater swamps, lakes and waterfalls. Much of the island is covered in forest, of which some is primeval forest. Some 570 hectares (1,400 acres) have been reserved as a national park.

The park's rich diversity of flora and fauna includes 21 species of birds – among these the hornbill – reptiles, and 28 species of mammals, including wild cats, boar, porcupines, monkeys, deer and gibbons. Human remains and stone tools from the neolithic era have been discovered in some of the island's caves. Submerged vegetation, hot springs and limestone lakes add to the attractions.

Boats from Hai Phong also leave for **Cat Hai Island** and the **Do Son Peninsula** east of the city, where palm-fringed sandy beaches set against pine-forested hills stretch far out into the clear waters

of the **Tonkin Gulf (Vinh Bac Bo)**. In the past, Do Son was exclusively reserved for the French, and for privileged Vietnamese holding high positions in the colonial administration. Today, Do Son is a popular weekend spot with local Vietnamese.

Vietnam's only **casino** (but not its first – there was a raucous gambling den in Saigon before President Ngo Dinh Diem outlawed it in the 1950s) sits alone atop the cliffs of Do Son, overlooking the South China Sea. It even has a helipad. What it doesn't have, yet, are gamblers, at least not many. Although Vietnamese themselves love gambling, the government doesn't allow them to visit the Do Son casino, financed and built in part by a Macau casino magnate. The casino is open to foreigners only.

Other possibilities here are visits to the **Nguyen Binh Khiem Temple**, a museum, the ancient Hang Kenh communal house, a carpet weaving shop and the small Den Ba De on Doc Mountain.

Bay of the Landing Dragon: No trip to northern Vietnam could be considered complete without a trip to **Quang Ninh Province**. This province shares a common border with China in the north, and harbors one of the wonders of the world with probably the most stunning scenery in Vietnam, **Ha Long Bay (Vinh Ha Long)**. The bay's tranquil beauty encompasses 4,000 square kilometers (1,500 sq mi), dotted with well over 1,000 limestone islands and islets, many of them without names. Bizarre rock sculptures jutting dramatically from the sea and numerous grottoes have created an enchanted, timeless world. The sails of the junks and sampans gliding on the bay add further to the beauty of the scene. Ha Long Bay was made famous to Westerners in the French film Indochine.

A boat trip from **Hong Gai** on the bay includes stops at some of the grottoes – the **Bo Nau (Pelican) cave**, the 2-kilometer-long **Hang Hanh tunnel** and the **Trinh Nu (Virgin) cave**.

Folklore claims that Trinh Nu cave was named after a young girl whose parents were poor fishing folk. They **Waiting for their boat to come in.**

could not afford to own a boat of their own and had to rent one from a rich man. When they could not pay what they owed him, the rich man demanded their beautiful daughter in lieu of their debt, and so forced her to marry him. The poor girl refused all his advances. He had her beaten, but still she would not submit to him, so he finally exiled her to a grotto, where she starved to death. She was immortalized in stone by a rock resembling her figure that emerged from her burial site.

The most spectacular of all the bay's grottoes is the beautiful **Dau Go cave**, with its stalactites and stalagmites resembling beasts, birds and human forms. It was christened the Grotte des Merveilles (Wonder Grotto) by the first French tourists who visited it in the late 19th century.

Ha Long Bay has been the setting of many historic battles against invasions from the north. It is believed that the sharp bamboo stakes that General Tran Hung Dao planted in the Bach Dang River to destroy Kublai Khan's fleet were stored in caves here.

The name Ha Long means the Landing Dragon, evoking an ancient dragon that in the mists of time is said to have descended in the bay.

In such a place it comes as no surprise to hear that some people claim to have seen the Vietnamese equivalent of the Loch Ness monster. It is said to be a black creature resembling a snake about 30 meters (100 ft) long, which supposedly inhabits the bay.

Within view of Ha Long Bay is the beautiful **Mt Yen Tu**. Minorities such as the San Chi, Dao, Tay and Hoa live in the vicinity. Perched on the summit of this mist-shrouded mount is the 13th-century pagoda built by King Tran Nhan Tong. After vanquishing the Mongols, the king abdicated in favor of his son, Tran Anh Tong, and retired to a retreat at Mt Yen Tu, where he founded the Thien Tong sect (or Vietnamese Zen) of Truc Lam Dhyana (the bamboo forest), a unique form of Buddhism.

Forty-five stupas containing the bones of retired bonzes lie scattered amidst a shady pine forest, carpeting the mountainside along the rather tortuous route up to the pagoda.

Along the coast: To the east is **Cam Pha**, famous for its black gold, coal. This is a grimy place where the people and town and everything else are blackened by coal dust.

Northeast is **Mong Cai**, situated on Vietnam's northeastern border with China, is a bustling town growing fat on trade, much of it illegal, with its neighbor to the north. The town was destroyed by retreating Chinese troops in 1979, and reconstruction began only when the border was reopened in 1991. This is one of three land border gates to China open to foreigners, but special permission is needed to cross.

A few kilometers to the east, on an island separated from the mainland by a narrow sea channel, is **Tra Co**, which has one of the most beautiful stretches of golden-sand beaches. Today, most visitors are Chinese, and there are numerous guest houses. At the southern end of the island is **Mui Ngoc**, a haven for local smugglers.

WEST AND SOUTH OF HANOI

To the south and west of Hanoi, the flat delta gives way to craggy mountain peaks inhabited by ethnic minority tribes. In this region, which includes the western-most part of Vietnam that borders Laos, are traditional craftsmen living in the shadow of a modern hydroelectric dam. Ancient kings and warriors are honored here, as is the site for the decisive battle of Vietnam's war against French colonialists, Dien Bien Phu.

West of Hanoi: Leaving Hanoi and traveling southwest, towards plateaus and mountains once inhabited by the prehistoric Lac Viet people, the road enters **Hoa Binh Province**. Many relics from the Hoa Binh culture of the ancient Lac Viet people have been discovered in the province. A number of ethnic groups – including Muong, Hmong, Thai, Tay and Zao – make up the local population. The province's diverse landscape is of plains, midland and mountainous regions.

The **Dao Pagoda**, 30 kilometers (20 mi) from Hanoi, dates from the 13th century. It is a bit off the beaten track, but the trip is well worth it, for the route passes through picturesque countryside and affords a glimpse of traditional village life. The pagoda houses two lacquered statues that contain the mummified remains of two bonzes, the brothers Vu Khac Minh and Vu Khach Truong, who lived there three centuries ago.

About 40 kilometers (25 mi) from Hanoi, in Sai Son village, the **Chua Thay** (Pagoda of the Master) nestles against the Sai Son hillside. (Its official name is Thien Phuc; pagodas often have more than one name in Vietnam.) Built in 1132 by King Ly Thai To, the pagoda is dedicated three ways: to Ly Than Tong, king of the Ly dynasty from 1127 to 1138; to the sect of Sakyamuni Buddha and his 18 disciples; and to the venerable bonze Dao Hanh (the Master) of the Ly Dynasty.

Dao Hanh was a great herbalist who had been a medical man in his native village before entering the pagoda. He was also very fond of the choreographic arts, particularly the traditional water puppet theater, which he taught in the artificial lake in front of the pagoda, still used today for water puppetry. The two arched, covered bridges spanning the lake date from 1602.

Within the pagoda is a large and white sandalwood statue of Dao Hanh, which can be moved like a puppet using cleverly-intertwined strings. Wooden statues of Buddha and various guardians are also housed in the temple's enclosures. A climb up the hillside leads to two more small shrines, and a superb view of the pagoda, lake, village and surrounding countryside. This idyllic place is an excellent spot for a picnic. Several limestone grottoes in the vicinity are worth exploring, notably **Hang Cac Co** (The Mischievous).

Nearby, in the picturesque village of **Thac Xa**, the **Tay Phuong Pagoda** (West Pagoda) perches on the top of the 50-meter Tay Phuong hill. The pagoda dates from the 8th century and is famous

for its 73 wooden lacquer statues, which are said to illustrate different stories from the Buddhist scriptures – their facial expressions reflect the different attitudes and faces of human nature. The pagoda is reached by climbing 262 laterite steps, where incense and fan sellers will be hot on your trail hoping to be rewarded for their efforts, if not on the way up, then while you're catching your breath at the top.

Built of ironwood with bare brick walls, the pagoda with its round windows is built in three parts: the Bai Duong (Prostration Hall), the Chinh Dien (Central Hall) and the Hau Cung (Back Hall), which together form the Tam Bao (Three Gems). The overlapping roofing of the halls is richly decorated with engravings and terracotta figures of dragons and animals. Valuable examples of traditional Vietnamese sculpture are here, including beautiful wooden statues of *arhat*, which are considered to be the best examples of Vietnamese 18th-century sculptural art.

If the effects of the winding, unpaved roads and last-minute kamikaze maneuvers of the traffic that rockets over them leave your nerves shattered and your body aching, then a trip to the **Kim Boi hot springs** would be in order. Located 100 kilometers (60 mi) from Hanoi, these springs produce hot water at a constant temperature of 36°C (97°F), and are reputedly therapeutic in treating anything from muscular pain to stomach troubles and tension.

Hoa Binh, the provincial capital, is home to Southeast Asia's biggest hydroelectric project. The dam, built with technical assistance and money from the former Soviet Union, displaced approximately 50,000 ethnic minority people from the Da River Valley, which is now under the **Song Da Reservoir**. Electricity generated is the main source for the country's newly-developed, high-power transmission line that runs north to south and supplies places as far away as Ho Chi Minh City in the south.

The **Mai Chau district**, further down the road, is a stunningly beautiful highland valley populated mostly by the **Dusk over flooded rice paddies.**

White Thai ethnic minority. Surrounded on all four sides by jagged peaks, the valley, less than 30 kilometers (20 mi) from the border with Laos, has intensive rice paddy cultivation. Visits can be arranged to a village, where one might partake of the home-brewed rice wine through long reed straws, while acquainting yourself with some of the other customs of your hosts. It is possible to stay in the traditional stilt houses of some of the White Thai villages for a small fee. Handicrafts include delicate hand embroidery, textiles and fabrics, traditional musical instruments and crossbows. For centuries, gold panning has been practiced here; today, tourism is becoming the main income generator.

Continuing west, the road, while scenic, becomes progressively more difficult to traverse. About 15 kilometers from **Mai Chau**, one area of primary forest has been preserved, which provides a glimpse of what the entire area was once like. But increasingly, the eye is met with barren hills, with only the craggy mountain peaks still forested.

Many areas have been denuded by minorities searching for timber, to use as firewood or wood to build their houses.

The far western **province of Son La** shares a common southern border with Laos. The region is home to many ethnic minorities, including Thai, Mnong, Tay, Muong, Mun, Kho Mu, Zao, Xinh and Hoa. Forests and mountains cover 80 percent of the province, which is one of the largest cattle-breeding centers in northern Vietnam. Two distinct seasons are experienced here, the rainy season that lasts from May to September, and the dry season from November to April. During the coldest months, January and February, the temperature can fall to 3°C (27°F). To the west, the White Thai are less prominant, and the Black Thai predominate.

The deep **Mai Chau Valley**, in Son La, is the main area settled by the Black Thai minority. They live in villages, known as *ban,* which include as many as 50 dwellings. Black Thai women are characterized by tight blouses held together with silver clasps running down

nall
bacco
tch, and
ave of a
eo girl.

their chests, and delicately-embroidered black headscarves. For more than a century, gold panning in the streams has provided the locals with a better livelihood than they can attain in the city. Between May and October, the road beyond Son La is often washed away or impassable due to mountain slides caused by the excessive rains.

Moc Chau district, set on a highland plateau, is known for its tea and dairy herds. The provincial capital, **Son La**, is situated 600 meters (375 ft) above sea level, on the southern bank of the Nam La River. The prison, built in 1908 by the French to hold revolutionaries, still stands on Khau Ca Hill, in the middle of town, a reminder of war.

Continuing to the west, **Lai Chau Province** shares a border with China in the north and borders Laos in the west. Among the ethnic groups here are Thai, Hmong, Xa, and Ha Nhi. Much of the land – about 75 percent – is covered in forest containing valuable timber and animals – some of them rare, including tigers, bears, bison and pheasants.

Eighty kilometers (50 mi) south of Lai Chau township, on the route to Laos, the famous battle site of **Dien Bien Phu** lies in an immense gorge 20 kilometers long (12 mi) and three kilometers wide, which opens onto the **Muong Thanh Valley**. Bordered on the west by mountains and on the east by the 1,900-meter (6,160-ft) Phu Xam Xan, the valley forms a natural barrier blocked off from Laos. It was here that the French met their defeat at the hands of Gen. Vo Nguyen Giap's Viet Minh forces in 1954.

The road south: The old Mandarin Route heading south from Hanoi was renamed **National Highway 1** after independence in 1945. It stretches the length of the eastern coast for more than 2,000 kilometers (1,240 mi), from Nam Quan at the Chinese border to Ha Tien in the Gulf of Thailand.

Heading south out of Hanoi, the road passes through the varied landscape of Ninh Binh and Nam Ha provinces, which contain every terrain imaginable – mountains, limestone hills, low lying plains, rice fields and long stretches of sand.

Catholic church on road to Nam Dinh, and boats for pilgrims at Huong Son.

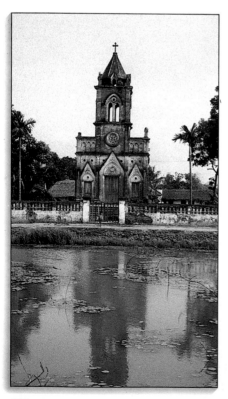

Nam Dinh, the provincial capital of Nam Ha, lies 90 kilometers (60 mi) from Hanoi. Under the French, it became a center for the textile industry that continues to flourish today as the largest in the country.

Just to the north of Nam Dinh is the village of **Mac**, and the **ancient Tran ruins**. These ruins are all that remain of the palaces built by the kings of the Tran Dynasty, who defeated the Mongol-Yuan invaders three times in the 13th century. Among these are the **Thien Truong temples**, which were dedicated to the 14 Tran kings, and the **Co Trach Temple**, which was dedicated to Gen. Tran Hung Dao. The only buildings left intact are the beautiful **Pho Minh Pagoda** and the 13-story Pho Minh tower, built in 1305, which contains the remains of King Tran Nhan Tong.

Nearby is the **ancient capital of Hoa Lu**. This picturesque site was once the ancient capital of Vietnam – or Dai Co Viet, as it was then known – under the Dinh, Le (10th century) and Ly (11th century) dynasties. Remains of the citadel, covering an area of 300 hectares (740 acres), border the Hoang Long River. An enormous stone column engraved with Buddhist sutras, dating from 988, was recently discovered here. Although the original palaces themselves have long since disappeared, temples have been built on the original sites.

After the capital was transferred from Hoa Lu to Thang Long (now Hanoi), two temples were built, one dedicated to King Dinh Tien Hoang and the other to his successor, Le Dai Hanh. Dinh Tien Hoang's temple, first built in the 11th century, was reconstructed in 1696. Statues of mythical animals stand guard outside the temple, where King Dinh Tien Hoang is worshipped at a central altar. The large characters written in ancient Vietnamese script translate as, "From this day onwards we have our independence." Also written on the pillars is Dai Co Viet, the name King Dinh Bo Linh gave Vietnam. In the temple's back room are statues representing Dinh Bo Linh and his three sons.

The **Dragon Bed**, once an area used

Plowing rice paddies the time-honored way.

for sacrifices, lies in the center of the courtyard, in front of the main building. Gifts and food offerings are placed on the slab during festivals.

The **Le Hoan Temple** is a miniature of the Dinh Hoang. The statues in the back room are those of King Le Hoan, his queen, Duong Van Nga, and his sons, Le Long Dinh and Le Long Viet.

Another scenic spot well worth visiting in Hoa Lu district is the **Chua Bich Pagoda**, in the mountains. Built in 1428, the pagoda is renowned for its beautiful bronze and marble statues, and for its huge bronze bell. From the same area, it's a leisurely boat ride to the three magnificent **grottoes of Tam Co**, nicknamed Vietnam's inland Ha Long Bay. These wonderful caverns, with their huge stalagmites and stalactites, recede into the depths of the mountain.

To the southwest, **Cuc Phuong**, a national park since 1962, is one of the few remaining tropical primeval forest reserves in the world. The park shelters 64 species of fauna and nearly 2,000 species of flora, including trees no longer found in other parts of the world. The fauna is particularly remarkable. Flying lizards, yellow monkeys and other bizarre animals roam around more than 25,000 hectares (61,000 acres), three-quarters of which are covered by limestone mountains.

These mountains form two parallel ranges that enclose a valley, with a micro-climate quite different than that of the surrounding region. Many caves and grottoes lie within the mountains. Three tombs, excavated in one of the grottoes in 1966, contained shells, animal teeth, rudimentary stone tools and even some human remains.

For a therapeutic warm dip, try the park's thermal springs. These remain at a constant temperature of 37°C (99°F) and contain more than 20 chemical elements believed to have healing properties. Accommodation – in the form of wooden houses on stilts in traditional Muong style – is available in the park.

The **Phat Diem Cathedral**, built in 1865, remains today an important center for Christian pilgrims from all over Vietnam. This remarkable cathedral, built of ironwood in Sino-Vietnamese style, was one of the earliest Catholic churches to be built in northern Vietnam.

To the east, **Thai Binh Province** has the highest population density in the country – over 1,000 people per square kilometer. Salt fields cover extensive areas on the coastal shores. In addition to rice, jute, rushes, mulberry, sugar cane and ground nut are also cultivated.

Among the crafts found in Thai Binh, carpet making, silk weaving, wickerwork and embroidery are common.

The 11th-century **Keo Pagoda**, located some 10 kilometers (four mi) from Thai Binh township, is considered one of the finest examples of traditional Vietnamese architecture in the northern delta. It is dedicated to Buddha, his disciples and the bonze superior. No metal nails were used in the construction of this impressive wooden pagoda and its three-story bell tower. Many traditional rituals and diverse forms of entertainment are performed here, some of them centuries old, particularly during the Tet holidays.

Left, poppies near Lai Chau. **Right**, an ancient tree in Cuc Phuong.

NORTHCENTRAL COAST

The rich and beautiful province of **Thanh Hoa** is the first in an almost unbroken succession of seven coastal provinces hemmed in between the South China Sea and the Indochinese mountain range.

Thanh Hoa, the cradle of the Dong Son culture, harbors a great many historical sites, and is an important settlement area for the Vietnamese Muong minority.

At the beginning of the 20th century, archaeologists discovered many relics of the Dong Son civilization dispersed the length of the **Ma River Valley**. Among the finds were bronze drums, musical instruments, statues, jewelry, various tools and domestic objects. The Muong still adhere to their ancient Vietnamese language and use the bronze drums inherent to their unique culture and festivals.

Lord Trieu's invasion in 208 BC was responsible for the Viet southward migration, and these first emigrants settled in the Phu Ly and Dong Son regions.

Before reaching Thanh Hoa, in Nam Ha Province south of Hanoi, **Phu Ly** is where the first bronze drum was discovered in 1902. Other similar drums were acquired from the Long Doi Son Monastery and the village of Ngoc Lu. The figurative and stylized designs on the drums depict birds, animals and scenes from everyday life. The Ngoc Lu bronze drum, 80 centimeters (30 in) in diameter, is decorated with an image of the sun. Its many rays are surrounded by 16 concentric circles of various designs depicting deer, aquatic birds, people and aspects of daily life. The drum's surface is engraved with pairs of animals and birds heading east towards the sun. In 1924, a member of l'Ecole Francaise d'Extreme Orient unearthed several bronze drums and other bronze objects at Dong Son.

The **Mieu Than Dong Co** (Temple of the Spirit of the Drum) is found in the village of **Dan Ne**, on Mt Tam Diep in Thanh Hoa Province. The temple contains a bronze drum two meters (six ft) in diameter, which, according to popular belief, is said to have belonged to one of the Hung kings. The drum's face is decorated with nine concentric circles engraved with ancient characters.

The Muong minority village of **Lam Son**, in the Thanh Hoa highlands, was the native village of Vietnam's national hero, Le Loi, who became King Le Thai To. It was from here that Le Loi launched a decade-long uprising against the Ming occupiers of the country. The struggle – waged from 1418 to 1428 in this mountainous region – finally ended in complete victory for Le Loi and his troops. The temple here is dedicated to Le Loi and contains his bronze likeness, cast in 1532. Nguyen Trai, Le Loi's advisor, penned the epitaph on the large Vinh Lang stele, dedicated solely to the life and works of Le Loi, in 1433.

Other memorials document 12 reigns of the Le family. Remains of the royal palace's ancient **Lam Kinh Citadel** are still visible. The **mausoleum of Dame**

Preceding <u>pages</u>: slow traffic on Highway 1. <u>Left</u>: successful catch.

Trieu, at the foot of Mt Tung Son in Phu Dien village, is the final resting place of the national heroine, Trieu Thi Trinh, who led an uprising against the Chinese in 247, aided by her elder brother Trieu Quoc Dat. The attempt failed and Trieu, rather than have her fate decided by the victorious Ngo rulers, committed suicide. A temple was built in her memory, and today, a festival is celebrated here in her honor on the 24th day of the second lunar month every year.

The megalithic-style **Ho Citadel** in Tay Giai village, Quan Hoa district, was built in 1397 under the orders of the usurper king, Ho Qui Li. He named the new citadel Tay Kinh (Capital of the West). It was more or less a replica of the citadel of Dong Kinh (Capital of the East). But unlike the other citadels of Hoa Lu and Co Loa, whose walls were built of earth, the Ho citadel's huge walls, five meters (16 ft) high and three meters (10 ft) thick, were made of stone. Some blocks weigh an estimated 16 tons and show a high degree of quarrying and stone-carving skill.

Not far from the provincial capital of Thanh Hoa, the white sands of **Sam Son Beach** stretch for three kilometers along the coast, from the Lac Hoi River to Mt Truong Le. Superb scenery surrounds the clear waters of Sam Son, named after the coastal mountain of the nearby Truong Le Range.

In a cave on a rocky hillside near the mouth of the **Y Bich River** is a temple dedicated to An Tiem, the man who brought watermelons to Vietnam. An Tiem is said to have domesticated the wild melon seed, and to have grown his first melons here on the land near the temple. A beach in Nga Son district, where his descendants still live today, is named after him.

The **Doc Cuoc Temple**, halfway up Mt Truong Le, is dedicated to a one-legged deity said to have divided himself in half, and who is believed to have supernatural powers that protect and save swimmers and navigators in distress. It is also said to guarantee the fishermen a good catch, although the local fishermen may have a different

Moving harvest by water.

story. At the end of the range is another temple, the **Co Tien**, or Fairy Temple.

The hunting area of **Khoa Truong**, 50 kilometers (30 mi) southeast of Thanh Hoa, is a swampy place dotted with numerous ponds. It is the habitat of many aquatic and migratory birds that become fair game during hunting season, from October to February.

Numerous Muong villages lie scattered throughout the highlands of Thanh Hoa. Although the lowland Vietnamese, the Kinh, lost their original written script after 1,000 years of Chinese domination, the Muong have retained theirs. Known as *khoa dau van,* it is similar to Thai, Lao and Indian script and has an alphabet of 30 basic consonant signs similar to Arabic.

Cinnamon trees are indigenous to this highland region. The bark, a sought-after ingredient in Sino-Vietnamese pharmaceutical preparations, is collected in the forests by local inhabitants.

The **Ham Rong bridge**, which links the Ngoc and Rong mountains on either side of the Ma River, was first built in 1904. It was damaged during the war against the French and rebuilt in 1964, before 70,000 tons of bombs were dropped on it during the war with the Americans. The bridge was built for the third time in 1973.

South of Thanh Hoa Province lies **Nghe An Province**, birthplace of several revolutionaries: Phan Boi Chau (1867–1940) and Nguyen Ai Quoc (Ho Chi Minh, 1890–1969), and the national poet, Nguyen Du (1765–1820), author of *The Tale of Kieu.*

The findings of archaeologists revealed the existence of both a stone age and a bronze age culture in the province.

In Nghe An and its neighbor to the south, Ha Tinh, mountains and midlands give way to coastal plains along a 230-kilometer (140-mi) coastline, and forests cover three-quarters of the land. The harsh climate often causes rain storms and flash flooding. More than 100 rivers and streams, the longest of which is the **Lam Dong River**, feed the two provinces.

The Lam Dong is a busy waterway

Fowl deal in the market.

plied by boats, sampans and rafts carrying bamboo and timber. Deer, raised for their antlers, are a common sight grazing amongst the orange orchards. Lang Sen, Ho Chi Minh's home village, proudly preserves the mud-and-wattle palm thatched house where he is said to have spent his childhood. Nearby is Uncle Ho's memorial house, where memorabilia and photographs extol the virtues of the revolutionary struggle.

Vinh, Nghe An's main town, does not have much to offer, although even in Vinh, the beginnings of economic renovation can be seen with a revived commercial center. Twenty kilometers from here lies the fishing hamlet and sea pine bordered white sand beach of **Cua Lo**. The greatest attraction here is the spectacular sight at sunrise of the fishermen pulling in nets full of long, silvery fish.

The **Cuong Temple** occupies a site on Mo Da Mountain next to National Highway 1, and is dedicated to King An Duong Vuong, Vietnam's first king when the nation was known as Au Lac, in the third century BC.

Traveling southward, National Highway 1 crosses the coastal plains, then climbs the Hoan Son Hills before entering Quang Binh Province. A detour here from Highway 1 leads to the fishing village of **Mui Ron** in Quang Trach District. Vast quantities of sea slugs (*hai sam*) and abalone (*bao ngu*) are caught here.

At the mouth of the Roon River is **Canh Duong village**, a resistance stronghold during the war against the French. Today, the village is known for its silk weaving and jute tapestry. The **Mieu Ong Shrine** here is dedicated to whales, a creature this fishing community regards as friend and benefactor. During the American bombings, the shrine's whale skeleton was moved to the Canh Duong communal house.

The coastal village of **Ba Don**, in Quang Trach district, is well worth visiting on market day, when the place is absolutely inundated with all manner of local products, livestock and a multitude of food, not to mention people.

Further south lies the **Gianh River**,

Childhood
Home of Ho
Chi Minh.

which once served as the demarcation line (*ranh* or *gianh*) between North and South Vietnam. Its deep and turbulent waters defy any attempt to build a bridge across it. The 160-kilometer-long Gianh takes its source in the Huong Son mountains, in Nghe An Province, and flows through limestone mountains, in the process forming wonderful grottoes such as Minh Can, Lac Son and Phong Nha.

A visit to the beautiful **Phong Nha Caves** is not to be missed when in the area. These caves, with their wonderful stalactites and stalagmites, are incontestably Vietnam's second natural marvel after Ha Long Bay. The caves are entered via an underground river, reached by following the Gianh River back up towards its source, in the limestone massifs of the highlands.

Southeast of the caves lies the provincial capital, **Dong Hoi**, and the remains of the ancient Dong Hoi Wall at the mouth of the Nhat Le River. The wall served as a defense rampart against Lord Trinh from the north. It was the brainchild of the great Vietnamese states-

man, Dao Duy To (1572–1634), counsellor and prime minister to Lord Sai Vuong (1562–1635). A large stone stele inscribed with Dao Duy To's biography and works stands under the Quang Binh Arch in the citadel at Dong Hoi. Dao Duy To also built another wall, the Luy Truong Duc. Its ruins are still visible amongst the wild mulberry trees beside Xuan Duc, Quanh Ninh district.

The locals use the fruit from the trees to make delicious wine (*ruou dau*), aromatic liqueurs with vanilla, and some aperitifs with quinine that were widely-commercialized during World War II. Toward the Nhat Le river mouth lies the battlefield where much bloody combat took place during the 17th and 18th centuries between the Trinh lords of the north and the Nguyen lords of the south. The unfathomable waters of **Lake Bau Tro** nearby are contained within the crater of an ancient volcano.

On the other side of the Nhat Le River, immense sand dunes stretch all the way to the coast.

Heading south from the region of Dong Hoi, the road to the west leads in the direction of the rice-growing areas of Quang Ninh and Le Thuy. North of Hue, the road arrives at the **Hien Luong Bridge** spanning the Ben Hai River. Situated exactly on **the 17th parallel, or DMZ**, the river served as the natural demarcation line between North and South Vietnam for two decades, after the frontier was set by the Geneva Agreement in 1954. More than a simple geographical frontier, the river separated two ideologically-opposed political currents, spanned by a bridge that could not be crossed until the fall of the south in 1975 and the country's reunification. It was an oddly-named battlefield.

Quang Tri Province is composed of a series of small plains bordered by sand dunes in the east, and forests, valleys and the green plateaus of the Truong Son Mountains in the west.

A mountain trail built by North Vietnamese guerrillas runs parallel to the national highway. Part of the **Ho Chi Minh Trail**, it was used by the revolutionary forces as a supply route for their troops and arms to reach the south.

Left, not going in reverse. **Right**, digging for clams along the coast.

REUNIFICATION EXPRESS

The Thong Nhat, or Reunification Express, a somewhat misleading name in every sense, refers to the train that crawls along at an average speed of about 50 kilometers (30 mi) per hour, making the journey between Hanoi and Ho Chi Minh City in from 36 to 44 hours, depending upon which "express" you travel on.

In fact, today's slowest trains may average as little as 15 kilometers (10 mi) per hour. However, the trains themselves are not solely to blame for the lack of rapid movement.

Only one track runs between Ho Chi Minh City and Hanoi. Apart from a 300-kilometer-long (180-mi) stretch in the north, the entire track system is meter gauged and in very poor condition, especially considering the damage from American bombing in the north, and from Viet Cong sabotage in the south, during the Vietnam War.

Trains can pass each other only at the few points where there are parallel tracks. Thus, one train has to wait on the side-track for the other to pass, and if, as is often the case, one train is running late, then the other and any subsequent trains will likewise be late. Considering derailments, buffalos, stalled vehicles, floods and typhoons, it is a logistical feat that the trains run at all.

The Reunification Express trains first rattled down the re-repaired tracks between Hanoi and Ho Chi Minh City in 1976. The massive reconstruction campaign carried out to make this possible, one of the government's first rehabilitation programs after the war, included the repairing of some 1,334 bridges, 158 stations and 27 tunnels.

For all the speed and efficiency of modern-day express trains elsewhere, those speed demons lack the atmosphere and sense of the unexpected that accompanies a journey on one of the old mavericks plying the rails of Vietnam. What Vietnam rail travel lacks in comfort and speed, it certainly makes up for

Family smiles spilling from an open window.

in local color, and in a certain charm reminiscent of train journeys of a by-gone era. Be prepared for frequent un-scheduled stops, flickering lighting, and a sound system that crackles forth Viet-namese songs interspersed with an-nouncements.

To take in the sights, sounds and smells of a fascinating country at a leisurely pace, and in the company of an equally fascinating array of traveling compan-ions, is an experience that will provide those game enough to do so with a wealth of images, memories and stories.

If time is limited, one may feel tempted to give the train journey a miss, but think again, as you may be forgoing an experience of a lifetime, as this rather antiquated rail system may one day be replaced by something contemporary.

When the train heaves out of the sta-tion, its cargo is an unlikely hodgepodge of humanity, livestock and goods that are about to embark on a journey of 2,012 kilometers (1,250 mi), one of the most beautiful journeys in the world.

Compartments designed for four to six passengers are in train cars crammed with food vendors squatting in the isles – men, women and children slung in hammocks or curled up in whatever space is left. Bulky packages and bags, jutting limbs and bales of clothes clog any available space between the seats, spill over from luggage racks, hang sus-pended from the ceiling and turn the cigarette-strewn aisles into a veritable obstacle course. A challenge, indeed, should one pluck up the courage to brave a sortie to the washroom or the restaurant car. The scene is one of noisy animation, in which stamina and an unflagging sense of humor is useful and will see one through the trip.

Arm yourself for the adventure with a flashlight, toilet paper, bottled water, bread and fruit, plenty of small denomi-nation *dong* and cigarettes (for sharing).

The on-board vendors are a mafia unto themselves, descending onto the train as it slows from its average slow speed and grinds to a halt, scheduled or otherwise, at strategic wayside villages or in the middle of nowhere. With an

Not too fast to appreciate the scenery.

uncanny sense of timing, the vendors materialize out of bush, rubber plantations and paddy fields to swarm aboard and proffer their welcome glasses of green tea or freshly-cut sugar cane.

The tidbits offered vary from one region to the next as the train progresses; each province, town or village peddles its own particular local specialty. Stock up on finger bananas in Xuan Loc, dried squid in Nha Trang, prawn fritters at Dien Tri and soft-shelled crabs and conical hats in Hue. Woman attendants in railroad uniforms take orders for lunch. Rice with chicken, pork or tofu is cooked over open braziers in the train's lead car.

As the passing landscape becomes drier, cacti and giant anthills thrust their way up from a desert-like earth. The sun, a glowing fireball ready to roll behind the mountain range, casts its lasts ray on the massive limestone outcrops, upon which herald a glimpse of the ancient Cham towers. A half-hour stop at Nha Trang provides a welcome opportunity to stretch legs in the shabby *ga*, or station. Back on the train, bunk-ing down for the night means securing window shutters – a guillotine for the unwary – and locking doors to discourage unwelcome rocks and riders.

The crew dispense a blanket, sheet and pillow to each berth, but even the blanket provided may disappear at station stops. Thieves are now, unfortunately, common and have been known to carry off anything not tied down.

The unceremoniously-dumped bucket of water is for the purpose of night and morning ablutions. However, the majority clean their teeth in the corridor, spitting into the wind – anything to avoid extra time in the fetid washroom, which demands the nigh on impossible of one's sense of balance when squatting over a hole as the train lurches and jolts through intersections.

A cup of strong cafe *den* (black coffee) will ease recovery as the new day dawns over lush rice fields, where the conical hats of the villagers form intricate geometric patterns as they labor in the paddy fields, and fisherman cast their nets in the rivers amid buffalo wallowing in the mud.

At a half-hour stop in Da Nang, vendors jostle for customers, displaying their goods: boiled eggs, tropical fruits, sweet corn and spiced pork pate wrapped in banana leaf (*gio lua*) – delicious with the French-style bread. The train backs down towards the coastal track that snakes around mountains rising nearly 2,000 meters (6,000 ft), with a sheer drop to the sparkling turquoise sea and white sand beaches below. The snail's pace on this leg of the journey allows for breathtaking views of the Vinh Da Nang estuary, a scene teeming with boats. The train crawls into Hue at about mid-afternoon, time enough to make a few purchases and catch a glimpse of this former imperial city hugging the banks of the Perfume River. To the north, massive bomb craters scar the countryside – a legacy of the Vietnam war and the B-52 carpet bombings. These craters are now watering holes for buffalo.

Dawn breaks over the lush emerald paddy fields of the northern Red River Delta before arrival in Hanoi with the early morning sun.

Left, guard at Hai Van Pass Right, DMZ bunker, no longer needed.

THE DMZ BLUES

From the driver's tape deck oozes a song from 1967, its sad melody reminding the school teacher in the car of another time in Vietnam. It is a song of longing, the words of a woman waiting for her husband – off at war – to return home. "Why don't you come back?" she sings.

The song, like many romantic tunes from southern Vietnam, was banned by the Communist government after the end of the war in 1975. Today, however, these sentimental songs are making a comeback.

"In the north, the war songs were never sad like this," explained the teacher. "Only patriotic songs, upbeat and strong, were allowed. They were supposed to motivate the soldiers, never to make them think about home." The teacher, who grew up near the line that divided Vietnam into two countries for two decades, smiled at the coincidence of hearing this wartime music while touring the old DMZ – the demilitarized zone, where some of the bloodiest fighting of the war occurred. The song may evoke memories of an earlier time, but the teacher feels no nostalgia for that era.

The DMZ stretched for eight kilometers (five miles) on either side of the Ben Hai River, which was the line of demarcation between North Vietnam and South Vietnam, established during the Geneva Conference in 1954, after the end of the war against the French. Almost exactly following the 17th parallel, the border was supposed to be temporary, until elections could be held in 1956. The elections never were held, and Vietnam remained divided along this line until the two countries were officially reunified in 1976.

Today, there are still desolate stretches of earth scorched long ago by repeated bombings, and where only a few saplings of growth have appeared and the indentations of explosions are still apparent. Some bomb craters have been filled in, others turned into fish ponds.

South of the DMZ, in Quang Tri, the shell of a church building is riddled with bullet holes, the roof missing.

North of the DMZ, in Vinh Muoc, a series of tunnels are where an entire village camped out for several years to escape the constant bombings. Most of the people had evacuated to other parts of the country, but some stayed. For five years, from 1966 to 1971, 300 people lived in the 2,000-meter-long network of tunnels. Seventeen babies were born in the tunnel; two decades later, two of them were married.

"We thought it was fun to live here, to run around the tunnels," said one man, now approaching 40 years of age.

Just south of the Ben Hai River, Highway 9, which runs west toward Laos, passes sites of some famous Vietnam War battles, and, too, some old US military bases – Con Thien, the Rockpile, Khe Sanh. Little remains of them today, however.

Near the Dakrong Bridge, villagers live in houses built on stilts. One of the men confides that he worked for the Americans during the war, dropping into remote locations to scout for the enemy. He doesn't tell his neighbors, who he thinks probably know about his past anyway. To remind them would be to force them to disown him. Nowadays, he doesn't speak the English he learned from Americans during the war.

The school teacher, a student at the time of the war, remembers the days when Agent Orange was sprayed, with the loudspeakers assuring people that the chemical defoliant would hurt only the plants.

"At that time," he said, "I often wished that I could have one day without war. Just one day. It seemed like then my wish would never come true." ∎

199

CENTRAL VIETNAM

A long string of coastal provinces, linking the vast rice-growing regions of the Mekong Delta in the south and the Red River Delta in the north, forms the narrow neck of central Vietnam.

At the heart of Vietnam's center lies Hue, the imperial city of the Nguyen kings. It is a magnificent city, despite the damage of war, with majestic citadels, fortresses and imperial mausoleums. Threading through its center is the River of Perfume, Song Huong, a name that teases with its promise. Centuries ago, after the Champa kingdoms fell to the invading Viets from the north, Hue was called Thuan Hoa: *thuan,* meaning allegiance or submission, and *hoa* meaning transformation. The name Hue is believed to have come about through the common mispronunciation of hoa.

Outside of Hue to the north, the skinny central coastal provinces of Quang Tri and Dong Ha suffered mightily during the Vietnam War, as they were directly south of the DMZ, or demilitarized zone.

South of Hue, the Hai Van Pass funnels into Da Nang, an active port city and Vietnam's third-largest urban center, with bustling commerce and lovely beaches nearby. Da Nang is the gateway to Quang Nam Da Nang Province and the ancient kingdom of Champa. The distinctive red-brick Cham towers and sacred sites, built between the 8th and 12th centuries, stand as silent testimony to the kingdom that flourished here, before its absorption by the Vietnamese descending from the north.

Nearby is the charming 15th-century town of Hoi An, which was the biggest seaport and most important center of trade in the country during the 17th and 18th centuries. Its beautifully-preserved communal houses, pagodas and other places of worship reflect the presence and influences of Chinese, Japanese and Westerners who later settled in the region.

Preceding pages: pagoda by the Perfume River, Hue; shimmering twilight teases a fading day, Perfume River. Left, at Thien Mu Pagoda, Hue.

HUE

Hue, the ancient imperial city of the Nguyen kings, is located 12 kilometers (7 mi) from the coast on a narrow stretch of land in Thua Thien Hue Province, which borders Laos in the west.

The first noble to reach Hue was Lord Nguyen Hoang (1524–1613), in the spring of 1601. He found a particularly good location to build a capital and erected the Phu Xuan Citadel.

The Nguyen lords administered the whole region with the agreement of the Trinh lords. This arrangement operated smoothly at first, but rivalry flared up as the territory was extended southward. Bloody battles broke out between the two rival families. Each side was fiercely determined to consolidate and assert its own sovereignty, but eventually the Nguyen lords gained the upper hand. As a result, Hue became a new kingdom under the reign of Lord Vu Vuong (1739–1763), independent of the north.

Nguyen Hoang also built the **Thien Mu Pagoda**, which remains intact on the left bank of the **Perfume River**. The seven tiers of the temple's octagonal tower each represent a different reincarnation of Buddha. Six statues of deities guard the Buddhist pagoda, which contains a gilt statue of the laughing Buddha, happy in prosperity, and three superb, glass-enclosed statues of Buddha.

Many generations have heard the tolling of the pagoda's enormous 2,000-kilogram (4,600 lb) bell since it was cast in 1701. The main temple, **Dai Hung**, is found in an attractive garden of ornamental shrubs and trees. A statue of Maitraya Buddha presides over the first room. Behind this temple is the Quan Vo Temple (God of War Temple), and behind that another, the Quan Am Temple, dedicated to the goddess Quan Am.

Nguyen Hoang was the first in an uninterrupted succession of 10 feudal lords to rule over the area of Hue until 1802. That year, after quelling the Tay Son uprising, the 10th Nguyen lord proclaimed himself Emperor Gia Long and founded the Nguyen Dynasty, which would last for 143 years, until 1945. But just 33 years into dynasty's reign, the French invaded Hue.

A quick succession of emperors graced the throne. The anti-French demonstrations and strikes of the colonial era were followed by the Japanese occupation in 1945 and the abdication of Bao Dai, the last of the Nguyen emperors, in August of the same year.

The relative peace that reigned after 1954, when Hue became part of South Vietnam following the country's division into two parts, was shattered under Ngo Dinh Diem's regime. Repressive anti-Buddhist propaganda sparked off a series of demonstrations and protest suicides by Buddhist monks in 1963.

Hue's imperial city suffered extensive damage during the Tet Offensive of 1968. Although many priceless historical monuments and relics were destroyed, amazingly, many survived.

Always an important cultural, intellectual and historical city, Hue remains one of Vietnam's main attractions. The charm of this timeless old city lies not

eft, tomb of mperor Tu uc. **Right**, uardian at 1ien Mu agoda.

only in its historical and architectural value, but also in the natural beauty of its location along the banks of the Perfume River. Today, there is a quiet grace to the city, as the pace of traffic on the wide avenues is slower and more leisurely than the bigger hubs of Hanoi and Ho Chi Minh City.

Nguyen legacy: The **Imperial City (Dai Noi)** of Hue is made up of three walled enclosures. The Hoang Thanh (Yellow Enclosure) and the Tu Cam Thanh (Forbidden Purple City) are enclosed within the Kinh Thanh (exterior enclosure). Stone, bricks and earth were used to build the exterior wall, which measured 8 meters (26 ft) high and 20 meters (65 ft) thick, and was built during the reign of Emperor Gia Long. Later, ten large and fortified gates, each topped with watch towers, were built at various points along the wall.

The Yellow Enclosure is the middle wall enclosing the imperial city and its palaces, temples and flower gardens. Four richly-decorated gates provided access: Ngo Mon (South or Noon Gate),

Hoa Binh, Hien Nhan and Chuong Duc. Ngo Mon, first built of granite in 1834 during the reign of Emperor Minh Mang, was repaired in 1921. The gate is topped by the Lau Ngu Phung, the Five Phoenix Watch Tower, with its roofs brightly-tiled in yellow over the middle section and green on either side. From here, the emperor used to preside over formal ceremonies and rites.

Through the Ngo Mon, walk across the Golden Water Bridge, which at one time was reserved for the emperor. It leads to the **Thai Hoa Palace** (Palace of Supreme Peace), the most important place in the imperial city. Here, the emperor received the high dignitaries of the land and foreign diplomats. The royal court organized important ceremonies here, as well. Built in 1805 during Gia Long's reign, the palace was renovated first by Minh Mang in 1834 and later by Khai Dinh in 1924. Today, it stands in excellent condition, its ceilings and beams decorated in red lacquer and gold inlay.

The emperor used to rest in the Truong

View of the river from Thien Mu Pagoda.

Sanh Palace (Palace of Longevity) and read the classics in the Van Palace or the Co Ha Garden.

The temples within the enclosure are dedicated to various lords: the temple of Trieu Mieu to Nguyen Kim, the Thai Mieu to Nguyen Hoang and his successors, the Phung Tien temple to the emperors of the reigning dynasty, and the Hung Mieu to Nguyen Phuc Lan, emperor Gia Long's father. The well-preserved The Mieu, dedicated to the sovereigns of the Nguyen Dynasty, houses the shrines of seven Nguyen emperors, plus monuments to the revolutionary emperors Ham Nghi, Thanh Thai and Duy Tan, which were added in 1959.

In front of the temple, completely undamaged, stands the magnificent **Hien Lam Cac** (Pavilion of Splendor), with the nine dynastic urns lined up before it. The urns, cast in 1822 during Minh Mang's reign, are decorated with motifs of the sun, moon, clouds, birds, animals, dragons, mountains, rivers, historic events and scenes from everyday life. Hundreds of artisans from all over the country were involved in their casting. Each urn represents an emperor of the Nguyen Dynasty and weighs up to 2,500 kilograms (5,600 lbs).

The **Dien Tho Palace**, built by emperor Gia Long in 1804, served as the Queen Mother's residence.

In the first enclosure of the royal city, towards the Chuong Duc Gate, are Sung Than Cong, or the Nine Deities' Canons. Five on one side represent the primary elements – metal, water, wood, fire, earth – and the other four represent the seasons. Each canon weighs 12 tons.

Tu Cam Thanh (The Forbidden Purple City) was reserved solely for the emperor and the royal family, who resided here behind a brick wall four meters (13 ft) thick. Seven gates set into the wall each had a special function and name glorifying the ancestral virtues. This area was extensively damaged during the Tet offensive, but has been undergoing extensive renovation.

The main building in the enclosure is the **Can Thanh Palace** (Celestial Perfection). The other once-grand palace,

art of Thien
u Pagoda.

Can Chanh, now sadly in ruins, was used by the emperor to receive dignitaries and settle the affairs of the kingdom. Its remaining walls, riddled with shell and bullet holes, stand as a crumbling reminder of the weapons that wrought such destruction to this once-splendid complex. Beyond lies an empty stretch of ground where the royal apartments once stood. The most modern palace in the enclosure was the Kien Than Palace that Emperor Khai Dinh (1916–1925) had built, complete with all the western comforts. Unfortunately, this too was a casualty of the war, and the palace still awaits reconstruction.

Another world lies beyond the walls of the citadel, which is surrounded in the south and east by Hue's commercial area. This is confined mainly to the area around the arched Trang Tien Bridge, which spans the Perfume River, and the Gia Hoi Bridge. Both bridges lend their names to the areas surrounding them. Located in Phu Cat, with its mainly Chinese and Minh Huong (Vietnamese-Chinese) population, is the lively **Dong Ba market**. The market has been around since the beginning of the century and offers a great variety of local products and gastronomic delights. Vi Da District, on the other side of the river, is renowned as a popular refuge for artists, poets, scholars and assorted mandarins.

Of an entirely different character is the district of Phu Cam, best known for its cathedral and the fervor of its predominantly Catholic community.

For those who like to look around old cemeteries, there are two rather interesting family grave sites in Hue, one belonging to the Ngo Dinh and the other to the Ho family.

Near the Forbidden Purple City, the **Imperial Museum**, built in 1845 under Emperor Thieu Tri, houses treasures bequeathed by the royal family and nobility. (It has been under renovation and some parts of it are closed to the public.) Sadly, many objects have disappeared without trace in the course of revolution and war since December 1946.

Across the street, an expanded **Military Museum** that was opened in 1975

Dynastic urn in the royal citadel.

is one of the finer collections related to the Vietnam War. The displays, photographs and maps must be viewed with a jaundiced eye, for they read as propaganda. However, the English translations are superior to those of other museums around the country, and the setting is brightly lit, air-conditioned and clean. The guides are helpful, as well. There is a large topographical map with lights showing the movements of the American troops, South Vietnamese military and Viet Cong during the Tet Offensive of 1968. Outside, in a yard overgrown with weeds, are pieces of military hardware. Next to the museum is a small natural history museum.

Royal tombs and pagodas: Unlike the other dynasties, the Nguyen Dynasty did not bury its members in their native village, Gia Mieu, in Thanh Hoa Province. Instead, their **imperial tombs** lie scattered on the hillsides on either side of the Perfumed River, to the west of Hue. Although the dynasty had 13 kings, only seven of them reigned until their deaths. And only they are laid to rest in this valley of kings: Gia Long, Minh Mang, Thieu Tri, Tu Duc, Kien Phuc, Dong Khanh and Kai Dinh.

Their tomb sites generally are patterned with the same configuration. Each has a large brick-paved courtyard (*bia dinh*) containing stone figures of elephants, saddled horses, soldiers, civil and military mandarins. In front of this stands the stele pavilion, containing the tall marble or stone stele engraved with the biography of the deceased king written by his successor. (Except in the case of Tu Duc – he wrote his own.) Beyond this is the temple (*tam dien*), where the deceased king and queen are worshipped and their royal belongings displayed. The king's widows would keep incense and aloe wood perpetually burning before the altar until their own deaths. Behind and on either side of the temple are the houses built for the king's concubines, servants and soldiers who guarded the royal tomb. The emperor's body is laid in a concealed place (*bao thanh*), enclosed by high walls behind well-locked bronze doors.

In certain mausoleums – Gia Long's and Thieu Tri's, for example – a special pavilion was built in the center from where the emperor himself would direct the construction work on his tomb, or simply relax on hot days. Tu Duc's tomb is something of an exception, as it comes complete with a lake-side pavilion, which served as both a place to bathe and as somewhere to relax for a spot of fishing.

Setting foot in any of the tombs, one feels a sense of admiration for the noble grandeur and elegant style of the architecture. This sense of awe is described by one of Vietnam's celebrated writers, Pham Quynh, a former minister of national education:

"This tomb is the general blending of all the colors of the firmament and of all the tints of water; it is an amalgamation of high mountains, of thick forests, of wind blowing through foliage. This tomb is a spectacle of nature, a marvel of great beauty, added to another sight, created by the hand of man, of a beauty no less marvelous. It is the patient and inspired work of the artist whose intention was to color the countryside to awaken the awaiting soul, soaring in the silence of this mournful place or whispering in the top of the lone pine tree. There are not the words to express the bizarre sensation, both gentle and of tender exhilaration, which grips one with an eagerness for poetry in this scenery charged with depth and mystery."

Minh Mang's tomb can be reached by hiring a small motorboat from any of the local owners opposite the Perfume River Hotel. Alternatively, take a car to Ban Viet village and from there, take a boat across the Perfume River. Minh Mang was Gia Long's fourth son and the Nguyen dynasty's second king. He built the Imperial City and was highly respected for his reforms in the sphere of customs, traditions and agriculture. His mausoleum is located where the Ta Trach and Huu Trach tributaries of the Perfume River meet. Its construction was begun a year before his death, in 1840 and was finished by his successor Thieu Tri in 1843. The setting blends the beauty of nature with the majestic architecture and superb stone sculpture created by its many anonymous craftsmen. The setting is at its best in mid-March, when the Trung Minh and Tan Nguyet lakes bloom with a mass of beautiful lotus flowers.

Tu Duc's tomb, just a bit southwest of Hue, can be reached by a very pleasant cycle ride through pine forests and lush hills. The mausoleum construction, begun in 1864, took three years to complete. The result resembles a royal palace in miniature and harmonizes beautifully with the natural surroundings. A work force of 3,000 men was used in its construction. Tu Duc, the son of Thieu Tri and the Nguyen Dynasty's fourth king, reigned for 36 years, the longest reign of any of the Nguyen kings. He spent his leisure hours in the two pavilions beside the lake, Luu Khiem. Here, he wrote poetry, no doubt inspired by the beauty of his surroundings, fished and enjoyed the fragrance of the lotus. The more popular of the two lake-side pagodas is the Xung Khiem Pavilion, which dates from 1865.

Entrance to Emperor Minh Mang' tomb.

A staircase leads to the Luong Khiem mausoleum, which contains a collection of furniture, vases and jewelry boxes. Further on is the terrace leading to the tomb, with its stone elephants, horses and mandarins. The tomb itself, ritually inaccessible, is covered by dense pine forest. The tombs of Tu Duc's adopted son, Kien Phu and Queen Le Thien An, lie beside the lake.

Thieu Tri's tomb is located nearby. Thieu Tri, Minh Mang's son, was the third Nguyen emperor and reigned from 1841 to 1847. His tomb was built between 1947 and 1948, and in the same elegant architectural style as his father's, but on a much smaller scale.

Khai Dinh's tomb is completely different from any of the other Nguyen tombs. If anything, it resembles a European castle, its architecture a blend of the oriental and occidental. Made of reinforced concrete, it took 11 years to complete and was finally finished in 1931. Khai Dinh, Bao Dai's adopted father, ruled for nine years during the colonial era. A grandiose dragon stair-case leads up to the first courtyard, from where further stairs lead to a courtyard lined with stone statues of elephants, horses, civil and military mandarins. In the center of the courtyard stands the stele inscribed with Chinese characters composed by Bao Dai in memory of his father. The exterior lacks the tranquil charm and beauty of Minh Mang's or Tu Duc's mausoleum, and the giant dragons flanking the staircase appear rather menacing.

Once inside, however, the contrast is striking. Colored tiles pave the floor, a huge "dragon in the clouds" mural, painted by artists using their feet, adorns the ceiling of the middle chamber. Jade green antechambers lead off to the left and right. Colorful frescoes composed of many thousands of inlaid ceramic and glass fragments depict various themes. Animals, trees and flowers provide a visual feast after the less-inspiring blackened exterior of the mausoleum. A life-size bronze statue of Khai Dinh, made in France in 1922, rests on a dais on top of the tomb.

Gia Long's tomb, 16 kilometers (10 mi) from Hue on the Bach hillside, is somewhat inaccessible by road; a more pleasant way to reach it is by boat. The tomb, began in 1814, was completed a year after his death in 1820. Unfortunately, the site was in the middle of a guerrilla zone during the war and the tomb has been considerably damaged by bombs. It has since become rather neglected, but the wild beauty of the site itself, with its backdrop of Mt Thien Tho, makes the effort to get there well worth while.

The **Minh Thanh Temple**, also in very bad shape, is dedicated to Gia Long's first wife, Queen Thua Thien Co. On the left is Gia Long's sepulchre, where he and his first wife are buried side by side.

Other attractions: Boats can be hired from the landing stage at the Pavilion of Edicts to travel up the Perfume River as far as the Van Mieu (Temple of Literature), dedicated to Confucius, and the Vo Mieu (Temple of Martial Arts), dedicated to the god of war, Quan Cong, and

certain Vietnamese marshals. In the evenings, boats offer dinner and traditional music performances.

Toward the mausoleums and below the Thien Mu Pagoda is the temple known as both **Dien Hin Chen** and Ngoc Tran Dien, where the goddess Po Nagar, protector of the Champa Kingdom, is worshipped. Po Nagar, greatly venerated by the Chams in the past, is also to a lesser extent worshipped today by the Vietnamese, who supplanted them in the narrow stretch of land that was once the Kingdom of Champa.

A festival takes place here on the 15th day of the seventh lunar month every year, when worshippers march in a long procession, accompanied by ceremonial music and a heavy cloud of incense.

On the west bank of the river lie the **Ho Quyen arenas**, where tigers and elephants were forced to fight against each other in bloody performances staged to amuse the king and his court. This type of arena is extremely rare in Southeast Asia. The village of Nguyet Bieu nearby is known for its excellent grapefruit and longans.

Surrounded by a park of pines and conifers, the **Nam Giao esplanade**, (Terrace of Heavenly Sacrifice), built by Gia Long in 1802, was in its day considered the most sacred and solemn place. Composed of three terraces – two square and one circular – as a whole the esplanade represents the sky and the earth. From here, the emperor paid homage to heaven in his capacity as the privileged mandatory on earth.

Every three years the Nam Giao (Festival of Sacrifice) took place at the center of the circular esplanade. A buffalo would be sacrificed to the god of the sky, who is believed to govern the destiny of the world. Unfortunately, the whole area has been turned into a hideous monument to the dead.

Hue and the surrounding area have many beautiful gardens with lakes, miniature mountains and trees, roses and a variety of flowers. The villages of Vi Da and Kim Long, in the suburbs, are worth visiting for their trees and gardens. Near Hue lie the lagoons and beaches of Pha Tan Giang, Thuan An and Tu Hien.

Left, market day in Hue. Right, royal stone guardians, Hue.

RUSH TO PRESERVE

For a country with a long and rich history, Vietnam boasts relatively few architectural landmarks. Those that have survived the centuries of war, typhoons and harsh climate have suffered from human neglect. Historical preservation, after all, is something of a luxury for a country preoccupied with fending off invaders and, later, grappling with poverty.

Today, however, Vietnam has begin to show an interest in saving its historical sites. Some of this has to do with the economy. Vietnam's economy is improving, so the country can begin thinking about more than filling the people's basic needs.

In part, too, this movement is a facet of the government's emphasis on nationalism – in politics, culture, and entertainment. (Recently, a karaoke contest had one rule: the contestants had to sing a patriotic song.) Restoring architectural ruins is one way to develop national pride.

More importantly, however, restoration is commercially viable. All government officials needed to do was look at tourists climbing about China's Great Wall or Cambodia's Angkor Wat to figure out there is money in a pile of old rocks.

If the rocks are well maintained, that is. And until now, Vietnam's architectural gems have lacked historical lustre.

The Citadel and tombs of Hue, however, recently grabbed international attention when they were included on a list of endangered sites. "This will make Vietnamese feel they have more responsibility in preserving the site," says one hopeful historian in Hanoi.

The government has pledged to spend at least US$1 million a year on the Hue conservation effort. Foreign organizations, notably from Japan and also from UNESCO, have also contributed funds. Vietnam does not have many trained restoration workers, but it is attempting to use native crafts people stone cutters, wood carvers, pottery makers and the like – to learn advanced skills from overseas experts. Again, this reflects the bent for nationalism: Vietnam, as one expert said, likes to do things on its own.

Right now, conservationists have their work cut out for them. Many of the stone pillars and statues have crumbled; the wood structures have been badly damaged by termites and water. Damage from the Vietnam War was severe. There are bullet-ridden stone walls visible on the grounds of the Citadel. Many statues and artifacts were destroyed. There are still standing reminders, however, that look as if the fighting just ended last week, such as a broken mirror in a house behind the Thai Hoa Palace.

Hue is not the only place drawing the interest of historic preservationists. Others include Hoi An, the shipping village with considerable Chinese and Japanese architecture; the Cham towers along the south-central coast, near Nha Trang; pagodas throughout the country; the monuments of My Son, in Quang Nam–Da Nang Province (which suffered war damage).

Historians also are keen to preserve the cultural traditions that are threatened with extinction, because older practitioners have either died, or they have not passed down their knowledge. So there are efforts to research and preserve traditional music, festivals, handicrafts, and even royal cuisine. Much of this tradition, of course, is linked to Vietnam's old dynasties, a royalist tradition fought against by the Communists. But reviving interest in royalist traditions doesn't seem to faze the government. "This is our history," said one official. "We must not lose it." ∎

DA NANG AND HOI AN

Quang Nam Da Nang Province lies about 800 kilometers (500 mi) between both Hanoi and Ho Chi Minh City, separated from Laos by the western Truong Son mountains. Forests of valuable timber – rose wood, iron wood and ebony – cover more than 60 percent of the land.

The drive from Hue to Da Nang is one of the most spectacular in Vietnam, as Highway 1 follows a vertiginous route up, down and around mountains that hug the coastline. The climate becomes noticeably warmer and less humid after descending the 1,200-meter (4,000 ft) summit of **Deo Hai Van** (**Hai Van Pass**), which adjoins another mountain, Bach Ma (White Horse), and descends to the scenic coastal region.

To the north of Da Nang and Hai Van Pass on the road to Hue, the palm-shaded peninsula of **Lang Co** rates as one of the most superb spots in the country. To one side lies a stunningly clear lagoon, and on the other, miles of unspoiled beach washed by the South China Sea. The town, dependent on fishing, is heavily Catholic.

The provincial capital, **Da Nang**, located on the west bank of the Han River, has grown from a fishing village into an important port and the country's fourth-largest city, with 400,000 people.

While it is not quite as hectic as the capital, Hanoi, or the southern commercial hub, Ho Chi Minh City, Da Nang is rapidly becoming a thriving city. Officials here are banking on tourism to revive the economy, and there are plans to offer international flights in and out of Da Nang's airport. Right now, there are not many high-end accommodations, however. Overseas developers have been planning for years to build resorts along the coastline south of Da Nang, in an area known to American GIs from the war as China Beach. Those plans, however, have faced a myriad of obstacles; actual construction and opening of hotels, golf courses and condominiums probably won't be completed for years.

That may be a good thing for tourists

who wish to avoid huge crowds; for now, Da Nang is a rather sleepy destination. People here are generally quite friendly, and many speak English because of Da Nang's development as an American military town during the war. Don't be surprised to meet middle-aged men and women who worked for the Americans as interpreters, mechanics, bartenders or in the many businesses that sprung up to offer all kinds of services to soldiers – everything from laundries to brothels.

Because of its location in the center of the country, Da Nang also found itself a city divided during the war. Many people supported the South Vietnam regime, but others quietly (until after 1975) worked for the Viet Cong. Sometimes families themselves had split allegiances; it's not uncommon to meet brothers who fought against each other.

There are a few relics of the war-era still standing. North of town, along the shoreline, are the rusted shells of an old air base, now used by the Vietnamese military for training. The Da Nang air-

port runway is lined with revetments. The old American consulate is on Bach Dang Street, parallel to the Han River.

Known as Tourane under the French, Da Nang is perhaps best remembered abroad from the role it played at the beginning and end of the Vietnam War. The first 3,500 US Marines came ashore here in 1965. Ten years later, Communist troops rolled into town facing little resistance as South Vietnamese soldiers shed their uniforms along the side of the road and fled. Two American 727 jets evacuated refugees, most of them soldiers, in a scene of panic broadcast around the world. So many people tried to climb onto the planes that, as one of them took off, people clinging to the wheels fell into the South China Sea.

Other foreigners came here long before the Americans, however. In the 17th and 18th centuries, the first Spanish and French landings were made here. Subsequently, Da Nang became the scene of battles between the Vietnamese who fought, first, the Spanish and later the French. In the course of the

19th century, it had superseded Faifo (Hoi An) as the most important port and commercial center in the central region.

Among the specialties produced in the province are cinnamon from Tra Mi, pepper from Tien Phuoc, tobacco from Cam Le, silk from Hoa Vang, saffron from Tam Ky and sea swallow nests from the islands off the coast.

The *nuoc mam* produced in the fishing village of Nam O, about 15 kilometers (9 mi) from the city toward the Hai Van Pass, is reputedly the best in Vietnam. (But then, too, supposedly is the nuoc mam from Phan Thiet and from Phu Quoc Island.)

Cham, Mnong, Hoa, Ka Tu, Sedang and Co are among the many minorities found in the province.

Vestiges of an ancient culture: The ancient kingdom of Champa once stretched all the way from Hue, in central Vietnam, to Vung Tau in the south. The kingdom incorporated the five provinces of O Ri, Amaravati, Vijaya, Kauthara, and Panduranga.

The Quang Nam Da Nang area was the center of the Cham civilization for many centuries. The most ancient capital, Singhapura (Lion Citadel) at Tra Kieu, was built during the course of the 4th century. Early in the 8th century, the capital was moved south to Panduranga.

In the late 8th century, it was transferred back to Quang Nam Da Nang and renamed Indrapura (City of the God of Thunder). Indrapura lasted until the early 11th century.

The ancient site of Singhapura – at Tra Kieu, 40 kilometers (25 mi) southwest of Da Nang, with its dozens of monuments, hundreds of statues and bas reliefs – attests to the rich culture that once flourished here. A stelek, erected by the eighth Champa king to the memory of Hindu poet Valmiki, author of the *Ramayana,* stands intact.

The sacred Buddhist-inspired site of Indrapura, now known as Dong Duong, lies 60 kilometers (40 mi) from Da Nang. The site's scattered monuments – some of them Buddhist and others Brahman-inspired – are engraved with texts about a line of nine kings and their deeds.

Archaeologists have discovered many

Cham sculpture, Da Nang Museum.

artifacts at the site, including the 2nd-century bronze Dong Duong Buddha that now resides in the National Museum, in Ho Chi Minh City. A large Buddhist monastery and many holy shrines also are located here.

The **My Son Valley**, southwest of Da Nang, was chosen as a religious sanctuary by King Bhadravarman I, and from the 4th century on, many temples and towers (*kalan*) were built. Most were dedicated to kings and Brahman divinities, including the god Shiva, who was considered the creator, founder and defender of the Champa kingdom and the Cham royal dynasties.

Some 12th-century stelae discovered here attest to a unified religious belief practiced in the sanctuary's first temple, which was erected for the worship of Shiva-Bhadresvara. More than 70 architectural works of different styles and eras once stood in this ancient valley. Today, less than 20 remain. My Son fell in a free-fire zone for B52 strategic bombers during the Vietnam War and was almost destroyed by bombs.

The Cham towers were ingeniously constructed of dried bricks, placed together with resin from the *cau day* tree. Once the tower was completed, it was encircled by fires kept well-stoked for several days.

The intense heat fired the whole structure, completely melding and sealing the bricks and resin together to form a structure able to withstand the combined onslaught of time and the elements – but not, unfortunately, 20th-century bombs.

The Chams were divided into two groups: the Dua, who inhabited the provinces of Amarvati and Vijaya, and the Cau, from the provinces of Kauthara and Pandaranga. The two clans differed in their customs and habits, and conflicting interests led to many clashes and even war. But they usually managed to settle disagreements through intermarriage between the two clans.

The influences that shaped the culture and history of the Cham people are revealed through their sculpture and carvings. An insight into the Cham peo-

ple is provided at the excellent **Museum of Cham Sculpture**, in Da Nang. The museum was set up in 1936 by the Ecole Francaise d'Extreme Orient. Its extensive collection is displayed in rooms featuring four different periods according to their origins: My Son, Tra Kieu, Dong Duong and Thap Mam.

South of Da Nang, towards the coast, stand five large hills known as the Marble Mountains, or **Ngu Hanh Son**, Mountains of the Five Elements: Kim Son (metal), Thuy Son (water), Moc Son (wood), Hoa Son (fire) and Tho Son (earth). These mountains were once a group of five offshore islets, but because of silting over the years, they became part of the mainland. Mysterious caves within the mountains shelter altars dedicated to Buddha, Bodhisattvas and the different deities created in stories of the area's inhabitants.

The most famous of these is Thuy Son. Used by the Cham for their rituals, these caves today still serve as religious sanctuaries. One can visit the Tam Thi Temple, built in 1852, the Linh Ung Temple and the Huyen Khong Grotto. Children in the area descend upon visitors who come to climb Thuy Son and its caves. While they appear to be pests, they actually are quite helpful and entertaining, shouting out a funny assortment of English-language words: "Awesome," "Don't worry be happy," "I'm cool," and the ubiquitous "America number one." They will direct travelers in and out of a maze of steps and hidden caves, and up a final ascent that provides a good view of the area. Of course, at the end of the hike, the children expect you to buy something: water, soft drinks or a trinket. A flashlight is helpful for the climb. The mountains are also a valuable source of red, white and blue-green marble. At the foot of the mountains, skillful marble carvers chisel out a great variety of *objets d'art*.

Alongside Marble Mountain is a long stretch of beautiful, quiet beach. To the south is **Bai Bien Non Nuoc**, known to foreigners as **China Beach**, near the village of Non Nuoc. China Beach was a place American GIs went for rest and

Slow going o
China Beach.

recreation during the war. However, some people contend the real China Beach is to the north, at My Khe.

Architectural melting pot: About 25 kilometers (15 mi) southeast of Da Nang, the ancient town of **Hoi An** nestles on the banks of the Thu Bon River, a few kilometers inland from the coast. This charming old town was once a flourishing port and meeting place of East and West, in what was central Dai Viet under the Nguyen lords.

Hoi An appeared in western travelogues in the 17th and 18th centuries as Faifo or Hai Po. Originally a sea port in the Champa Kingdom and known as Dai Chien, by the 15th century it had become a coastal Vietnamese town under the Tran Dynasty. In the beginning of the 16th century, the Portuguese came to explore the coast of Hoi An. Then came the Chinese, Japanese, Dutch, British and French. With them came the first missionaries – Italian, Portuguese, French, Spanish. Among them was Alexander of Rhodes, who developed the roman alphabet for Vietnamese.

For several centuries, Hoi An was one of the most important trading ports in Southeast Asia, and an important center of cultural exchange between East and West. By the beginning of the 19th century, Hoi An's social and physical environment had changed drastically. The conflict between the Trinh and Nguyen lords and the Tay Son caused Hoi An considerable damage. Rivers changed course as the mouth of the Thu Bon River silted up and prevented the flow of sea traffic. Another port was built at the mouth of the Han River; that port, Da Nang, replaced Hoi An as the bustling center of trade.

Today, Hoi An is a quiet town of about 75,000 people – 12,000 of them living in the **old quarter** that has been restored and renovated as something of a historical showpiece for tourists. Many of the older homes, built with wood beams, carved doors and airy, open rooms, have been turned into souvenir shops fronting as museums.

In the early 1980s, UNESCO and the Polish government took the initiative

and funded a restoration program to classify and safeguard Hoi An's ancient quarters and historic monuments. The town faces yearly floods, as water spills over the river banks and submerges some streets in two to three meters of water. That, of course, damages the timber construction of the houses.

Hoi An has become a popular tourist spot, so popular that it can seem crawling with foreigners at times. In fact, older residents worry that the very thing that makes Hoi An attractive – its quiet charm – is being ruined. People will kindly invite visitors into their homes to look at the architecture. But then some of them hit people up for a donation.

But for better or worse, Hoi An is stuck with the tourists. Today, in the old part of town, nearly 80 percent of the people derive their income from tourism. The rest of the residents work primarily as fishermen.

The oldest part of town is in the southern section, bordering the Thu Bon River. Le Loi Street was the first street to be built, four centuries ago. The Japanese quarter, with its covered bridge, Japanese-style shops and houses, followed half a century later, followed by the Cantonese quarter in another 50 years.

Hoi An's ancient past is superbly preserved in its architecture. The old quarter is a fascinating blend of temples, pagodas, community houses, shrines, clan houses, shop houses and homes.

One of the most remarkable historical architectural examples is the covered **Japanese Bridge**. Built by the Japanese community in the 17th century, it links the districts of Cam Pho and Minh Huong. The bridge's curved shape, and undulating green-and-yellow tiled roof, give the impression of moving water. In the middle of the bridge is a square pagoda dedicated to Dac De and Tran Vu, two legendary figures.

Some pagodas and 20 clan houses stand in the center of the ancient town. The **Chua Phuc Kien**, on Tran Phu Street and built in 1792, has been the meeting place of many generations of the same clan, who arrived from Fukien. Here, they remember their origins and worship their ancestors. The temple is dedicated to the cult of Lady Thien Hau and contains many exquisite woodcarvings. Most of these temples and houses were built by the Chinese migrant community over a span of 40 years, between 1845 and 1885.

Also on Tran Phu Street, the **Mieu Quan Cong**, built in 1904, is dedicated to Quang Cong, a talented general of the Three Kingdoms period in Chinese history. Many of the temples venerate Buddha, along with Confucianism, Taoism and a diversity of other gods and beliefs. The 15th-century **Phuc Thanh Pagoda**, on the outskirts of Hoi An, contains many beautiful statues and is one of the oldest in the region.

Although many of the old homes and monuments have been restored over the years, they retain their original wooden framework, carved doors and windows and sculpted stuccos, as well as very rare and ancient furniture from Vietnam, China, Japan and the West.

The most characteristic examples of Hoi An's architecture are the old houses along **Nguyen Thai Hoc Street**, particularly at Number 1001. These elongated houses front onto one street and back on to the street behind. All the houses are built of precious wood in a very refined, two-story style. The front facade serves as a boutique and the area behind is generally used as storage space. The interior is terraced for living, and an inner a courtyard is open to the sky with a veranda linking several living quarters. One of the most remarkable features of these old homes is the diversity in their architectural structure. This varies greatly from one house to another in terms of space distribution, sculptural art, decoration and inner courtyard gardens. Space is creatively utilized to the utmost.

The unique crabshell roof style extensively used is typical of Hoi An. Walking in the streets of this beautiful and charming town, one can observe the influence of the architecture, sculpture and decorative styles of China and Japan, and the skill of the Vietnamese architects who have absorbed these outside influences and created something similar yet somehow different.

Fishing on China Beach.

THE SOUTH

Far removed from the more traditional north and center, southern Vietnam has a character all of its own. Saigon, the former capital of South Vietnam until it collapsed in 1975, now bears the name of Ho Chi Minh City, a change that many of its residents (and foreigners) still resist. Traditions and habits die hard.

But whatever one calls it, this furiously active and commercial city is definitely going somewhere. The streets are filled with new motorbikes and new taxis, and construction is adding a glittering shimmer to the downtown boulevards.

It's always been an entrepreneurial center, and for decades, people from all over the country have flocked here to make their fortunes. This is Vietnam's city of dreams – and sometimes, nightmares. Many become disillusioned, and they may be seen on the streets, looking for a job or a place to sleep. But the effort and luck needed to find fortune has done little to deter the flow of hopefuls, young and old alike. And, indeed, their spirit gives the city an optimistic edge. In fact, southern Vietnam, especially Ho Chi Minh City, has always been noted for its business acumen. Cholon, the city's long-established and thriving Chinese community, never seems to sleep. It's here that Vietnam's economic revival awoke.

An increasingly important facet of Vietnam's economic growth, however, can be found some 125 kilometers (70 mi) east of Ho Chi Minh City, in Vung Tau, the center of the country's growing oil industry. One of the country's major ports, Vung Tau bathes in a mild climate, and is a popular weekend seaside resort.

Although oil portends a prosperous future for Vietnam, for the moment its export powerhouse is the rice-growing region of the Mekong Delta (and, too, the north's Red River Delta). The vast Mekong Delta stretches from the eastern coast to the western border with Cambodia, and as far south as Ca Mau Point, the southernmost tip of the country. An extensive network of waterways, irrigation canals and rivers crisscrosses the region, which is plied by ferries and every type of sailing vessel imaginable, linking the various towns and provinces to Ho Chi Minh City.

Rice fields stretch as far as the eye can see, creating a many-hued and textured patchwork. It is a quiet, isolated life, one that apparently makes many a person restless and thus drawn to the bright lights of Ho Chi Minh City, or Saigon, if one prefers.

Preceding pages: fowl for dinner, Ho Chi Minh City; the lingering dusk over Nha Trang harbor. **Left**, rice factory outside of Ho Chi Minh City.

NHA TRANG
AND THE COAST

Along the southcentral coast, travelers can get a glimpse of two sides of life in Vietnam: the relaxed beach life of the picturesque Nha Trang, and then the hardscrabble existence of the desolate areas around Phan Rang and Phan Thiet. The drive along the coast, from Da Nang to Nha Trang, provides spectacular vistas of beaches, coves, cliffs and mountains jutting out into the sea, with miles and miles of rice paddies bordered on one side by blue-tinted mountain sides, and on the other, by the sea.

Vietnam's most picturesque coastal town and beach resort, **Nha Trang**, is the ideal place to break a journey, relax and soak up the sun.

Established on the orders of a Nguyen king in 1924, Nha Trang, with its population of 200,000, is now the provincial capital of **Khanh Hoa Province**, which lies to the east of the Central Highlands. According to popular belief, the town derives its name from the Cham word *yakram,* meaning bamboo river.

Nha Trang is a good place to idle. The beaches are clean and generally empty, although the beach town is becoming a popular weekend getaway for the wealthy of Ho Chi Minh City. In recent years, there has been a considerable amount of construction of new hotels along Tran Phu Street, which runs parallel to the shoreline. But the beach itself has been left reasonably undisturbed, and most of the hotels are small family operations, although eventually, large hotels will change the small-town feel of Nha Trang's beach. A small amusement park, with a ferris wheel and a fun house, fronts the beach.

There are several good restaurants right on the beach, serving everything from pizza baked in a brick oven to the expected fresh seafood; the large shrimp is especially good.

The attitude here is generally more relaxed and carefree than elsewhere in Vietnam. Visitors will find pick-up soccer games on the beach, the sky filled with kites, and vendors peddling fruit, steamed corn, crabs, T-shirts, massages and manicures on the beach. It's possible to sell and trade books in English, French and German. Generally, the vendors are friendly and not terribly pushy; they seem to sense that visitors are here to unwind.

Besides risking a sunburn, reading a book and napping – in other words, doing not much of anything – there are things to see in and around Nha Trang.

At the town's northern entrance stand the majestic towers of the famous Brahman sanctuary and temple, **Po Nagar**. The main tower is dedicated to the Cham goddess Po Ino Nagar, the Lady Mother of the Kingdom, reputedly Siva's female form. Today, she is still worshipped, adopted by Vietnamese Buddhists who refer to her as Thien Y A Na. Her statue resides in the main temple, but it was decapitated during French rule, and the original head now resides in the Guimet Museum, in Paris.

Only four of the sanctuary's original eight temples, all of which face east,

remain standing. These date from between the 6th and 11th centuries. From the top of **San Hill**, behind the ancient Cham towers, a superb panoramic view looks out over Nha Trang.

Palm trees line the dazzling, fine-white sands and clear waters of the city's gently curving bay. Idyllic islands, easily accessible by boat, lie just off the coast. Boat excursions can be arranged to visit the islands and coral reefs, where snorkeling is excellent. Deep-sea fishing is also possible.

The islands, particularly **Hon Yen** (Salagande Island), are home to sea swallows, whose famous nests, gathered in vast quantities, constitute a valuable source of both nutrition and income. The nests are collected twice a year here, in spring and autumn. They vary in color from grey and white to the greatly appreciated and much rarer orange and red nests. These are more valuable and are believed to have certain therapeutic properties, no doubt hiking the price.

A huge white Buddha statue commands an excellent view from his seat at the top the hill behind the **Long Son Pagoda**. The pagoda was established in the latter part of the 19th century and has been reconstructed several times since. Glass and ceramic mosaics depicting dragons adorn the main entrance and roofs, and colorful dragons are entwined around the pillars of the main hall.

The **Pasteur Institute**, on the sea front, was founded in 1895 by Dr Alexandre Yersin, a French microbiologist and military doctor who had worked as an assistant to Dr Pasteur in Paris. He arrived in Vietnam in 1891 and was among those Europeans who first appreciated Da Lat. Yersin was also responsible for introducing and establishing Brazilian rubber trees and *quinquina* plantations – quinine-producing trees – in the region of Suoi Dau, about 25 kilometers (15 mi) southwest of Nha Trang. He is buried here among his rubber trees, according to his wishes.

(While at Suoi Dau, it's possible – and worthwhile – to visit **Hon Ba Hill** and a lagoon known as **Ho Tien**, the

Harbor at low tide.

Lagoon of the Immortals. The lagoon is formed by a stream that tumbles down the Hon Ba hillside. According to legend, the flat rocks that jut above the surface of the lagoon were once a meeting place for immortals, who gathered there to play chess and inscribe wins and losses on the rocks.)

Dr Yersin's library and office have been converted into a museum, where some of his laboratory equipment and personal affects are displayed. Many of his books are kept in the library opposite the museum. Today, the institute still produces vaccines and carries out research, with a very limited budget and equipment that looks as if it should join the exhibits in the museum.

The **Oceanographic Institute** is located south of the town, in the fishing village of **Cau Da**. The institute was founded in 1927 on the initiative of a biologist, Armand Krempf. Today, it houses a collection of aquatic flora and fauna. Its aquariums are a bit dilapidated – nothing but rows of small fish tanks lined up along the walls, and a few

specimens preserved in jars. Outside, there is an open-air pool with a few fish swimming about.

Cau Da does a brisk business in shells, coral and tortoise shell items – necklaces, bracelets and the like – at reasonable prices. The ever-present Vietnamese condiment, *nuoc mam,* is produced here in large quantities. Five tons of a sardine-like fish, *ca nuc,* dried in two tons of salt will yield 70,000 liters of nuoc mam and an overpowering odor in the process.

Just north of Cau Da, Emperor Bao Dai's five villas are set among well-manicured trees and shrubs on three hills. The villas were built in the 1920s, their location obviously chosen for the superb views over the sea, the bay and the port.

Three cycles of Vietnamese leadership have used the site for rest and relaxation. Bao Dai and his family came here until the royalty was ousted. From the mid-1950s until 1975, high-ranking officials of the South Vietnamese government enjoyed the accommodations.

Life is best with an empty beach.

After 1975, they were supplanted by Communist leaders from Hanoi. The *hoi polloi* can now enjoy the site, too. The villas have been restored, with a new restaurant, and are open to the public for surprisingly reasonable prices.

Cyclos and motorcycle taxis (*xe om*) regularly ferry visitors up and down the highway in and around Nha Trang.

During the day, one can catch the interesting sights and smells of Nha Trang's main market, **Cho Dam**, which was built in 1972. Goods include everything from fruit and vegetables to items ingeniously made from old aircraft parts.

A guaranteed sight is the return of the local fishing fleet to shore as the evening sun is setting. One place to watch is from the **Xom Bong bridge** that spans the **Cai River**. The Cai, which joins several waterways from the western forests, flows to the Nha Trang River mouth. The province's largest river, the 300-kilometer-long (180-mi) **Da Rang River**, is the longest in central Vietnam. Canals branch off, carrying water to the vast fields of rice, maize and beans.

The three hills at Nha Trang's western exit each sport a pagoda. The most important of these is the **Hai Duc**, a religious center that was started by leaders of the now-outlawed South Vietnamese Buddhist organization.

Ten kilometers (6 mi) further west lie the remains of the old vauban-style **Dien Khanh Citadel**, built in 1793 by French engineers employed by Lord Nguyen Anh, who became Emperor Gia Long in 1802. Little is left of it today, apart from a few sections of the walls and gates.

Not far from the town, the **Hon Chong rocks** jut out into the clear aquamarine waters of the South China Sea. Northeast of here is **Mt Tien Co**, or Fairy Mountain, so named because its three summits are thought to resemble a fairy lying on her back.

To the north, National Highway 1 traverses the Minh Hoa Plain, crossing the Ro Tuong and Ru Ri passes before climbing the sinuous **Deo Ca Pass** over Mt Dai Lan. Here, in 1470, King Le Thanh Tong and his troops stopped and erected a stele to mark the boundary

Along the road, near Nha Trang.

236

between Dai Viet and the Kingdom of Champa. Today, this spot marks the boundary between Phu Yen and Khanh Hoa provinces.

About 80 kilometers (50 mi) northeast lies **Cap Varella** (Vinh Van Phong or Bien Nho); in the west, the famous **Mother and Child Mountain** reaches a height of 2,000 meters (6,600 ft). The mountain can be seen on a clear day by fishermen far out at sea, and was named because from a distance its silhouette resembles a women carrying a child.

From Cap Varella, the road descends sharply towards the market town of **Tu Bong**, and from there to **Van Gia**, just a little over 70 kilometers (40 mi) north of Nha Trang. The **Long Son Pagoda** at Van Gia made headlines in 1963 after one of its officiating bonzes, Thich Quang Duc, immolated himself in the center of Saigon.

The pagoda's enormous white Buddha, erected in 1963, commemorates the Buddhist struggle against the repressive regime of Ngo Dinh Deim. Images of the Buddhist nuns and monks who laid down their lives as a final protest are at the foot of the statue.

North of Nha Trang, near the village of Phu Huu, is a quiet, isolated park with a stream and waterfalls called **Ba Ho**. The area is generously endowed with thermal springs, and the scenery is varied and quite magnificent.

Forests in the northern part of the region produce many kinds of wood, including sandalwood, aloe wood, eaglewood, barian kingwood, rosewood and ebony. An abundance of high-quality sea salt is produced at **Hon Khoi**, the Smoking Mountain.

Leaving Nha Trang to the south, the coastal road passes **Cam Ranh Bay**, the deep-water bay used as a naval base, first by the Americans and later by the Soviets. The base remains a sensitive military area and absolutely no photography is permitted. The sand from the bay is of a quality much sought after for manufacturing lenses and high-quality crystal. Before the Vietnam War, enormous quantities of the sand was exported to Japan, Europe and America.

ha Trang shing fleet.

The area of Cam Ranh alone has more than 750 acres (300 hectares) of salt marsh that yield around half a million tons of salt per year. Immense sugar cane plantations cover certain areas of the province. Molasses produced from the sugar residue is combined with sand and lime to produce an inexpensive but excellent mortar used in construction.

South of Cam Ranh, the road enters **Ninh Thuan Province**. The coastal road passes through a rather monotonous, sand-covered landscape. Mountains and forest cover two-thirds of Ninh Thuan and Binh Thuan to the south. Together, they remain one of the country's poorest areas, due to its lack of agricultural resources – just 10 percent of the province is suitable for farming.

The town of **Phan Rang**, capital of Ninh Thuan, is an ancient Cham principality on the **Chai River**. The town lies in an extremely arid landscape dotted with menacing-looking cacti and poinciana trees. From here, a scenic inland road leads to the Central Highlands resort of Da Lat. A few kilometers down

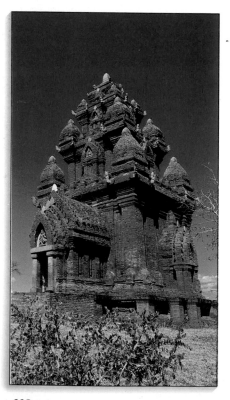

this road, four 13th-century Cham towers known as **Po Klong Garai** stand on an arid hill. These brick towers were built under the reign of the Cham King Jaya Simhavarman III. The entrance to the largest tower is graced with a dancing, six-armed Shiva, and inside a statue of a bull known as Nandin is the recipient of offerings brought by farmers to ensure a good harvest. Under a wooden pyramid is a *linga* painted with a human face. A rock on a nearby hill bears inscriptions commemorating a linga's erection by a Cham prince in 1050.

Further down the road, 40 kilometers (25 mi) from Da Lat, is **Krong Pha**, with the crumbling remains of two old Cham towers.

Even more interesting are the colorful, traditionally-clad Cham people who live in the foothills around this extremely poor area. This region is renowned for its grape production, and foreign wineries are developing vineyards here.

About 15 kilometers (10 mi) south of Phan Rang is the Cham tower of **Po Ro**, named after the last King of Champa, Po Ro Me, who ruled from 1629 to 1651 and died a prisoner of the Vietnamese.

The lovely white-sand beaches and turquoise waters of **Ca Na Beach**, roughly 30 kilometers (20 mi) south of Phan Rang, is an excellent place to break a journey.

Phan Thiet, the provincial capital of Binh Thuan, has a population of 76,000. Fishing is the mainstay of Phan Thiet and the province as a whole. A great many different varieties of fish are caught in the region. Visit the fishing harbor early in the morning, when the fishermen are unloading their catch, and you'll be treated to an unusual – and quite spectacular – sight.

As in many other towns along the coast, the unpleasant odor of nuoc mam hovers over the town. Among the other products of the region are mineral water from Vinh Hao Spring, cashew nuts, grapes and cuttlefish.

There is an impressive stark beauty to the graceful sculptured forms of the **Mui Le sand dunes**. The dunes, and a beach of the same name, are located 20 kilometers (12 mi) east of Phan Thiet.

Left, Cham tower, Phan Rang. **Right**, shy giggles at the beach.

CENTRAL HIGHLANDS AND DA LAT

A cool, tranquil and lush retreat from the bustle of Vietnam's cities, **Da Lat** was first developed as a getaway by the French. Located in **Lam Dong Province**, Da Lat, the city of Eternal Spring, is today Vietnam's most popular mountain resort and escape.

Da Lat's name comes from two words: *da,* meaning river or source, in reference to the Cam Ly River, and *lat,* the name of an ethnic minority living here.

Although accessible by several inland routes from the coastal provinces of Khanh Hoa and Ninh Thuan, the most used route is the 300-kilometer-long (180 mi) route via Bien Hoa from Ho Chi Minh City, about a five-hour trip. Another route from Nha Trang, on Highway 11, passes through areas with the residue of Cham relics.

Da Lat is nestled amongst mountains, pine-covered hillsides, lakes and forests on the Lam Viet plateau, beside the **Cam Ly River**. With a population of about 125,000, the city's economy is based on agriculture and tourism. The average annual temperature of about 17°C (63°F), fresh mountain air and tranquil beauty first attracted the French, who developed the resort and built holiday villas on the hillsides. Da Lat has long been a favorite destination for lovers and honeymooners. Many natural beauty spots await visitors in and around this charming old town, whose colonial-era villas and buildings are decorated with attractive gardens of roses, poppies, sunflowers and gladioli.

Da Lat was at one time projected to become the capital of the French colonial Indochinese State Federation. In the late 19th century, the French governor of Cochin China sent a delegation to explore the region. On the strength of their findings, the governor established a meteorological and agricultural research center here.

There is still something of a French colonial air about the place. The grand Dalat Palace Hotel commands a prime location in town, above a vast green lawn (perhaps the only such piece of grass anywhere in Vietnam) overlooking the central lake, Xuan Hoang. The hotel, built by the French in 1922, was renovated in 1995 and reopened by the French Sofitel chain.

On Tran Hung Dao Street, more than two dozen villas built by the French in all manner of European styles stand under tall trees, looking out over the valley and the mountains surrounding it. Villas built as summer residences for Vietnam's last emperor, Bao Dai, and one for the French governor-general are nestled among the pine trees.

A large Catholic cathedral, painted coral pink, tolls its bells early every morning to signal morning mass. Small houses are cozily perched, side by side, on the town's hilly terrain.

The beauty and serenity have made Da Lat a popular retreat. But its appeal has a downside. All around town, especially at many of the parks, lakes and villas, the tacky side of tourism has sprung up – photographers with hilltribe

eft, standing nch, Da at. Right, aying espects, uddhist emple.

costumes for visitors to don while posing for a picture by a lake, young men dressed as American cowboys leading children on pony rides, souvenir stands selling all manner of kitsch.

The risk, of course, is that the sideshow of schlock will upstage Da Lat's main attraction: its natural landscape, beauty and quiet.

The **old French quarter**, near the bridge spanning the Cam Ly River, has lost none of its charm or character. From a distance, this area of town looks like a village plunked out of the French Alps. Here are the Catholic cathedral, or **Nha Tho Con Ga**, built in 1931. Its stainedglass windows were made by Louis Balmet, in Grenoble.

Another Catholic church, **Du Sinh**, rests on a hilltop up Huyen Tran Cong Chua Street, where it commands a superb view of the surrounding area. It was built in 1955 by northern Vietnamese Catholic refugees.

The **imperial summer residence** of Vietnam's last emperor, Bao Dai, is tucked away under the pine trees, a few kilometers southwest of the center of town. Construction was begun in 1933 and finished five years later. Inside, there is a room with photographs of Bao Dai, his wife and children, and a desk with two telephones, one supposedly used by Bao Dai, the other by the former president of South Vietnam, Nguyen Van Thieu. (South Vietnamese leaders used the villa after Bao Dai left Vietnam; Communist government officials have used it since 1975.) Today, visitors can rent rooms here. There is a large lacquer map of Vietnam, a grand piano and frayed furniture covered in red velvet. Although guides say the furnishings were used by Bao Dai, in fact, much of his belongings have been carted away over the years.

In an upstairs bedroom, many Vietnamese visitors like to pose talking on a telephone. Outside, visitors will be amused to see young men and boys dressed up in animal outfits, ready to pose for photographs. One boy sometimes wears a Santa Claus suit. Another one may be dressed as a cowboy.

Garden at the Linh Son Pagoda, Da Lat.

242

Not far from here, on Thien My Street, is the **Lam Ty Ni Pagoda**, founded in 1961. The pagoda's attractive flower beds and garden, and much of its wooden furniture, are the handiwork of the pagoda's sole monk, Vien Thuc.

The pink **Evangelical Church** on Nguyen Van Troi Street was built in 1940. Since 1975, Vietnam's Protestants have suffered persecution, and even today the government restricts the activities of this church, whose congregation is composed mostly of hilltribe people. Also pink, the **Domaine de Marie convent**, built between 1940 and 1942, perches on a hilltop on Ngo Quyen Street. There are just a few nuns remaining, although they do operate a school and sell hand-made ginger candy.

The **morning market** in the heart of Da Lat is an ideal place to encounter some of the ethnic minorities, distinctive in their traditional dress, who come from the surrounding villages to sell their produce. Here also are the great diversity of fruit, flowers and vegetables produced in the region. Da Lat's

strawberries, and the jam made from them, are famous throughout the country. Avocados, artichokes, mushrooms, tomatoes, asparagus – just about any fruit, flower and vegetable found in Europe or America can be bought here. Flowers from Da Lat are sent to all parts of Vietnam. In fact, several foreign enterprises – from Japan, Taiwan and America – are setting up vegetable-growing ventures for export, as conditions for cultivation are ideal in this temperate region.

A wide range of handicraft items find their way to the market from various parts of the country, including bamboo handbags, rattan boxes, pressed flowers, fur hats and clothing.

Da Lat's **Ethnic Minority Museum** exhibits traditional costumes, ornaments, jewelry, baskets, hunting implements and musical instruments. The museum's archaeological display features a statue of the Hindu goddess Uma, 12th- and 14th-century Cham pottery vases, rice wine jars more than 200 years old, an unusual stone xylophone, and tools used in the province more than 1,500 years ago.

Ethnic minorities: Visits can be arranged to hillside minority villages and hamlets, where villagers make a meager living from the rice, corn, pumpkins, squash, tobacco and, sometimes, cotton that they grow on hillsides. They also work in tea and coffee plantations. The Ma minority women are excellent weavers and dye their cloth using natural bark extracts. The men use simple traps and spears to hunt and fish. A toxic substance extracted from leaves is sometimes used in fishing. This stuns the fish but is apparently harmless to humans.

Be warned that nothing is free in Da Lat, including a visit to a hilltribe village. Visitors need a permit, not free, to visit some villages. Once there, visitors are surrounded by villagers selling their goods, and they can be persistent.

Xuan Hoang Lake, formerly part of the town's golf course during the colonial era, lies in the heart of the town. The surrounding low hills, villas and pine forests provide a lovely backdrop, although the water itself is muddy with red clay most of the year, as the surrounding hillsides, bare of trees, are eroding. Drivers offer rides in horse-drawn carts from the edge of the park.

On the north side of the lake, a golf course originally built for Bao Dai has been renovated and expanded, supplanting what had been a public park. Near the golf course is the small campus of Da Lat University.

Not far away, the well-manicured **Flower Gardens** offer a nice quiet retreat. Established in 1966, a walkway winds through the gardens and around a small pond.

Just outside of town, in **Thung Lung Tinh Yeu** (Valley of Love), one can wander in the forest where Bao Dai used to hunt. Colorful sailboats can be rented on the artificial lake, formed during flooding in 1972. Visitors must pass through a gauntlet of souvenir stands.

Ho Than Tho (Lake of Sorrows) lies five kilometers (3 mi) northeast of Da Lat. It derives its name from the patriotism of a young couple, Hang Tung and Mai Nuong. When Hang joined Quang Trung's resistance forces against the Tsin invaders, Mai, believing Hang would be better able to serve his country unencumbered, drowned herself in the lake. Since then, the lake has been known by its present name, sometimes translated to mean Lake of Sighs – which is what visitors might do when they see the tacky gift stands that have sprouted on the lake's edge, not to mention wooden cutouts of a heart where couples can pose for a photo.

The French governor-general's palace, similar to Bao Dai's summer palace, is on Tran Hung Dao, southeast of the center of town. Rooms can be rented here as well, although as at Bao Dai's villa, there are daily pilgrimages of tourists tromping in and around the villa.

Waterfall haven: Several waterfalls liberally sprinkle the landscape in and around Da Lat. In a park about a few kilometers from the city, visit the **Cam Ly Falls**, which may also filled with young men and boys dressed in cowboy outfits. The falls are best visited during the rainy season; at other times the dry

Da Lat's coo climate is excellent for growing produce.

244

bed emits a foul odor. Further on and to the south, the **Da Tanla Falls** cascade into a pool enclosed by high rock walls and surrounded by luxuriant greenery.

Enclosed within the Thousand Flowers Valley and pine-covered hills south of Da Lat, the Prenn Falls, also known as **Thien Sa**, descend 15 meters (50 ft) across the mouth of a cave, entered from behind the falls via a small bridge.

Water from the Ankroet, or Golden Stream Falls, drops from a height of 15 meters (50 ft). Some 30 kilometers (20 mi) from town are the Lien Khuong Falls, and eight kilometers (five mi) further on, the silvery waters of the Gougah, or Pot Hole Falls, drop from a height of 20 meters (60 ft), creating rainbows on sunny days. The Pongour Falls, 50 kilometers (30 mi) from Da Lat, lie deep within thick primeval forest. The sound of the waters falling from a height of 30 meters can be heard even from several kilometers away during the rainy season.

The **Lang Biang mountains**, which flank the town to the north and north-east, consist of five volcanic peaks that are over 2,000 meters in height. A three- or four-hour hike up to the top will reward with a splendid view. Another good place for trekking is Mt Nui Ba. The waters in the area are said to cure many ailments.

The road heading south from Da Lat passes through pine forests and into the Di Linh district, where pineapple plantations and tall elephant grass line the roadside. Here, and also in Bao Loc district, it is not uncommon to see members of the Ma minority walking along the road carrying large stick baskets supported by head straps.

The **Bao Loc Mulberry and Silkworm Farm**, one of the largest in the world, is well worth a visit, but here again, special permission must be obtained from the authorities before a visit can be arranged. New silkworm hybrids, bred to survive the cooler highland climate, are raised year-round. The silkworms dine on the farm's mulberry plants; they spin silk cocoons, producing 37 tons a year.

egetable lots outside Da Lat.

HO CHI MINH CITY

Built on the site of an ancient Khmer city, Ho Chi Minh City was a thinly-populated area of forests, swamps and lakes until the 17th century. By the end of the 18th century, Ben Nghe, as the area was known, had become an important trading center within the region.

Different theories expound on the origins of the name Saigon – what Ho Chi Minh City was called before the Communists changed the name. Saigon is still used by many people, even in official capacities: the river coursing through the city remains the Saigon River, for example, and the state-owned tour company is Saigon Tourism.

Some say the name derives from the former name Sai Con, a transcription of the Khmer words, Prei Kor (the kapok-tree forest), or Prei Nokor (the forest of the kingdom), in reference to the Cambodian viceroy's residence, located in the region of present-day Cholon.

In the 19th century, southern Vietnam, particularly Saigon, prospered despite the incessant fighting between the Vietnamese and Cambodians, and between the Vietnamese themselves, who were divided in their support of either the Nguyen lords from Hue or the Tay Son insurgents from Binh Dinh.

In 1859, French and Spanish ships landed in southern Vietnam. The French unloaded troops and weapons and embarked upon their conquest of the country. Saigon itself was captured later the same year and became the capital of the French colony of Cochin China. Modernization accompanied colonization, and the French filled in the ancient canals, drained marshlands, built roads, laid out streets and quarters, and planted many trees. The city developed rapidly, acquiring something of the character of a French provincial town, served by two steam-powered trams.

After the division of the country in 1954, Saigon became the capital of the Republic of South Vietnam, until it fell to the Communists in April of 1975. The revolutionary authorities renamed it Ho Chi Minh City, after the founder of the modern Vietnamese state, who was, of course, anathema to supporters of the southern regime that lost the war. To many of its five million inhabitants, the city remains Saigon.

Today, 80 kilometers (50 mi) inland from the coast, Vietnam's largest city and river port sprawls across an area of 2,000 square kilometers (760 sq mi) on the banks of the Saigon River. The city is divided into 12 urban and six rural districts. Here, the dry season lasts from November to April, and the rainy season endures for the rest of the year.

The city appears to be a city on the move, although it is disorderly movement, bordering on chaos. Everywhere there is construction. So many new hotels are under construction in the city's center that officials are talking about a glut of hotel rooms. The streets and sidewalks overflow with the business of commerce, something that has always come quite naturally to the Saigonese. After a decade or so of having their entrepreneurial talents suppressed by a

Preceding pages: busy night, Ho Chi Minh City. Left, front garden of Reunification Hall, and Le Duan Blvd. Right, French facade on the City Hall.

socialist system, the business tycoons are out in full force again. Much of this comes from the city's large ethnic Chinese community, centered in the Cholon district, but branching throughout to other parts of the city.

Called *viet kieu*, Vietnamese who now live in the United States, Australia, France and other countries have much to do with fueling the economic boom here, as well, but on a smaller scale than the overseas Chinese. On many streets and in many neighborhoods, it is easy to pick out the families with relatives overseas – they have newer houses, nicer clothes and more amenities, and often, they are the ones who have opened new shops and restaurants. The city is quickly taking on the air of a modern, yet still developing, Asian city.

All over the city, there are new restaurants, bars and cafes catering to the naturally-sociable Saigonese, who stay up until late at night partying and relaxing, in contrast to early-to-bed Hanoi.

But, in fact, the darker side of life – prostitution, drugs and drinking – has begun to emerge again. There are massage parlors and drinking clubs with private rooms, and prostitutes advertise themselves on some street corners.

The streets are crowded with an endless stream of humanity on motor scooters, bicycles, cars and cyclos. While few Vietnamese can afford a car, some nevertheless own them. There are four or five taxi fleets, with meters, radios and clean air conditioned comfort.

Although not to the degree that one finds in Hanoi, the French presence still remains in this southern city, lingering not only in the minds of the older generation but physically in the legacy of colonial architecture, and the long, tree-lined avenues, streets and highways they left behind.

But the French era is quickly being overwhelmed by today's rush to open a business, make money, get rich. Although visitors may encounter disgruntled soldiers who fought on the losing side of the war, in fact, most people today have stopped living the war and are consumed with the task of making a

Dockside, Saigon River.

life. Most people are no fans of the Communist government, but they nonetheless appreciate recent economic reforms and have learned to simply ignore the government, with the hope that the government will ignore them. Now, they say, is not the time to talk of politics.

Yet politics still looms within Vietnam's public buildings and museums. While some of the anti-American rhetoric has been toned down, there are still reminders of the war that divided the country for so many years.

Prominently located in the city's District 1 is a building that symbolizes, to the Communists, the decadence of the Saigon regime. The former Presidential Palace of South Vietnam is now called **Thong Nhat (Reunification Hall)**, and is open as a museum. It is frequently used as a setting for lavish parties and receptions for foreign companies introducing their products to Vietnam.

Surrounded by large gardens, this large modern edifice rests on the site of the former French governor's residence, the Norodom Palace, which dated back to 1868. After the Geneva Agreement put an end to French occupation, the new president of South Vietnam, Ngo Dinh Diem, installed himself in the palace.

In 1963, the palace was bombed by a South Vietnamese air force officer and a new building known as the Independence Palace was erected to replace the damaged structure. The present structure was designed by Ngo Viet Thu, a Paris-trained Vietnamese architect, and completed in 1966. (He continues to live the city.)

The left wing of the palace was damaged by another renegade pilot in early 1975, and before the month was out, on April 30, tanks from the Communist forces crashed through the palace's front wrought-iron gates and overthrew the South Vietnamese government.

Today, the former palace can be visited as a museum, with everything left much as it was on 30 April 1975. The ground floor includes: the banquet room; the state chamber, from where the South Vietnamese government surrendered; and the cabinet room, which was used

South along the Saigon River.

for the daily military briefings during the period leading up to the overthrow of the South Vietnamese government.

On the first floor is President Tran Van Huong's reception room and President Thieu's reception and residential domain, complete with a Catholic chapel, dining room and bedroom. The second floor hosts the reception rooms of the president's wife. A private theater and a helipad are found on the third floor, which commands an excellent view over **Le Duan Boulevard**.

In back of the palace is **Cong Vien Van Hoa Park**, a nice and shady green spot. In front, Le Duan is bordered by a large park shaded with trees, where street vendors from the countryside gather to sell their wares. On one side, near Thai Van Lung Street, men who fought for the former regime gather most mornings, still plotting for a way to leave Vietnam. The offices of the American Orderly Departure Program, established in 1980 to help Amerasian children and political prisoners immigrate, is nearby.

Further down Le Duan is the **Cathedral of Our Lady**, with two bell towers, standing in the square across from the **post office**. Construction of this cathedral began in 1877, and it was consecrated in 1880. A statue of the Virgin Mary stands in front of the cathedral, looking down **Dong Khoi Street**.

Dong Khoi, a busy shopping street that was called Tu Do before 1975 (and rue Catinat before 1954), has evolved from a seedy strip of hustlers, bars and two-bit souvenir stands into a glitzy parade of shops selling designer clothes, watches and perfume.

Further down Le Duan, the compound of the weed-infested **former US embassy** stands much as it did in 1975, when the American ambassador and last US troops escaped from the rooftop by helicopter, as Communist troops were advancing toward Saigon.

Today, a small plaque on the front gate commemorates an earlier event that was a turning point of the war, the Tet Offensive of 1968, when Viet Cong guerrillas attacked southern cities and even ambushed the American embassy. The property, however, has been re-turned to the United States for a future consular mission.

At the end of Le Duan, **Thao Cam Vien (Botanical and Zoological Gardens)** provides a welcome alternative to the noisy chaos of the streets, and constitute the most peaceful place in Ho Chi Minh City. The attractive gardens were established in 1864 by two Frenchmen – one a botanist, the other a veterinarian – as one of the first projects the French embarked upon after they established their new colony. The zoological section, although somewhat rundown, houses rather dejected-looking birds, tigers, elephants, crocodiles and other indigenous species in cages built during the colonial era.

Vien Bao Tang Lich Su (National History Museum), located just within the entrance of the botanical gardens, was built by the French in 1927. It documents the evolution of Vietnam's various cultures, from the Dong Son Bronze Age civilization through to the Funan civilization, the Chams and the Khmers. Among its exhibits are many

The cathedral in downtown Ho Chi Minh.

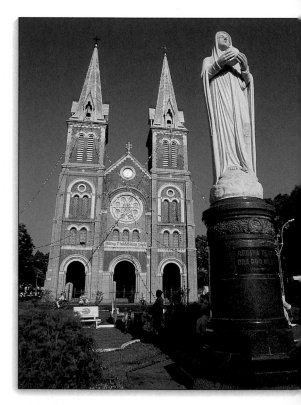

252

stone and bronze relics, stelae, bronze drums, Cham art, and ceramics, and a display of the traditional costumes of ethnic minorities. Behind the building, on the third floor, is a research library with an interesting and quite extensive collection of books from the French era.

Just opposite the museum is the **Den Hung**, a temple dedicated to the ancestors of Hung Vuong, the founding king of Vietnam.

Across Nguyen Binh Khiem Street, outside the zoo, the tired **Military Museum** displays American, Soviet and Chinese military hardware.

If Reunification Hall is a symbol of the former South Vietnam regime, then **City Hall**, at the top of Nguyen Hue Street, is the symbol of the French colonial era. Decorated by Ruffier, it was finished in 1908 after almost sixteen years of ferment over its style and situation. Its ornate facade and equally ornate interior, complete with crystal chandeliers and wall-size murals, is now the headquarters of the Ho Chi Minh City People's Committee. Illuminated at night, the building is a lure for insect-hungry geckos.

Across the street, there is a plaza with a **statue of Ho Chi Minh** in his role as favorite uncle to all children. Near the **Rex Hotel**, the plaza is crowded on weekend nights with young people, parents with children, and hustlers trying to sell souvenirs or cyclo rides to tourists. Watch out for pickpockets here, and for passing motorcyclists grabbing backpacks, purses, even eyeglasses.

Nguyen Hue is being developed into a broad boulevard lined with fancy hotels and upscale restaurants. This area of town buzzes with energy, especially at night. At the corner of Le Loi, there is another plaza with a fountain that is crowded with a carnival-like atmosphere into the evenings. Near the end of Le Loi is the **Nha Hat Thanh Pho (Municipal Theater)**, which faces Dong Khoi Street between the Caravelle and the Continental hotels. The theater was originally built in 1899 for opera, but was used as the fortress headquarters of the South Vietnam National Assembly.

National History Museum.

These days, it serves its original purpose, and every week, a different program is on show there – anything from traditional Vietnamese theater to acrobatics, gymnastics and disco music. Bars have opened in the basement.

The former War Crimes Exhibition, now called the **War Remnants Museum**, occupies the former US Information Agency building on Vo Van Tan Street, near Reunification Hall. Among items on display here are American tanks, infantry weapons, photographs of war atrocities committed by the Americans, and the original French guillotine brought to Vietnam in the 20th century, which saw a lot of use between late 1959 and 1960. A visit here is likely to jolt the senses, as many pictures depict shocking atrocities committed during the war. Particularly distressing is the display on the effects of chemical defoliants like Agent Orange. The museum shows graphic pictures of deformed children.

The **Vien Bao Tang Cach Mang (Museum of the Revolution)**, one block from Reunification Hall on Ly Tu Trong Street, is found in a white neoclassical structure once known as Gia Long Palace. The walls of the former ballrooms of this colonial edifice, built in 1866, are now hung with pictures of the war and displays of the flat-bottomed boats Viet Cong soldiers used to hide guns.

A network of reinforced concrete bunkers stretching all the way to the Reunification Hall lies beneath the building. Within this underground network were living areas and a meeting hall. It was here that President Diem and his brother hid just before they fled to a church in Cholon, where they were captured and subsequently shot.

At the junction of Ham Nghi, Le Loi and Tran Hung Dao boulevards, in the center of town, is the busy **Ben Thanh market**. The market covers over 118,400 square feet (11,000 square meters) and was opened in 1914. Here is an amazing collection of produce, meat, foods, CD players, televisions, cameras, calculators, refrigerators, fans, blue jeans, and leather bags, all imported

Rex Hotel's tennis courts and club.

from around the world. The smell of spices and dried seafood assails the nostrils, and the color of the many varieties of fresh fruit and vegetables provides a veritable feast for the eyes. At the back of the market, small food stalls serve a wide variety of local dishes.

Not far from the Ben Thanh market, down Duc Chinh Street, is the **Fine Arts Museum**, housed in a grand colonial-era building built about a century ago by a wealthy Chinese merchant.

The first floor features changing exhibitions. On the second floor, the rooms display what can be described as revolutionary – or war – art, such as a lacquer painting depicting guerrillas in the jungle and a bronze statue of a man collecting rice for the war.

On the third floor, labeled the contemporary wing, the art is actually much older: porcelain pots, statues of Buddha and Cham, Thai and Khmer sculpture.

Near the museum, on Le Cong Kieu Street, is the city's **antique street**. Here, two dozen or so shops sell old clocks, silver, glass and ceramics; much of it once belonged to wealthy Saigonese, who fled the country after 1975. One shop has a set of silver flatware engraved with the insignia of the U.S. Navy. There is quite a bit of junk for sale here, too, but also some valuable furnishings. Two nearby shops on Nguyen Thai Binh do a good business refinishing finely-carved wood furniture.

Down Nguyen Thai Binh, near the corner of Yersin Street, is the Dan Sinh market, known by its informal name, the American market. In the back, a few stalls sell old U.S. Army jackets, gas masks and GI dog tags – no doubt fake.

A few blocks away, on Ben Chuong Duong Street, which runs parallel to the Saigon River, a market does a brisk business selling animals: dogs, birds, snakes, monkeys, and even small bears.

Directly across the river on Nguyen Tat Thanh Road, there is a memorial to Ho Chi Minh, the **Nha Rong (Dragon House)**. Documents and pictures relating to Ho's life and revolutionary activities are displayed here. The house was built in 1862, and was originally

Morning routine in *tai chi*.

used as the head office of a French shipping company. It was from this place that Ho Chi Minh, then going under his given name of Nguyen Tat Thanh, left Vietnam in 1911 as a cook on a French merchant ship.

Hotbed of commerce: Ho Chi Minh City's Chinatown, **Cholon**, was formerly a separate sister city, but is now in the city's 5th District, thanks to the outward growth of the suburbs. As the name indicates, Cholon remains a thriving commercial center in its own right.

With a population of around half a million Hoas – Vietnamese of Chinese origin – Cholon has come a long way since 1864, when it was home to just 6,000 Chinese, mostly shopkeepers or traders, 200 Indians and 40,000 Vietnamese. Today, countless small family businesses operate in this bustling Chinatown. Day and night, Cholon's streets, markets and restaurants are scenes of noisy animation and much activity. The many richly-decorated Chinese temples and pagodas found here are distinctly different from their Viet-namese counterparts, and are best visited in the morning if you wish to see the faithful at their prayers. The **Cholon Mosque**, on Nguyen Trai Street, was built by Tamil Muslims from the French enclave of Pondicherry in 1932.

One of the largest churches in the city is the **Cho Quan Church**, on Tran Binh Trong Street. Built in the late 1800s by the French, it has a belfry with an excellent view. The neon halo that glows around the head of the statue of Jesus is glaringly late 20th-century.

At the end of Tran Hung Dao Boulevard is **Cha Tam Church**, where President .i.Ngo Dinh Diem;Ngo Dinh Diem was captured and, shortly afterwards, assassinated along with his brother in November of 1963. The church was built around the turn of the century. Not far west of here, on Hau Giang Boulevard, is the large **Binh Tay market**, Cholon's main marketplace.

As fast as the French, and later the Americans, were establishing their ways in Saigon, the Vietnamese were retaliating with the many pagodas, shrines and

Slack time on the road to Cholon, and in the rainy season, a taxi is preferred.

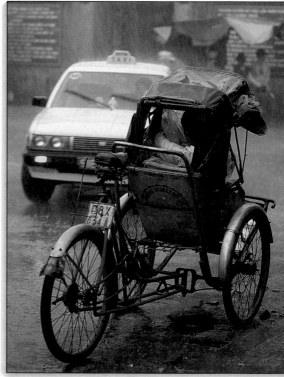

temples that sprung up all over the city: Buddhist temples, Indian temples and Muslim mosques. Many of the Vietnamese and Chinese temples are not actually Buddhist, but instead are dedicated to the worship of certain legendary or historical heroes.

The **Giac Lam Pagoda** in Tan Binh district, thought to be the oldest in the city, dates from the end of the 17th century. Reconstruction work was last carried out on it in 1900. Carved wooden pillars within the main building bear gilded inscriptions in old Vietnamese nom characters, which have also been used on the red tablets that record the biographies of the monks of previous generations, whose portraits adorn the left wall. The pagoda houses many beautifully-carved jackwood statues. Buddha, reincarnations of Buddha, judges and guardians of hell and the goddess of mercy are all present here.

The more recent Buddhist **Vinh Nghiem Pagoda** on Nam Ky Khoi Nghia, district 3, is the newest and largest of the pagodas in the city. Built with aid from the Japanese Friendship Association, this Japanese-style pagoda was begun in 1964 and finished in 1973. Each stage of its seven-story tower contains a statue of Buddha. In the huge main hall stands a large statue of Buddha surrounded by his disciples. Behind are altars consecrated to the dead, where tablets and photographs of the deceased are placed for the first one hundred days after their death.

The temple's screen and large bell were made in Japan. The bell, a gift from Japanese Buddhists, was presented during the Vietnam War as the embodiment of a prayer for an early end to the conflict. The large three-story funeral tower behind the main temple holds ceramic burial urns containing the ashes of the dead. The pagoda becomes the scene of great animation and color during the Buddhist Ram Thang Gieng festival, which takes place on the 15th day of the first lunar month.

The small Sino-Vietnamese **Phuoc Hai Tu**, or Ngoc Hoa Pagoda (Emperor of Jade Pagoda), at 73 Mai Thi Luu,

Motos in front of Binh Tay market.

dates from the early 1890s. It was built by Cantonese Buddhists and is one of the city's most colorful pagodas. A haze of heady incense and candle smoke envelops a fascinating array of weird and wonderful wooden statues, some Buddhist, others Taoist-inspired. The elaborately-robed Taoist Jade Emperor surveys the main sanctuary. Just to his right, the triple-headed, 18-armed statue of Phat Mau Chau De, mother of the Buddhas of the Middle, North, East, West and South, looks out in three directions from her encasement.

A door off to the left of the Jade Emperor's chamber leads to the Hall of Ten Hells, where carved wooden panels portray, in no uncertain detail, the fate that awaits those sentenced to the diverse torments found in the ten regions of hell. Despite the hellish scenes and prolific number of strange deities, an atmosphere of calm pervades the temple and its surrounding garden.

Interesting temples can be visited on Nguyen Trai Street, near Cholon. At number 710 is the richly-decorated

Thien Hau Temple (Heavenly Lady), more commonly known as Chua Ba (Women's Pagoda). This Chinese temple, dedicated to the Goddess Protector of Sailors, was built by Cantonese Buddhists at the end of the 18th century. The temple is frequented by women, mostly, who bring their offerings to the altar of the Heavenly Lady with its three statues of Thien Hau located at the back of the temple. Votive paper offerings are burnt in the big furnace to the right of the altar.

Among the other altars is one dedicated to the protection of women and newborn babies, and yet another to sterile women or mothers who have no sons. Ceramic figurines, attired statues, and a model boat commemorating the arrival of the first Chinese from Canton are among items of interest here. The pagoda's bronze bell was cast in 1830.

Nearby at 678 Nguyen Trai is Chua Ba's counterpart, **Chua Ong**, the men's pagoda. (Its official name is Nghia An.)

The smaller **Ha Chuong Pagoda** at number 802 contains wooden sculptures and statues, including a statue of the god of happiness and an altar for sterile women.

The Buddhist **Giac Vien Pagoda** on Lac Long Quan Road was built in 1803. It was formerly known as Chau Ho Dat (Earth Pit Pagoda), due to the vast amounts of earth required to fill in the site before its construction. Some 153 beautifully-carved statues are housed within the pagoda. One of the most valuable items in the pagoda is a decorated palanquin, presented to the pagoda's founder, Bonze Superior Hai Tinh Giac Vien, by the Nguyen court. His statue stands near the rear of the temple's second chamber.

A large and elegant **mosque** on Dong Du Street serves the city's Islamic community. It was built on the site of an older mosque by southern Indian Muslims in 1935. Only a handful of Indian Muslims remain, since most fled the country after 1975. The **Mariamman Hindu Temple**, three blocks from the Ben Thanh market, on Truong Dinh Street, was built at the end of the 19th century and caters to the city's small population of 70 or so Hindu Tamils.

Left, the best baguettes outside of France. Truly. **Right**, interior of the former Presidential Palace, now Reunification Hall.

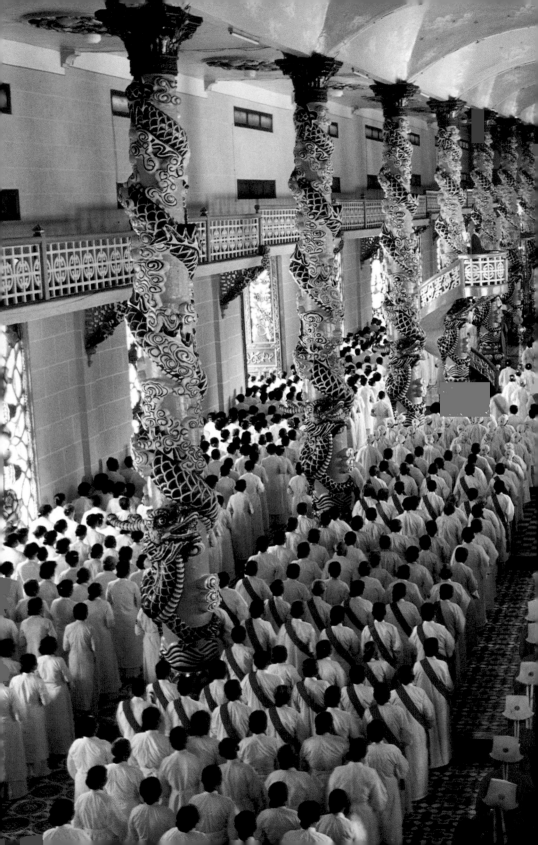

BEYOND HO CHI MINH

To see Ho Chi Minh City and its suburbs from a different perspective, take a boat trip on the **Saigon River**. The picturesque village of **Thanh Da**, in the countryside five kilometers (3 mi) to the north, is a pleasant destination and an ideal picnic spot.

To the northwest, **Tay Ninh Province** shares a border with Cambodia. The province's main river, the Vam Co Dong, separates Vietnam from Cambodia. From the 7th to the 14th centuries, Tay Ninh belonged to the powerful Funan empire. Later, it became part of the Chen La kingdom, the forerunner of the Champa kingdom. In the early 18th century, the Nguyen lords defeated the last remnants of Champa and established the province of Gia Dinh, which integrated and administered Tay Ninh.

During the war against the French, Tay Ninh was a hot bed of anti-colonial resistance, and in the 1950s, bearing the standard of the Cao Dai religious sect, a hero of the armed resistance forces conducted his efforts against the central government in the Nui Ba Den (Black Lady Mountain) area.

Tay Ninh's greatest attraction is found approximately 90 kilometers (50 mi) northwest of Ho Chi Minh City, in the township of Tay Ninh itself. Here, resplendent in all its glory, stands the holy see of the **Cao Dai** religious sect. This surreal temple has to be seen to be believed. The best time to arrive is before the daily ceremony at noon. The interior is like something out of fantasyland, and the followers in their colorful ceremonial gowns of azure, yellow and white cut striking figures in their procession towards the altar.

Photography was once restricted within the temple, but nowadays the taking of photographs is readily accepted, and even flash can be used without problems.

The most outstanding natural feature in the province, **Mt Ba Den** – the Black Lady Mountain – overshadows the town. The mountain is dotted with many temples and pagodas, and it shelters a black stone statue of a Brahman goddess, the Bhagavati protectress of the region. More than 1,500 steps – a 300-meter climb – lead up to the **Linh Son Pagoda**, at the mountain's summit, from where a splendid view takes in the region and the Mekong Delta beyond. The Nui Ba Den, or Black Lady Mountain Festival, takes place here during the spring months, from February through May. Within the mountain is a beautiful grotto that is the source of pure, crystal-clear water. At the foot of the mountain is a monument to the soldiers killed in the fierce fighting in the province during the Vietnam War.

Leaving Ho Chi Minh City via the east-northeast exit, the road passes through **Ba Chieu**. A temple dedicated to Le Van Duyet, the ancient viceroy of Cochin China under Emperor Gia Long's reign, is located here.

Quite a story surrounds this historical figure, who loomed even larger than life after his death. According to numerous records, this respected person is said to

Preceding pages: interior of the Cao Dai cathedral. Left, Vung Tau's relaxed beach. Right, Cao Dai believer.

have manifested his presence throughout the Mekong Delta area after his death, performing miracles.

This phenomena caused quite a stir, as might be expected, not only among the Vietnamese, but also among the equally-superstitious Chinese community, particularly those in Cholon. And anyone who perjured an oath that was made before the tomb of this revered individual could expect death shortly.

In serious cases, when mortal judges were unable to decide a person's guilt or innocence, justice would move to the temple. Here, the course of justice would be pursued in the ritual manner, which involved the two contesting parties having to slit the throat of a hen and drink its blood. In doing so, they were obliged to repeat the ritual formula, "If I lie, I will die like this innocent hen whose blood I have drunk."

The temple, built within the enclosure of the tomb itself, is set in a park shaded by old trees. Emperor Minh Mang destroyed the tomb, after Le Van Duyet was posthumously tried and found guilty of treason. Later, Emperor Tu Duc repaired the injustice, and restored the marshall's tomb and standing through a royal decree.

The **Ba Chieu Temple**, better known as the Lang Ong, is easily recognized from a distance by its large triple entrance gate. Inside the temple are several altars dedicated to various cults. A portrait of Le Van Duyet in full court costume hangs over the central altar. During the Tet festivities, thousands of Vietnamese and Chinese pilgrims visit the temple for their horoscopes.

From Ba Chieu, the road continues to the market town of **Thu Duc**, 20 kilometers northeast of the city. Thu Duc is a rapidly-growing suburb that is congested with truck traffic along the main road leading to Vung Tau. The area was popular with South Vietnam's leaders; former President Nguyen Van Thieu had a weekend retreat here that he reached by helicopter. Today's new elite – wealthy entrepreneurs – are turning the area into a haven for the rich, complete with a golf resort.

Bananas at the market.

264

Further along the road, a village path leads off to the right to several ancient tombs belonging to the Ho family, the family of Emperor Minh Mang's wife, Queen Ho Thi Hoa.

Traveling north from Thu Duc, the road crosses into **Song Be Province**, renowned for its orchards of Lai Thieu and Thu Dau Mot. From May to July, these orchards are an absolute haven for tropical fruit lovers. Here, one can feast on the diverse textures and succulent flavors of a huge variety of freshly-picked fruit.

The pottery kilns surrounding the church at **Lai Thieu** were built by Chinese immigrants, who put the region's clay reserves to good use.

The **Cat Tien nature reserve** lies in an area adjacent to the three provinces of Dong Nai, Song Be and Lam Dong. This primeval forest, covering an area of roughly 10,000 hectares (25,000 acres), is the natural habitat of some rare and unusual creatures – various species of pythons and crocodiles, and the nearly-extinct Asian rhinoceros.

Dong Nai Province, the eastern gateway to Ho Chi Minh City, is a rural area growing a variety of agricultural crops that is quickly transforming into a loud, boisterous, dusty industrial zone. The highway leading through the province and the provincial capital, **Bien Hoa**, is lined with new factories. There is a large concentration of Catholics here, too, evidenced by the number of Catholic churches lining the highway. Many of the people originally migrated from Hanoi and elsewhere in the north, in 1954, when Viet Minh forces defeated the French colonialists and the Communists came to power. The province also had a large number of refugees who tried to flee as part of the "boat people" exodus during the 1970s and 1980s.

Dong Nai River originates in the Central Highlands, flowing through the province for 290 kilometers (120 mi). The fertile red soils produce sugar cane, rubber, maize, tobacco, coconut palms and peanuts. The fields of such diverse vegetation contribute to the greatly varied texture and color of the scenery.

Fish at the beach.

Mountainous forests, rivers, lakes, waterfalls and jungle give way to long stretches of white, sandy beaches along the coastline of the neighboring province to the east, **Ba Ria-Vung Tau**.

From the palm trees, raffia plantations produce the brilliant yellow strands that lie drying by the roadside. These are then woven into hats, baskets, and mats, and used also as a roofing material. Rubber plantations here originally were established by the French.

The attractive town of **Bien Hoa** is an important industrial center lying 30 kilometers (20 mi) from Ho Chi Minh City, on the banks of the Dong Nai River. In the 15th and 17th centuries, Bien Hoa was a focal point for Chinese emigration. One of their leaders, Tran Thuong Xuyen, built a fort on **Cu Lao Pho**, an island in the Dong Nai River.

The tomb of Trinh Hoai Duc – the minister that Emperor Gia Long sent to China to negotiate the country's change of name to Viet Nam – will be found on the island. Toward the wharf, on the left bank of the river, stands a large temple dedicated to Nguyen Huu Canh (1650–1700). In true Vietnamese fashion, this national hero, better known in southern Vietnam as Chuong Binh Le, has acquired the status of a saint and is venerated by the population as their protector. Several times a year, notably on the general's birthday, and during the spring and autumn seasons, festivities are held at the temple.

Classical theater performances are a major form of entertainment during the festivities. The temple rests in the shade of two huge trees, many centuries old, their heavy tops appearing to bow before their heavenly protector.

The town's **Buu Son Temple** shelters a 15th-century Cham statue. A school attached to the temple teaches pottery and bronze work.

From Bien Hoa, Highway 51 heads southeast towards the coast and the **Vung Tau Peninsula**. Further on, the road passes through **Long Hai**, a coastal district with beautiful scenery and a beach stretching for several kilometers. Some ancient pagodas stand near Mt Minh

Vung Tau, known as the Bay of Boats.

Dam, not far from the beach. **Dinh Co**, near the beach, is dedicated to a young lady, who, as the story goes, was carrying a letter to Emperor Quang Trung when huge waves sank her boat. Local people reputedly built the temple in memory of this patriotic girl.

The waters are believed to possess curative properties. **Vung Tau**, the Bay of Boats, is located on a peninsula 125 kilometers (80 mi) southeast of Ho Chi Minh City. In the 15th century, after Le Thanh Tong had conquered the Kingdom of Champa, Portuguese merchant ships were already anchoring in the bay of Vung Tau. Known as Cap Saint Jacques under the French, this popular seaside resort is bathed in sunshine year-round. This seaport and economic center has a growing oil and gas industry.

Restaurants, colonial villas and cafes line the resort's largest beach, **Thuy Van**, which stretches for seven kilometers (4 mi) along the eastern coast. Here, for a small fee, relax on deck chairs under gaily-colored umbrellas. Thuy Van is very popular with the locals and becomes quite crowded at weekends. For those who prefer a little more privacy and natural shade, head for the quieter tree-lined beaches, or the small **Tam Duong Cove** on the west coast. The beach opposite the main hotel area is full of silt due to its proximity to the mouth of the river.

Aside from the beaches, Vung Tau has over one hundred Buddhist pagodas and temples. A visit to the **Lang Ca Ong**, the Whale Temple, on Hoang Hoa Tham Avenue is a must. Built in 1911, the temple is dedicated to a whale cult. Its most frequent visitors are fishermen who revere the whale as man's savior from the perils of the high seas. Skeletons of whales that have been beached on the shores in the region are kept in huge cases, some of them four meters (13 ft) long. Some of the skeletons date from 1868. The Vietnamese adopted the whale cult from the people of Champa, who worshipped the whale deity. Every year, on the sixteenth day of the eighth lunar month, fishermen gather at the temple to make offerings to

The beach and town of Vung Tau.

the whales. Indeed, thousands of anecdotes occur in Vietnamese folklore about whales as saviors.

In the northeast of the peninsula, a winding track leads inland across **Mt Nui Lon** to the **Cakya Mouni Pagoda**, the Pagoda of the Buddha. The pagoda was built in 1957 and was later enlarged in 1963. An enormous white statue of the Grand Buddha sitting on a pedestal looms in the distance. The **Bao Thap Tower** has four urns placed at its four corners. These are said to contain lumps of earth taken from the four places in India relating to Buddhism – Buddha's birthplace, and his places of enlightenment, preaching and attaining Nirvana.

Set in lovely grounds of frangipani, bougainvillea and rare trees on the Nui Lon hillside, the **Villa Blanche (White Villa)** commands a superb view over Vung Tau. It was built by the French administration, who referred to it as the governor-general's palace. King Thanh Thai resided here between 1907 and 1916, until he was packed off to exile with his son, King Duy Tan, to Reunion

Island. Later the villa became the seaside residence of two of South Vietnam's presidents, Diem and Thieu. The Lam Son cafe next door provides a panoramic view of the sea along with refreshments.

The scenic coastal road in the southwest of the peninsula, the former Route de la petite Corniche, follows the contours of Mt Nui Lon.

As if giving a sermon on the mount, a 30-meter (100-ft) statue of Jesus looks out across the Pacific Ocean at the peninsula's southern point. The statue was erected by the Americans in 1971.

Inland from **Bai Dua Beach** is the most celebrated of Vung Tau's pagoda's, the **Niet Ban Tinh Xa**. *Niet ban*, Vietnamese for Nirvana, is symbolized in the pagoda's long reclining Buddha, who, having attained niet ban, can lie back and enjoy it. The statue is made of concrete overlaid with marble. Each of the Buddha's 12 meters represents one of the twelve stages of reincarnation, all of which are engraved on the Buddha's feet. The goddess Quan Am is also represented here. The statues standing at the entrance gate are those of Than Thien, the good deity, and Than Ac, the evil deity, who are believed to guard the entrance to Nirvana.

From Vung Tau, a 13-hour boat trip, or 50-minute plane trip, links the mainland with the **Con Doa archipelago**. The archipelago comprises 14 islands, which boast unspoiled beaches, coconut groves, corals and clear waters. Sea turtles laboriously make their way onto the beaches here to lay their eggs. Between the months of February and July, they are captured for their shells.

Dense virgin forest, rich in precious woods, covers the island's interior. Today's image of unspoiled natural beauty is a far cry from that of the dreaded penitentiary of **Poulo Condore (Devil's Island)**, run by the French on the main island for almost a century, and later by the South Vietnamese regime as a prison for Communist sympathizers. Reminders of the island's less attractive past are present in the remains of the penal colony, a museum and the Hang Duong cemetery.

Left, statue of Jesus. **Right**, interior of the White Villa.

THE MEKONG DELTA

The vast delta of the **Mekong River** (**Cuu Long**) is formed by the alluvium deposited by the multiple arms and tributaries of the river. The Mekong descends from its source high in the Tibetan plateau and follows a 4,500-kilometer (2,800-mi) course through China, Burma (Myanmar), Laos, Cambodia and southern Vietnam, and then into the South China Sea.

The Mekong's Vietnamese name, Cuu Long, means Nine Dragons; it branches into nine mouths that empty into the sea.

The **Mekong Delta**, an ancient Khmer territory, was an area of marshlands and forest before the first colonizers arrived by sea in the 16th century. During the rule of the Nguyen lords, great expanses of marshlands were reclaimed, and a network of small canals was built. By the end of the 18th century, two huge canals – the Thai Hoa, which linked Rach Gia and Long Xuyen, and the Vinh Te, linking Chau Doc and Ha Tien – were in use.

The Delta region is still populated by a large percentage of people of Khmer origin, Chinese and Chams as well as Vietnamese. Among them are followers of diverse religious beliefs, including Buddhism, Catholicism, and sects of Cao Dai, Hoa Hao and Brahmanism.

The Delta's eleven provinces – Long An, Dong Thap, An Giang, Kien Giang, Tien Giang, Ben Tre, Vinh Long, Tra Vinh, Can Tho, Soc Trang and Minh Hai – are served by more than 100 ferries and an adequate road network. On the whole, the roads are in good shape – by Vietnamese standards – and the comprehensive waterway network carries a busy and greatly varied flow of traffic. However, crossing the river at its main points can take hours, as there are no bridges, and while waiting for a ferry, traffic backups can be long.

The best time to travel in the Delta is between January and March, when the temperature ranges between 22–34°C (72–93°F). From May onward, the rainfall and humidity increase. During the wettest months, between July and October, some provinces are badly flooded and travel is considerably restricted.

In contrast to northern Vietnam, the people here appear well clothed and fed, although there is great poverty in some of the most isolated areas. Many villages have no clean drinking water or electricity, and it's not uncommon to see families collecting water for drinking and cooking from the same canal in which they bathe.

The region has greatly recovered from the ravages of the chemical defoliants and bombs dropped on it during the war. The markets in the region are abundantly supplied with fish and a variety of produce yielded by the Delta's rich alluvial soil: rice, soybeans, maize, sesame, peanuts, pineapples, pumpkins, potatoes, tangerines, melons, cabbages, durians and tobacco. The area is known as Vietnam's bread basket, or more aptly, rice bowl, because the region produces much of the country's rice. In many places there are three full harvests during the year.

The **province of Long An**, which stretches from the Cambodian border in the west straight across the country to the east coast, is more of historical than scenic significance. It was here, at **Nhat Tao** on the Vam Co Dong River, that the French battleship *l'Esperance* was completely burnt by the Vietnamese in 1861. This decisive battle cost the life of everyone on board and forced the French out of the south, at least temporarily.

The northern part of Long An is slightly hilly, although most of the province occupies a level plain a few meters above sea level. The Vam Co Dong, Vam Co Tay and Saigon rivers flow through the province, bringing rich alluvial silt to the extensive rice fields. Plantations of pineapple, cassava, coconut, sugar cane and banana are a common sight. So, too, are freshwater aquaculture farms.

The western provinces: Dong Thap Province can be reached by the ferry from My Thuan or via Highway 49. Bordering Cambodia in the north, it is one of the three provinces lying in the marshy area known as **Dong Thap Muoi**, or the Plain of Reeds. The province takes its name from the 10-story Thap Muoi Tower, built in the commune of An Phong. The tower, no longer here, was used as a lookout by the resistance forces against the French.

The province was formerly inhabited by the ancient Phu Nam kingdom and later the Chan Lap (Tchen La) civilization, a people who, in the 1700s, exchanged the area of Sa Dec with Vietnam for military aid that restored order to the area. The Chen Lap were subsequently wiped out and assimilated by the Vietnamese, and today the area is populated primarily by people of Chinese, Khmer, Cham and Thai origin.

Archaeological remains have been uncovered in the area of Dong Thap Muoi and the ancient alluvial area of Duc Hoa. **Binh Ta**, 15 kilometers from Ben Luc township, produced the richest finds. Among the objects unearthed were gold artifacts, precious stones, fine ceramic pieces of the Oc Eo civilization, and iron objects – all attesting to the earlier presence of the Phu Nam (Funan)

kingdom. Among the golden artifacts was a plate engraved with ancient sanskrit, in the southern Indian style, recording the Phu Nam king's order to withdraw troops in 550 AD.

Excavations at the **Go Xoai Temple** revealed the exact location of the troop withdrawal ceremony: the center of Dac Muc, capital of the Phu Nam kingdom.

This excavation marked the first time Vietnamese archaeologists uncovered evidence linking the Phu Nam kingdom and the Oc Eo civilization. A large number of prehistoric remains were found within a 10-kilometer (6-mi) radius of the temple.

Among the other archaeological discoveries in the province are the remains of a town buried perhaps 1,000 years ago, excavated at the archaeological site of Go Thap.

In addition, Dong Thap Province is famous for its scenery, particularly its extensive reed beds, lakes and ponds, where lotus grows in profusion. Its cajeput forests are home to many species of rare birds and animals.

Geese on the Delta.

To the south, **An Giang Province** borders the Cambodian province of Takeo. This border remains a somewhat politically-sensitive area. Here, the Mekong enters the province and splits into two branches, forming the Tien and Hau rivers, which every year deposit millions of cubic meters of alluvium in the adjacent areas. This prosperous region, rich in natural resources and fertile land, produces many varieties of fruit trees and crops of soya bean, tobacco, groundnut, tobacco and mulberry.

Phu Tan village in the north of the province is the birth place of Huynh Phu So, founder of the Hoa Hao religious sect. Its male followers are easily identified by their long beards and long hair tied into a bun.

Long Xuyen, the provincial capital located in the east of the province, has a population of about 100,000 people. Its Catholic church can seat 1,000 and is one of the largest in the Delta. From here, a road heads west to Ba Chuc, passing many fishing villages built beside the canals. Flimsy bamboo "monkey bridges" stretch across the canals. These were built for the lighter and more agile Vietnamese and are to be avoided, or negotiated with extreme care, unless one wants to end up in the canal, an all-too-easy feat.

Some 30 kilometers (20 mi) from Long Xuyen, in the hilly area of Ba Thi, are the **ruins of Oc Eo**, which was a major trading port during the first centuries AD. Oc Eo lay submerged for centuries until it was rediscovered in the 1940s. Traces of architectural structures and other finds made by researchers here indicate that it was a city closely linked with the ancient kingdom of Phu Nam (Funan), which dates back to the first century AD and reached its peak in about the 5th century.

Most of what we know about this ancient civilization – gleaned from excavations at Oc Eo – reveals evidence of contact with the Roman Empire, Persia, China, Thailand, Malaysia and Indonesia; in addition, there are the written accounts of Chinese travelers and emissaries. Oc Eo's elaborate and intricate

canal system was used, not only for irrigation, but also for transportation.

The **An Giang Museum** displays some of the artifacts found in the ruins. It is also possible to visit the ruins themselves; however, during rainy season the area tends to be flooded and is impossible to visit.

The province is renowned for its unglazed black pottery, pieces of which were excavated at Oc Eo. This is produced using diato-mocaolinite, a type of clay formed from the dried remains of living creatures. After firing, the pottery is so light that it can float on the surface of the water.

The early-morning market on the canal in An Chau is a lively and very visual affair. Not far from here are the long irrigation canals of the district of Tri Ton, where a great percentage of the population is now Khmer, including the thousands of refugees who poured into the area during the late 1970s, fleeing Pol Pot's forces in Cambodia.

The town of **Chau Doc**, not far from the Cambodian border, is situated on the right bank of the **Hau Giang River**. The **Dinh Than Chau Phu** (Chau Phu temple) in the township was built in 1926. Here, the locals worship Thai Ngoc Hau, the man responsible for the nearby Chau Doc Canal, which opens the frontier between Cambodia and Vietnam. He held a high official rank under first the Nguyen lords, and then later, during the Nguyen Dynasty.

Mass is held twice a day in the town's small Catholic church, built in 1920. From the Chau Giang terminal, a ferry crosses the Hau River. On the other side is the **Chau Giang Mosque**, which serves the district's Muslim Cham community. From here, travelers can pick up a lift to Tan Chau district, famous throughout the south for its silk industry and prosperity. The market there offers many imported goods from Thailand, which are brought into the country through Cambodia.

Five kilometers (3 mi) from Chau Doc stands **Mt Nui Sam**, so named because, from a distance, the hill resembles a king crab, called *sam* in Vietnamese. This beautiful site holds many important monuments and relics, among them the **tomb of Thoai Ngoc Han**, which holds his remains plus those of his two wives.

Sharing the Nui Sam hillside are the Indian-style **Tay An Pagoda**, which dates from 1847 and is famous for its many finely-carved religious figures, and **Den Thanh Mau** (Temple of the Goddess Saint), where a granite statue left by the Cambodians is worshipped.

Every year on the 22nd day of the fourth lunar month, a large procession of religious followers begins a week-long series of festivities and ceremonies to celebrate their pilgrimage.

About half way up Mt Nui Sam's western flank, set apart from the main body of religious buildings, is a pagoda, **Chua Phuc Dien Tu**, which backs onto a cave containing a shrine dedicated to the Quan Am, a goddess of mercy.

Kien Giang Province, in the southwest of the Delta, shares a common border in the northwest with Cambodia, and in the west is washed by waters from the Gulf of Thailand. Forests, plains, offshore islands and a 200-kilometer-long (125 mi) coastline contribute to Kien Giang's rich scenic diversity. It features one of the most beautiful of all the towns in the Delta, **Ha Tien**. Located just a few kilometers from the Cambodian border, this charming town of Chinese origin was founded in around 1670 by Mac Cuu, a Chinese immigrant from Canton who arrived here after the fall of the Ming Dynasty. He refused to serve the Manchu rulers and instead explored the South Seas with his men. After procuring the agreement of the Cambodian kings and the Vietnamese Nguyen lords, he and his men installed themselves at Ha Tien, transforming it in no time into a prosperous principality equipped with a maritime port.

In 1714, Ha Tien was given to Lord Nguyen Phuc Chu, from Hue, who compensated Mac Cuu with the title generalissimo of Ha Tien. The principality prospered with the revenue accumulated from a gambling house and a tin mine. The governor used the tin to make coins for commercial exchanges. His son, Mac Thien Tu, continued his father's work in improving administration, and thus social and economic development. He organized an army equal to the task of repelling the Cambodian and Siamese invasions, and also founded an academy of arts, the Chieu Anh Cac (Pavilion of Quintessential Welcome).

The journey to Ha Tien begins in the provincial capital, **Rach Gia**, an active fishing port with a population of around 120,000. It is bordered by marshlands, much of which have been drained for rice cultivation.

The town has quite a number of interesting temples and pagodas. The large Khmer **Phat Lon Pagoda** was established about two centuries ago. **Ong Bac De Pagoda,** on Nguyen Du Street in the town center, was built by the local Chinese community about a century ago. The central altar is occupied by a statue of Ong Bac De, the reincarnation of the Jade Emperor of Heaven. To his left is Ong Gon, the guardian spirit of happiness and virtue, and on his right is Quan Cong. **Nguyen Trung Truc Temple**, at

18 Nguyen Cong Tru Street, is dedicated to Nguyen Trung Truc, who led the resistance campaign against the French during the 1860s. In fact, he led the attack on the French ship *l'Esperance*. Although the French repeatedly tried to capture him, it wasn't until 1868 that they succeeded, after taking his mother and a number of civilians hostage. Truc eventually gave himself up and was executed by the French in the Rach Gia marketplace, on 27 October 1868.

The small **Pho Minh Pagoda** on the corner of Co Bac and Nguyen Van Cu streets was built in 1967. A garden full of trees pruned in the shape of animals surrounds the **Tam Bao Pagoda**, near the corner of Tran Phu and Thich Thien An streets. The town also has a small Cao Dai temple, near the bus station on Nguyen Trung Truc Street, and a Protestant Church further along the street in the direction of the river.

Rach Gia is well known for its seafood, and it has a good selection of restaurants serving both Chinese and

One for the album at the Tay An Pagoda.

Vietnamese food, and also specialties such as eel, turtle, snake, frog legs, deer and cuttlefish.

Ferries leave for Chau Doc, Long Xuyen and Tan Chau from the Muoi Voi ferry terminal on Bach Dang Street.

The road from Rach Gia to Ha Tien is a bit rough, but it passes many duck farms and provides an interesting look at life on the canal. The Khmer **Soc Soai Temple** in Hon Dat district stands in a beautiful setting of lush tropical vegetation. Completed in 1970, it houses many monks. The temple's interior – with its old-fashioned furnishings – has a well-worn charm.

Many Khmer people live in this area, and a little detour off the main road leads to the Khmer village of **Binh An**.

The **Chua Hang Grotto** and **Cua Duong Beach**, one of the best beaches in the area, lie about 100 kilometers (60 mi) from Rach Gia and 30 kilometers (20 mi) from Ha Tien. The grotto is entered from behind the altar of the pagoda, which is set back into the base of the hill. The grotto's thick stalactites are hollow and give off a bell-like resonance when tapped. Inside the grotto is a plaster statue of the goddess of mercy, Quan Am.

The beach Bai Duong, next to the grotto, takes its name from the *duong* trees growing beside it. Its white, clear water and picturesque surroundings make it an ideal spot to break the journey and enjoy a swim.

A few kilometers further on is the **Hang Tien Grotto**, or Coin Grotto, which takes its name from the zinc coins found buried within it by Nguyen Anh, the future Emperor Gia Long, and his troops, who camped here while battling the Tay Son rebels.

About 17 kilometers (10 mi) from Ha Tien, and 3 kilometers (2 mi) from the main road, is the **Mo So Grotto**. During the wet season, it is accessible only by boat, but for the rest of the year it can be reached on foot. Be sure to take a flashlight, and a local guide, to explore the labyrinth of tunnels beyond the three main caverns.

A floating toll bridge completes the

On the beach at Binh An.

278

last watery stretch of the journey to **Ha Tien**. Nestling in a cove formed by the **Gian Thang River**, Ha Tien has a population of 80,000. The region belonged to Cambodia until 1708, when, unable to deal alone with the repeated attacks from the Thais, its Khmer-appointed governor, Mac Cuu, requested help from the Vietnamese. Thereafter, Mac Cuu acted as governor under the protection of the Nguyen lords. His son, Mac Thien Tu, succeeded him. In 1798, this region and the southern tip of the Delta came directly under Nguyen rule.

Ha Tien's unspoiled natural beauty attracts many visitors. Among the most picturesque spots are the **Dong Ho** (East Lake) and Ngu Ho and To Chau, peaks that dominate the mouth of the Giang Thanh River.

The town has several temples dedicated to the Mac family, and an even greater number of tombs that rest on the eastern flank of **Mt Binh San**. These are built of bricks – cemented together with vegetable resin from the *o duoc* shrub – and contain the remains of both Mac Cuu and his relatives. His own tomb, built in 1809, is the largest, and is decorated with finely-carved figures of the Blue Dragon and the White Tiger.

The **Bao Pagoda**, at 328 Phuong Thanh, was founded by Mac Cuu in 1730. A statue of Quan Am atop a lotus stands in front of the pagoda. Nearby is the **Phu Dung Pagoda**, which was founded by Mac Cuu's second wife in around the middle of the 18th century. Her tomb is built on the hillside behind the pagoda's main hall. The pagoda contains some interesting statues. In the center of the main hall is one of the newborn Sakymouni Buddha, in the embrace of nine serpents; on the main dais in a glass case is a bronze Chinese Buddha. Dedicated to the Taoist Jade Emperor of Heaven, the small temple beyond the main hall contains papier mache statues of a number of Taoist divinities, including the gods of the northern and southern stars, happiness and longevity.

Ha Tien does a lively trade in items handcrafted from the shells of sea turtles. These creatures are domestically reared in pools along the coastline. It is also famous for its seafood and black pepper. Looking out to sea from the headlands, you will see the Father and Son Rocks, whose grottoes are a favorite haunt of sea swallows.

The area also has beautiful white sand beaches such as Bai No, with a coconut palm-shaded shore, Mui Nai, just west of the city, and Bai Bang, with its dark sands lined with trees.

One of the main attractions located a few kilometers from town on Mac Tu Hoang Street is **Thach Dong Thon Van**, the Grotto That Swallows the Clouds. The grotto shelters a Buddhist sanctuary and funerary tablets, and altars to Quan Am and to Ngoc Hoang, the Jade Emperor of Heaven, are contained in several of its chambers. Nearby is a mass grave where 130 people, victims of a massacre by Pol Pot's troops in March 1978, are buried. To the left of the sanctuary's entrance is a stele known as Bia Cam Thu – the stele of hatred – that commemorates the victims.

The island of **Hon Giang** lies about

The Grotto That Swallows the Clouds.

15 kilometers (9 mi) off the coast of Ha Tien and can be reached by boat. Its lovely and quite secluded beach is well worth the trip.

A beautiful and forested archipelago known as **Phu Quoc** consists of 16 islands, about 30 kilometers (20 mi) west of Ha Tien. Phu Quoc, the largest island, is a 50-kilometer-long (30-mi) long island with a population of about 18,000, covering an area of 1,300 square kilometers (500 sq mi).

The future Emperor Gia Long was sheltered here from the Tay Son rebels by the French missionary Pigneau de Behaine, who himself had used the island as a base between the 1760s and 1780s. The French later used the island as a prison. Today, Phu Quoc is renowned for its bountiful fishing grounds and its quality *nuoc mam* production.

The eastern provinces: Tien Giang Province represents one of the country's main rice-growing areas. Land reclamation began in this extremely fertile region during the 17th century. This ancient Khmer territory was colonized by the Vietnamese towards the end of the 17th century, then taken over by the French in 1861.

Major rivers such as the Tien, Go Cong, Ca Han and Bao Dinh flow through the province. Combined with the extensive canal network, these provide excellent waterway access to Ho Chi Minh City and Phnom Penh. The sites of Rach Gam and Xaoi Mut, by the Tien River, are where the peasant hero Nguyen Hue won his first victory in an historic river battle, which claimed the lives of 40,000 Siamese troops in 1785.

My Tho, the provincial capital with its population of 90,000, lies on the left bank of the **My Tho River**, the northernmost branch of the Mekong. Founded in the 1680s by political refugees from Taiwan, the city is easily reached from Ho Chi Minh City by a one-and-a-half-hour bus journey, or a six-hour trip by river ferry.

This region is famous for its orchids, coconut palms and fruit, including mangoes, longans, bananas and oranges.

The old Saigon–My Tho railway, the earliest built in Indochina, no longer operates, but the province has a more-than-adequate road network. The central market is located on Trung Trac and Nguyen Hue streets and is closed to vehicular traffic. Stalls selling all manner of goods fill the streets.

The Catholic church here was built at the end of last century, and there is still a large Catholic congregation. The **Vinh Trang** (a real tourist trap) and **Quan Thanh** pagodas are monuments to kitsch and bad taste, not worth visiting.

From here, a boat can be taken to one of the nearby islands, an interesting and enjoyable excursion. **Phung Island** lies a few kilometers from My Tho and can be reached by either ferry or hired boat. This island was the home of the Coconut Monk, Ong Dao Dua, a charismatic character who founded a religion known as *Tinh Do Cu Si,* a synthesis of Buddhism and Christianity, and with Jesus, Buddha and the Virgin Mary forming an interesting triumvirate.

Born Nguyen Thanh Nam in 1909, the future Coconut Monk studied physics and chemistry in France between 1928 and 1935, before returning to Vietnam, where he married and had a daughter. In 1945, he left his family to live the life of a monk, and for three years is said to have sat on a stone slab beneath a flag pole meditating, and eating only coconuts. His philosophy advocated peaceful means of reunifying his country.

This concept did not go down at all well with the successive South Vietnamese governments, in whose prisons he was a frequent guest. He died some years ago, a prisoner of the Communist regime that arrested him for anti-government activities. After his arrest, his band of followers dispersed.

The island boasts the remnants of a bizarre open-air sanctuary where the Coconut Monk addressed his following. Today, its faded dragon-entwined columns and multi-tiered tower, with a great metal globe atop, stand rather forlorn and neglected.

Tan Long Island is a five-minute boat ride from the dock at the bottom of Le Loi Boulevard. Its shores are lined with lush coconut palms and many wooden fishing boats. The island is famous for its longan orchards.

Twelve kilometers (7 mi) from the town is a snake farm, where the snakes yield a variety of medical substances used in traditional medicines. Their flesh is believed to be an effective remedy against a number of ailments ranging from mental disorders to rheumatism and paralysis. Snake gall combined with other drugs is used to treat coughs and migraine. An excellent tonic alcohol is obtained by steeping three special varieties of snake in alcohol.

Ben Tre Province lies between the My Tho and Co Chien rivers. A ferry runs between Ben Tre and My Tho further south. The provincial capital, **Ben Tre**, is located on the Mi Long tributary. More coconut palms are grown here than in any other province in the country. These contend for space with the province's extensive rice fields.

Ben Tre was made famous during the Vietnam War when a village here was leveled by American troops who were trying to ferret out the Viet Cong. An American army officer was quoted as saying, "It became necessary to destroy the town to save it."

A boat trip along the Bai Lai–Ham Luong waterway provides an opportunity to become better acquainted with everyday life on the river. Ba Tri district's bustling market is a good place to buy locally-produced silk. The **Nguyen Dinh Chieu Temple** here is dedicated to a poet of the 19th-century who once lived in Ba Tri.

Many species of birds can be seen in the **Cu Lao Dat bird sanctuary**, which covers 30 hectares of forest, in the small village of An Hiep.

Vinh Long Province, further south, is crisscrossed by canals and lies just two meters above sea level.

A number of interesting temples and pagodas can be visited in the provincial capital, also named Vinh Long. Boats leave from in front of the Cuu Long Hotel for the An Binh and Binh Hoa Phuoc islands in the Tien River. The one-hour trip is a treat for fruit lovers, as it takes in villages whose gardens and

orchards produce a great variety of seasonal fruit, such as mangoes, mandarins, rambutans and plums.

Can Tho, the capital of Can Tho Province, is the most modern city in the Delta, and the only one with a university. This important commercial center and river port, with its population of 150,000, lies on the banks of the **Hau River**, the Mekong's southernmost tributary. Can Tho University, founded in 1966, conducts valuable agricultural research and development that has contributed substantially to improving production and pest control.

A visit to the animated **Can Tho market**, which spreads out along Hai Ba Trung Street, with its main building at the intersection of Hai Ba Trung and Nam Ky Khoi Nghia streets, reveals the rich variety and abundance of fruit, seafood and vegetables produced in the region. Several restaurants along the waterfront serve specialties of the region: frog, turtle, snake and fish.

The city has a friendly feel about it, but there is not a great deal of sightsee-

ing to be done here. The **Vang Pagoda**, on Hoa Binh Avenue in the center of town, is worth visiting.

Boat trips on the Hau River provide an opportunity to see life on the waterways. A lively floating market takes place at the junction of seven canals, where all manner of boats and sampans gather, their occupants busily engaged in buying or selling a wide variety of fruit, fish and vegetables.

About 35 kilometers (20 mi) southeast of Can Tho is **Soc Trang Province**. Many Khmer people live in the area, and just outside the town is a Khmer temple, richly decorated with elephants, griffins, tigers and statues of dancing girls. A *ghe ngo,* or rowing boat festival, is held here on the 14th day of the tenth lunar month. A 52-man crew displays its skills in a 200-year-old Cambodian war canoe, 25 meters (80 feet) long. Canoes from other neighboring villages race against them to the noisy accompaniment of a gong.

The deep south: The southernmost province of Vietnam, **Minh Hai**, is not best described as a tourist destination. **Ca Mau**, the largest town, lies 180 kilometers (110 mi) south of Can Tho on the Gan Hao River, in the heart of an immense, submerged plain covered in mangroves.

The **U Minh forest**, the largest of its kind in the world outside the Amazon, was seriously damaged by defoliants dropped by the Americans during the war. The dense and swampy undergrowth is home to many varieties of venomous snakes, leeches, unidentifiable things, and mosquitoes.

The locals catch the snakes and breed them at farms, selling them for pharmaceutical products, and for food. Another unusual animal eaten by the locals is the *te te.* The meat of this creature, which resembles a combination of a snake and a lizard, is reputedly delicious.

Large tortoise are found in the drier areas. Cajeput forests thrive in the brackish water, the cajeput collected for a variety of special oils. Honey is collected from wild bees' hives. **Ca Mau Point** marks the extreme southernmost tip of Vietnam.

Left, Can Tho market. **Right**, Ben Tree boats, all-seeing.

INSIGHT GUIDES
Travel Tips

FLY SMOOTH AS SILK TO EXOTIC THAILAND ON A ROYAL ORCHID HOLIDAY.

Watching exquisite cotton and silk umbrellas being hand-painted in Chiang Mai. Lazing in the shade in sun-drenched Phuket. This

what holidaying in Thailand is all about. Book the holiday of your choice now, flying Thai. Smooth as silk.

See the World with a different eye

The world's leading series
of full-colour travel guides

★ More than 300 titles

★ Three distinct formats
tailored for individual needs

★ Spectacular photography
and award-winning writing

APA INSIGHT GUIDES

TRAVEL TIPS

Getting Acquainted

Vietnam, like Laos, Cambodia and Thailand, lies in the zone seven hours ahead of Greenwich Mean Time.

The sun sets relatively early, around 5.30pm in winter and 8pm in summer.

Culture & Customs

The concept of tourism is very new to Vietnam. Even before reaching the country, you may encounter attitudes in official representatives that try your patience to the limit. However, firmness, perseverance and diplomacy will achieve a great deal more than losing your cool. Patience is a necessity in this long-suffering country. If misunderstandings do arise and things do not seem to be going the way you anticipated, or you don't feel you're getting what you paid for, raising your voice, shouting and loudly criticizing the offending party will only result in loss of face all round and make matters worse. If you have a complaint to make, do so in a manner that will not be taken as threatening or insulting. On the whole the Vietnamese are very friendly, polite, hospitable and helpful. Like anywhere else in the world, these attributes take a back seat during rush hour traffic and in the battle for space on the overcrowded public transport, situations that tend to bring out the worst in everyone.

Very direct questions about one's age, family status and income are quite natural topics of conversation and not considered rude or personal. Vietnamese who have not had much exposure to foreign visitors are often very shy but curious and those who speak English or French enjoy an opportunity to converse with foreigners and make friends. Be sensitive to anyone who may appear ill at ease or not wish to be seen talking to a foreigner, locals have been arrested for less and the past is hard to shake off. A gentle handshake is usual when you meet, but public demonstration of affection is not quite accepted.

The working day starts early in Vietnam; business meetings can begin as early as 7am. However, offices generally shut down at 11.30am for lunch and often do not re-open until 2 or even 2.30pm. Business generally ends for the day at 4.30pm. Offices are open on Saturdays, but usually only in the morning.

The Vietnamese often have a more relaxed attitude about office work. Business can be conducted at a pace that seems maddeningly slow to Westerners. In part, this is because of a group consensus process in making decisions. An individual is either reluctant or unable to make a decision on his or her own.

Gifts are much appreciated and it is a good idea to bring a supply of pens, lighters, shampoo, foreign cigarettes, spirits and perfume to give to the friends you will make in Vietnam.

People in the North are generally more reserved and have had less exposure to Westerners than those in the South have.

Tips are much appreciated, but bear in mind that whatever you do sets a precedence for those who follow and the average wage is very low. A small donation is much appreciated when you visit a temple or pagoda – there is always a little contribution box for this.

It is a matter of courtesy to ask before you take someone's photograph and to ask permission to take photographs in religious buildings, although permission is usually granted. Formal dress is expected when you visit religious buildings.

In Ho Chi Minh City particularly, you will be approached by beggars if you give anything, do so discreetly otherwise you will be plagued by a very persistent and ever increasing following. It is very difficult to ignore these people, whether their plight is genuine or not, but in the long run it does not help to foster an attitude whereby foreigners are seen as a soft touch and preyed upon as a source of easy income.

The Economy

Vietnam is essentially an agricultura country, with rice cultivation account ing for 45 percent of the GNP and em ploying 72 percent of the population Other major crops include tea, coffee maize, bananas, manioc, cotton, to bacco, coconut and rubber.

Industry represents 32 percent o the country's GNP and occupies 11 percent of the active population. Elec tricity, steel, cement, cotton fabrics fish sauce, sea fish, wood, paper anc the growing oil exploration and produc tion industry represent Vietnam's ma jor areas of industrial production.

Ho Chi Minh City now boasts a small oil refinery and has become Viet nam's economic capital, accounting for 30 percent of the national indus trial production.

The country's standard of living ranks amongst the lowest in the world Despite a protracted effort to revive the rural economy, disastrous eco nomic polices coupled with the drain o more than 50 percent of the country's budget on supporting its occupatior forces in Cambodia and Laos, have had devastating effects on Vietnam's economy. In an effort to revive the ail ing economy the country has recently opened its doors to encourage foreigr investment and tourism, while furthe reform policies have been geared to re-establish a market economy anc encourage production in the private sector, agriculture and light industry.

Recently there has been an infusior of consumer goods, many of them smuggled across the border from China. In the cities, particularly Ho Ch Minh City and Hanoi, there is a bur geoning consumerism, reflected in the number of motorcycles, electronics Western clothes and music for sale. Ir the two cities, an estimated 95 per cent of the households now own TVs Nationwide, about half the populatior regularly watches TV (although in the countryside most people cannot afforc such a luxury).

While there probably always has been a wealthy class, its members dic all they could to hide their prosperity fearing the wrath of the police anc party officials. Today, however, people begin to feel more relaxed. Young peo ple, in particular, flaunt their wealth and have embraced a materialistic cul ture. People accumulate wealth through trading goods (often illegally), buying and selling real estate and in a few cases, building successful manufacturing enterprises, like garment making and shoes. Salaries at government agencies and state-owned companies are low, so many people today are looking to work for foreign companies or to start their own businesses.

But the low wages also account for a nagging problem of corruption, as bureaucrats at all levels look for ways to supplement their meager incomes. Bankers, for example, often charge people extra if they want larger denomination dong notes when withdrawing money. Doctors sometimes insist on separate payments to treat patients, or insist that patients buy medicine from them. Teachers routinely extract bribes from students in exchange for good grades. At government ministries, licenses and permissions often requiring a "payment" from people. The government publicly criticizes these practices and has prosecuted several high-profile cases, but the problem persists.

Government

Vietnam is a socialist republic ruled by the Vietnamese Communist Party since the fall of Saigon in 1975, and the country's subsequent imposed reunification in 1976. Vietnam's domestic policy is shaped primarily by the party and its Secretary General, Mr Do Moui. The Prime Minister, Mr Vo Van Kiet, presides over drafting of laws and day-to-day governing. The President, Mr Le Duc Anh, oversees state policy, the military and internal police apparatus. There has been speculation that all three men may retire soon.

The government is nominated by the National Assembly, proposed by the party and theoretically elected by the people.

Although the National Assembly has in the past been something of a rubber stamp operation, recently it has become more aggressive in challenging government functions, implementing laws, debating policy and holding government ministers accountable.

The republic is divided into 53 administrative areas: three cities, Hanoi, Ho Chi Minh City and Hai Phong, and 50 provinces. Traditionally provincial officials maintain some level of independence in implementing state policy. Ostensibly there are elections at the local level for provincial officials, however, the candidates are all screened and are members of the Communist Party. In the Communist Party, the Politburo wields all power in decision making, directing party line and policies. The Party Congress, with about 1,200 members, meets every five years, although a first ever mid-term congress was held in 1994. The Congress appoints members to the Central Committee, which has about 160 members and meets twice a year. The Central Committee in turn delegates most of its power to the Politburo, which now has 17 members. Power in the country, then, is concentrated among this small group of older men. Vietnam has generally avoided major upheavals within its power structure. When high-level officials retire, they still maintain important advisory roles. For example three former leaders, Vo Chi Cong, Pham Van Dong and Nguyen Van Linh, are believed to have exerted strong influence long after they officially retired.

Party members do not automatically have the right to run for office, but must first be screened by appropriate executive committee levels before their names can appear on a list of candidates. They are then screened again when congresses evaluate those who meet the criteria set by the Central Committee. Although encouraged to exercise initiative, party members are not at liberty to disagree with party line, policies or decisions hailing from above. Re-education camps and other disciplinary measures ensure that party members toe the line, as expulsion from the only ruling party means losing the many privileges that go with the position. The party encourages criticism and self-criticism within its ranks through its media, but few voluntarily subject themselves to this form of public confession.

If there is any crisis in leadership in Vietnam today, it is that there does not appear to be a younger generation of leaders ready to step in and take the reins of power. Thus there is considerable speculation that the current leaders will continue in their positions for two more years instead of retiring as was earlier expected. Party leaders emphasize that there is no room for political pluralism at this point and that the Communist Party will maintain its hold on power.

Conflict within the party and government tends to be between reformers, like Prime Minister Vo Van Kiet, who have pushed for a transition to a market economy and increased contact with Western countries, and conservatives who want to hold onto a stricter Communist Party doctrine. The reformers appear to be in control, however, and there have been recent signs that the conservative element is flexing its muscles somewhat. There is also an element within the government that wants to encourage ties with foreign countries and investment from foreign firms – but wants to limit those ties to other Asian countries.

Historically, within the party, there has been a division between those aligned with China's Communist Party and those aligned with the former Soviet Union, a division that dates back to the very founding of the Vietnam Communist Party.

Planning The Trip

What to Wear

The main thing to consider is the weather, as it can be freezing cold in the mountainous North and at the same time hot and humid on the Central Coast. If you are traveling in the North or the Central Highlands during the winter months definitely bring jeans and a warm coat or sweater. It seems that it is always raining somewhere in Vietnam, so lightweight rain gear is essential.

In the hot months, dress cool but conservative. Many Vietnamese cannot understand why foreigners insist on wearing shorts, tank tops and sleeveless T-shirts when they have the money to dress well. For the Vietnamese, appearance is very important, so if you are dealing with an official of any rank make sure you are dressed appropriately.

It is best to travel light in Vietnam. One medium sized bag and a daypack will provide more than enough room to carry everything you'll need to survive, and enough space for the things you'll buy in Vietnam.

There is an extensive black market for smuggled consumer goods in Hanoi and Ho Chi Minh City, so don't worry about running out of something. However, there are two things that are difficult to find in Vietnam: sunscreen and tampons.

It is very difficult to get access to news in Vietnam, so you may want to consider bringing a small short-wave radio to keep up with the world. Film, both print and slide, is available in the cities, but look at the expiration dates and make sure it hasn't been sitting in the sun.

The voltage in the cities and towns is generally 220V, 50 cycles, sometimes 110V in the rural areas. Electric sockets are standard European or American. If you bring a computer to Vietnam, you must use a surge suppresser to protect your circuits. Large Taiwanese voltage regulators can be bought at computer stores in Vietnam to give greater protection.

It is a good idea to bring adapter plugs in case your plugs do not fit the sockets, which are sometimes two round pins, other times three pins. If you do not have the correct size plug, however, it is easy to buy one at many markets or electronics stores. Batteries are available in the major cities.

Visas & Passports

It used to be incredibly difficult for independent travelers to gain entry to Vietnam. Today, it is fairly straightforward to get a visa. It is possible to get a tourist visa for US$60 in four workings days from a number of travel agents in Bangkok and Hong Kong. Bangkok is definitely the best place in Asia to pick up a visa and many travel agents offer attractive round trip flight and visa packages.

Other types of visas available include: business, press, family visit, and official visit. To enter Vietnam on business, you must contact your Vietnamese sponsor who will then submit an application and letter to the embassy you are applying to. This process can often take weeks, so make sure you get a head start. Certain Vietnamese companies have the connections to have visas issued on arrival in Hanoi and Ho Chi Minh City for US$50. If you do enter Vietnam without a visa in hand, and there is a problem with immigration, remain calm. Usually the worst thing that will happen is you'll be put in the airport hotel for a night while your host hopefully secures your visa.

Without the right connections, it can be very difficult to get any type of visa issued for more than one month. Most visas must be used within one month of their issue. While it once was fairly easy to receive an extension to your visa in Vietnam, recently the government has changed its rules and tightened restrictions. Now, no extensions will be given for tourist visas. Foreigners who enter on tourist visas and conduct business or government activities will be deported when caught. They may also be fined.

Overseas Vietnamese may be granted extensions for as long as six months, but family reasons must be proven. Visa extensions may also be granted for foreigners working in joint-venture offices, foreign representative offices and who have proper visas.

You will be given a copy of your landing card on your arrival. This, along with your visa, must be kept with you at all times and handed back on your departure.

Foreign Registration & Internal Travel Permits

Internal travel permits are not required when visiting major tourist areas in Vietnam. In April 1993, Hanoi eased its internal travel policies and opened all provinces to tourists. However, each province has its own regulations. Many tourists have reported being arrested by provincial police in the Central Highlands and Mekong Delta for traveling in restricted areas. Occasionally innocent tourists walk unknowingly into sensitive border areas and military installations unaware that they are breaking the law. In Vietnam, ignorance of the law is no excuse. Regulations change daily and some provinces completely ignore directives from Hanoi. The best advice is to play it safe in remote areas and always contact the police. It may end up costing a few dollars, but it beats spending your vacation under house arrest.

Tourists staying in hotels and guesthouses do not need to register with the police directly. When you check-in at reception the staff will take your passport to the police for registration. Better to do it yourself.

If you plan on staying with family or friends you may want to visit the local police station to avoid any late night visits by the police, as nosy neighbors often report suspicious foreigners.

Although you may consider this a nuisance, you will be saving your hosts quite a bit of trouble from authorities. It is always important to consider what impact your visit and contact may have on your friends who will be living and working in Vietnam long after you have gone home.

Recently authorities have begun to crack down on foreign visitors. For example, people in Vietnam on tourist visas who are actually working are being told to leave. Journalists who attempt to work on tourist visas may encounter problems.

Also, visitors should keep in mind that your activities may be monitored by security police. Some tour guides have been told to report the activities of their clients: where they go, who they meet with. Some tour companies have members of the country's internal security apparatus working for them. Most foreigners working in Vietnam assume their phone lines may be tapped and faxes monitored. While visitors will not notice a heavy police presence – in fact, they will notice quite the opposite – be assured that there are many ways for the security police to keep tabs on visitors.

Hanoi Police Office for the Registration of Foreign Visitors, 63 Tran Hung Dao, Hanoi.

Ho Chi Minh City Police Station, 161 Nguyen Du, Dist 1. Tel: 829 9398, 829 7107. Opens 8–11am and 1–4pm.

Vung Tau Immigration Police, 14 Le Loi Street.

Immigration offices:

Hanoi, 40A Hang Bai. Tel: 826 0921.

Ho Chi Minh City, 254 Nguyen Trai, Dist. 1. Tel: 839 1701.

Hue, 43 Ben Nghe. Tel: 822134.

Da Nang, 1 Nguyen Thi Minh Khai. Tel: 821075.

Nha Trang, 5 Ly Tu Trong. Tel: 822400.

Can Tho, 5 Ly Tu Trong. Tel: 810811.

Hai Phong, 2 Le Dai Hanh. Tel: 841251.

Da Lat, 31A Tran Binh Trong. Tel: 822460.

Vung Tau, 422 Truong Cong Dinh. Tel: 852423.

Customs

Visitors to Vietnam are required to fill in a detailed customs declaration in duplicate upon arrival. Customs may inspect your luggage to verify that you have made a correct declaration. Although it is unpleasant to say this, authorities seem to cause more problems for overseas Vietnamese than for other foreigners. At times this is probably justified, as many overseas Vietnamese return loaded down with boxes and bags. The volume of baggage, as much as the nationality, may account for the extra scrutiny.

Currency, as well as most electronics items – cameras, radios, computers, video cameras – must be declared, as well as books, reading material and videos. Your items may be inspected to check for anything considered culturally or politically sensitive. Some travelers report having books and videos confiscated.

You must keep a copy of the customs declaration form to show customs officials upon leaving Vietnam. They may check to see if you are leaving with the items declared, such as computers and cameras.

Official authorization from the Ministry of Culture is required to export or take out antiquities. Visitors are not allowed to take ancient artifacts, antiques or items of value to Vietnamese culture. Travelers have reported problems in trying to leave with items that appear to be antiques, even if they are reproductions. It is a good idea to take a detailed receipt from the shop with a description of the item. But your goods still may be confiscated. Shop owners will often insist that what they sell can be exported; don't believe them. If you

have the time to receive official permission, it is best to do so.

On both arrival and departure luggage will be exposed to an X-ray examination. It is probably a good idea to keep film and software away from it.

When leaving Vietnam, you may be stopped to have film, video and reading materials inspected. Usually this is just an annoyance, but if you are a journalist, your film or tapes will be seized unless you have permission to take them out from the government's Foreign Affairs Press Department.

Health

The only vaccination required is for yellow fever, for travelers coming from Africa. Immunization against hepatitis (A & B), Japanese encephalitis and tetanus are strongly urged.

It is a good idea to consult a physician a month to six weeks before departing to leave enough time to obtain the immunizations.

Malaria is widespread in Vietnam, especially in the Central Highlands and the Mekong Delta. The best protection is prevention. Always sleep under a mosquito net when visiting rural areas, use a high concentrate DEET repellent and wear long sleeves and pants from dusk to dawn when malaria carrying mosquitoes are active. Lastly, consult with a knowledgeable doctor to determine what anti-malarial drugs are best suited for your travels. Opinion is divided about using prophylactics for malaria. Some doctors argue against taking the anti-malarial drugs because of the potential side effects, because the side effects can mask symptoms of other illnesses and because malarial strains have developed that are resistant to the drugs.

Do not drink tap water unless it has been boiled properly and avoid ice in drinks, especially in the countryside. Imported bottled water is available in most cities, but beware of bottles that are refilled with tap water.

Caution should be taken when eating, because food is often not prepared in sanitary conditions. Doctors advise abstaining from shellfish, especially shrimp. Fruit and vegetables should be peeled before eating. Cooking them is a better idea. Some doctors advise avoiding even raw vegetables like the herbs and lettuces served

with *pho*, the noodle soup, and spring rolls. Eat in restaurants that are crowded. Because most places do not have refrigeration, food is thrown away at the end of the day. If a place is crowded, it is a good sign that the establishment is not serving spoiled food. Avoid the usual suspects: mayonnaise, and eggs that have not been cooked thoroughly, for example.

Should you have an accident or an emergency health problem in Vietnam, you may want to consider evacuation to Singapore or Bangkok for treatment. Vietnam has no shortage of well-trained doctors, but hospital services and supplies are in very short supply.

Imported pharmaceutical drugs are widely available in Hanoi and Ho Chi Minh City, but it is best to bring a small supply of medicine to cope with diarrhoea, dysentery, eye infections, insect bites, fungal infections, and the common cold.

Money Matters

Vietnam's unit of currency, the dong (pronounced *dome*), currently circulates in bank notes of 50,000, 20,000, 10,000, 5,000, 2,000, 1,000, 500, 200 and 100 denominations. The dong has been relatively stable for the past two years. In October 1991, it hit a record exchange rate of 14,000 dong to one US dollar. Today, it is stable at around 12,000 dong to the dollar. Care should be taken when exchanging money or receiving change. The 20,000 dong notes and the 5,000 notes – both widely used – are the same size and color (blue) and easily confused.

Vietnam's black market for US dollars isn't what it used to be. The difference between the street rate and the bank rate is very small – if there is any difference at all.

Changing money on the street is a foolish proposition. Because the dong notes are the same size and same or similar colors, you can easily be given the wrong denomination. As the old saying goes, you get what you pay for. Better to stick to a bank or currency exchange booth, of which there are many in all the major cities.

After banking hours, it is possible to change dollars at almost any jewelry or gold shop; sometimes the rate is slightly higher than the bank rate. These shops are called *hieu van* or *hieu kim hoan* and are easily identifiable because their signs usually have bright, gold-color letters.

Be prepared to be offered two exchange rates: One for denominations of 50 and 100 USD, a lower rate for smaller denominations. Better to change larger bills.

Some banks will also exchange Vietnamese dong for other currencies: French francs, German marks, Japanese yen, Australian dollars, for example. But gold shops will not. Better to bring US dollars. Travelers checks in US dollars are accepted in most banks and in major hotels, but not in shops and not in smaller hotels and restaurants. Major credit cards are accepted. Sometimes a high commission – 4 percent is standard – is assessed when using credit cards, however.

Cash advances can be collected from major credit cards (again with the 4 percent commission) from major banks, including Vietcombank.

Although the government recently issued a decree that all transactions be conducted in Vietnamese dong, in reality the country still uses a dual-currency system. That is, most purchases can be made in US dollars, as well as Vietnamese dong. However, often shops, restaurants and taxi drivers insist on a lower conversion rate – 10,000 dong to 1 dollar is standard – when using dollars. To avoid haggling, it is better to carry some Vietnamese dong. (Sometimes this can work to your advantage. For example, if a shop owner says a bicycle costs 50 US dollars, they will tell you it costs 500,000 Vietnamese dong: 50 US dollars should actually convert to about 550,000 dong.)

One other potential problem is the quality of the notes themselves. Although the Vietnamese dong notes are often ripped, faded and crumpled, Vietnamese are reluctant to accept US dollars that are not crisp and new. Before taking US dollars from a bank, you should inspect them to make sure they have no stray marks or tears, or appear old. People may refuse them.

When you arrive in Vietnam, the custom form requires you to note currency brought into the country if it is worth more than 2,000 US dollars. However visitors no longer have to account for money exchanged or spent during their trips.

Holidays

The most important celebration of the year in Vietnam is Tet, or Lunar New Year, which falls either in late January or early February, on the day of the full moon between the winter solstice and the spring equinox.

Official Public Holidays
1 January – New Year's Day
3 February – founding of the Communist Party of Vietnam
8 March – Women's Day
26 March – Youth Day
30 April – Liberation of Saigon
1 May – International Labor Day
7 May – Victory over France
19 May – Ho Chi Minh's birthday
1 June – Children's Day
27 July – Memorial Day for war martyrs
19 August – August Revolution of 1945
2 September – National Day
20 November – Teacher's Day
22 December – Army Day

Getting There
By Air

The easiest way to get to Vietnam is by air. International flights are available to Hanoi and Ho Chi Minh City, and direct service is expected to be available to Da Nang in the near future.

HANOI

Noi Bai Airport is served by direct flights from Bangkok (Thai, Vietnam Airlines, Air France), Berlin (Vietnam Airlines), Dubai (Vietnam Airlines), Guangzhou (China Southern Airlines), Hong Kong (Cathay Pacific, Vietnam Airlines), Moscow (Aeroflot, Vietnam Airlines), Paris (Air France), Seoul (Vietnam Airlines), Singapore (Singapore Airlines), Taipei (China Airlines, Vietnam Airlines) and Vientiane (Lao Aviation, Vietnam Airlines).

There are bus and taxi services from the airport into central Hanoi. Vietnam Airlines operates a shuttle bus between its central Hanoi office and the airport for US$4 (US$2 for Vietnamese nationals), a bit more if you want to be dropped off at your hotel. An official Vietnam Airlines taxi costs US$20; tickets for a taxi and the shuttle can be purchased near the baggage claim area. Freelance taxi drivers will also swarm around visitors. They will

try to charge as much as they can; a car in good condition with air conditioning should cost around US$15. For an older car without air conditioning, US$10. Drivers will grab your arm and try to pick up your bags; negotiate the fare before letting anyone lead you away. If a driver refuses to come down in price, walk away. There are more than enough drivers. They may also try to charge you for a road toll. You should not pay this. If a driver insists, demand that you pay for the toll and keep the receipt. Also try to steer the driver onto the new highway; it will save you about 20 minutes of time. (Say: *Di duong Bac Thang Long – Noi Bai* or simply *Cau Thang Long*.) There are also metered taxis, although they are difficult to find at the airport. The fare should be about US$25.

HO CHI MINH CITY

The recently renovated Tan Son Nhat Airport is served by flights from Amsterdam (KLM Airlines), Bangkok (Thai, Vietnam Airlines), Berlin (Vietnam Airlines), Dubai (Vietnam Airlines), Frankfurt (Lufthansa), Hong Kong (Cathay Pacific, Vietnam Airlines), Jakarta (Garuda Indonesia), Kuala Lumpur (Malaysia Air), Manila (Philippine Airlines), Osaka (Vietnam Airlines), Paris (Air France), Phnom Penh (Vietnam Airlines, Cambodia Air), Seoul (Vietnam Air), Singapore (Vietnam Airlines, Singapore Airlines), Sydney (Qantas), Taipei (Eva Air, Vietnam Airlines, China Airlines).

Tan Son Nhat is located just 15 minutes from the center of the city. Here the taxi scene is not as chaotic as Hanoi. There is a somewhat orderly system for metered taxis, with an attendant directing taxis to passengers. A metered fare is reasonable and should cost less than US$10 to the city center; there are no extra charges for baggage or extra passengers. You can also hire a freelance taxi driver, but the fare will not be much less than a metered taxi, perhaps as low as US$5.

Vietnam Airlines has improved its service in recent years and also has added newer aircraft to its fleet. It still uses old Russian Tupelov jets on shorter hops within the country. The airport personnel working for the airlines tend to be gruff and unhelpful; ticketing personnel and on-flight attendants are generally more helpful. One consistent problem faced by people trying to fly within the country is an over booking of flights. Passengers are often told a flight is booked. But it is a good idea to go to the airport and try to fly stand-by, as generally the flights have many open seats. Traveling within the country is relatively inexpensive for Vietnamese nationals, so often people make reservations and do not bother to cancel them when their travel plans change.

Vietnam Airlines flies to the following cities within the country: Hanoi, Ho Chi Minh City, Da Nang, Hai Phong, Hue, Nha Trang, Da Lat, Vinh, Pleiku, Qui Nhon, Buon Ma Thuot and Can Tho. The airline has a two-tiered pricing system: one price for foreigners, another price for Vietnamese. For example, a roundtrip fare between Hanoi and Ho Chi Minh City is US$330 for foreigners, but only US$120 for Vietnamese. (Overseas Vietnamese pay the foreigner price; ticket sellers ask for passports or Vietnamese national identity cards, so overseas Vietnamese can't pass for local Vietnamese.)

By Sea
Cruise ships sometimes make stops in Ho Chi Minh City and Da Nang as part of South China Sea cruises, but there is no regular service at this time. Anyone considering arriving by sea on a freighter or private vessel should contact the Hanoi immigration office directly to receive authorization. It is possible to take a ferry between Cambodia and Chau Doc in the Mekong Delta, but travelers have reported difficulties with immigration officers upon arrival.

By Road
It is also possible to enter Vietnam from China (and vice versa) at the Lang Son border crossing. Border tensions between the two countries routinely flare, so find out what the situation is when making your travel plans.

A few travelers have managed to get permission to travel overland from Laos to Vietnam via the Lao Bao border crossing in Central Vietnam, but it is definitely not common practice to do so. Travelers also can enter Vietnam by crossing the border with Cambodia.

When applying for a visa, you must specify where you intend to enter and

exit Vietnam. If you do not do so the immigration police may turn you away from the border. Exit points can be changed by the immigration offices in Hanoi and Ho Chi Minh City.

Special Facilities
Doing Business
A growing number of foreign banks and trading companies provide various services for business people and visitors alike. Many of the trading companies are involved in tourist services such as tours to neighbouring countries like Cambodia and Laos, transport, visa services and form, import export services, hotel bookings, guides, rail, boat and even helicopter tours, foreign exchange and banking services and shipping.

HO CHI MINH CITY
Import Export Corporation of Ho Chi Minh City "IMEXCO", 1 Nam Ky Khoi Nghia, Dist 1. Tel: 829 5232, 829 5931. Telex: 8223, 8224 IMEX HCM.
OSC Tourism Transactions and Guide Office, 65 Nam Ky Khoi Nghia, Dist 1. Tel: 829 6658. Fax: 829 0195.
Riverway Transport Corporation, 94 Nam Ky Khoi Nghia, Dist 1. Tel: 822 4342, 822 4535.
Ocean Transport Company, 23 Nguyen Hue, Dist 1. Tel: 829 0197.
Vietnam Overseas Shipping Agent, 57 Nguyen Hue, Dist 1. Tel: 829 7694, 829 0194.
Ocean Shipping Company, 142 Nguyen Tat Thanh, Dist 4. Tel: 829 3124.
Transimex–Ministry of Foreign Economic Relations, 406 Nguyen That Thanh, Dist 4. Tel: 822 2415, 822 5663.

VUNG TAU
OSC (Oil Services Company), Head Office, 02 Le Loi Street. Tel: 897562, Telex: OSC SGN 307.

HANOI
Hanoi Foreign Trade Company, 56 Ly Thai To.

Tour Operators
Organized tours are available through a growing number of overseas agencies and both official and unofficial agencies within the country. You may feel that you are not getting what you paid for or have been misled, but try to deal with any misunderstandings that may arise with as much tact and patience as you can master, it will get you further in the long run. Many operators advertise their services, both within Vietnam and elsewhere, particularly Bangkok. It pays to shop around as prices vary considerably.

Visas may be acquired more easily, at a price, through a specialist agent or tour operator, who can arrange an all-inclusive package of visa, flight and hotel accommodation. Taking an all-inclusive package outside Vietnam is usually considerably more expensive than if you make your arrangements yourself once you have arrived.

Tourist Information Centers
Apart from Vietnam Tourism, some other state organizations offer much cheaper and more flexible organized tours. For example, Trung Tam Du Lich Thanh Nien Vietnam (Vietnam's Youth Tourism Centre), 31 Cao Thang, Dist 3, Ho Chi Minh City, tel: 829 0553, 829 4602, provides a very accommodating service and will tailor a guided tour to suit your requirements.

HO CHI MINH & THE SOUTH
Vietnam Tourism, 234 Nam Ky Khoi Ngia. Tel: 829 0776. Fax: 829 0775.
Saigon Tourist, 49 Le Thanh Ton. Tel: 829 8914. Fax: 822 4987.
Saigon Tourist Association, 112 Cach Mang Thang Tam. Tel: 823 8653. Telex: 811514 EPO-VT. Fax: 84824744.
Can Tho, Hau Giang Tourist Office in service of Shipping, 27 Chau van Liem. Tel: 20147, 35275.
Rach Gia, Tourist Office, 12 Ly Tu Trong. Tel: 2081.
Lam Dong – Da Lat, 12 Tran Phu, Da Lat. Tel: 2021, 2034.
Phu Khanh Hoa and Nha Trang, 1 Tran Hung Dao, Nha Trang. Tel: 22753, 22754, 22721.
Thuan Hai – Phan Thiet, 82 Trung Trac, Phan Thiet. Tel: 2474, 2475.
Vung Tau, Tourist Agency in Service of

Vung Tau Oil and Gas Enterprise, 2 Le Loi. Tel: 852405. Fax: 852834.

HUE & THE CENTER

Hue – Thua Thien Tourism, 51 Le Loi, Hue. Tel: 822369.
Binh Tri Thien Province Tourist Office, 51 Le Loi, Hue. Tel: 822288, 822369.
Quang Nam – Da Nang, 48 Bach Dang, Da Nang. Tel: 821423, 822213.
Binh Dinh – Quy Nhon, 4 Nguyen Hue, Quy Nhon. Tel: 2524, 2206.
Nghe Tinh, Truong Thi Square, Vinh. Tel: 692 VINH.

HANOI & THE NORTH

Hanoi Tourism, 18 Ly Thuong Kiet, Hanoi. Tel: 826 6714. Fax: 825 4209.
Green Bamboo Travel, 42 Nha Chung, Hanoi. Tel: 826 8752. Fax: 826 4949. E-mail: bamboo@netnam.org.vn
Hai Phong, 15 Le Dai Hanh. Tel: 842957.
Hoa Binh, 24 Tran Hung Dao, Ha Dong. Tel: 37.
Ha Long, Bai Chay Street, Ha Long City West. Tel: 846320. Fax: 846318.
Ha Nam Dinh, 115 Nguyen Du. Tel: 439, 362.
Thanh Hoa, 21a Quang Trung. Tel: 298.
Thai Binh Tourist Agency, Ly Bon Tel: 270.

Banks

There are several foreign banks now in operation in Hanoi and Ho Chi Minh City. It is possible to receive cash advances on a major credit card (usually with a commission of 4 percent), and to open bank accounts. Money can be wired into bank accounts from overseas banks.

HANOI

(Some foreign banks will provide services for account holders only.)
ANZ Bank, 14 Le Thai To. Tel: 825 8190. Fax: 825 8188.
Bank of America, 27 Ly Thuong Kiet. Tel: 824 9316. Fax: 824 9322.
Chinfon Commercial Bank, 55 Quang Trung. Tel: 825 0555. Fax: 825 0566.
Citibank, 17 Ngo Quyen. Tel: 825 1950. Fax: 824 3960.
Credit Lyonnais, 10 Trang Thi. Tel: 825 8102. Fax: 826 0080.
Indovina Bank, 88 Hai Ba Trung. Tel: 826 5516. Fax: 826 6320.
ING Bank, 17 Ngo Quyen. Tel: 824 6888. Fax: 826 9216.

Standard Chartered Bank, 27 Ly Thai To. Tel: 825 8970. Fax: 825 8880.
VID Public Bank, 2 Ngo Quyen. Tel: 826 6953. Fax: 826 8228.
Vietcombank, 47-49 Ly Thai To. Tel: 826 5501. Fax: 826 9067.
Vietnam Bank for Investment and Development, 194 Tran Quang Khai. Tel: 826 6963.
Industrial and Commercial Bank of Vietnam, 16 Phan Dinh Phung. Tel: 823 2008. Fax: 823 3452.
Vietnam Bank for Agriculture, 4 Pham Ngoc Thach, Dong Da. Tel: 852 5374.

HO CHI MINH CITY

(Several banks are located on or near Chuong Duong Street, which runs parallel to the Saigon River.)

Bangkok Bank, 117 Nguyen Hue, Dist. 1. Tel: 822 3416. Fax: 822 34221.
Credit Lyonnais, 17 Ton Duc Thang, Dist. 1. Tel: 829 9226. Fax: 829 6465.
Deutsche Bank, 174 Nguyen Dinh Chieu, Dist. 3. Tel: 829 9000.
Hong Kong Bank, 75 Pham Hong Thai, Dist. 1, next to the New World Hotel. Tel: 829 2288. Fax: 823 0530
Indovina Bank, 36 Ton That Dam, Dist. 1. Tel: 822 4955. Fax: 823 0131.
VID Public Bank, 15A Ben Chuong Duong, Dist. 1. Tel: 822 3583. Fax: 822 3612.
Vietcombank, 29 Chuong Duong, Dist. 1. Tel: 829 7245. Fax: 829 7228.
Vietnam Bank for Investment and Development, 134 Nguyen Cong Tru. Tel: 823 0125.
Industrial and Commercial Bank of Vietnam, 79A Ham Nghi, Dist. 1. Tel: 829 7266.
Vietnam Bank for Agriculture, 50 Chuong Duong, Dist. 1. Tel: 829 3516.

Airlines

HANOI

Vietnam Airlines, 1 Quang Trung. Tel: 825 0888.
(There are also several agents of Vietnam Airlines in town, including one inside the Metropole Hotel).
Air France, 1 Ba Trieu. Tel: 825 3484. Fax: 826 6694.
Cathay Pacific, 27 Ly Thuong Kiet. Tel: 826 7298. Fax: 826 7709.
Thai Air, 25 Ly Thuong Kiet. Tel: 826 6893. Fax: 826 7934.

Singapore Airlines, 17 Ngo Quyen. Tel: 826 8888. Fax: 826 8666.
Malaysian Air, 15 Ngo Quyen. Tel: 826 8820. Fax: 824 2388.
China Southern, 27 Ly Thai To. Tel: 826 9233.

HO CHI MINH CITY

Vietnam Airlines, 116 Nguyen Hue. Tel: 829 2118. Fax: 823 0273.
Air France, 130 Dong Khoi, Dist. 1. Tel: 829 0981. Fax: 823 0190.
Cathay Pacific, 58 Dong Khoi, Dist. 1. Tel: 822 3203. Fax: 825 8276.
Thai Airways, 65 Nguyen Du, Dist 1. Tel: 829 2810. Fax: 822 3465.
Malaysian Air, 65 Le Thanh, Dist 1. Tel: 824 2885. Fax: 824 2884.
Garuda Indonesia, 132/134 Dong Khoi, Dist 1. Tel: 829 3644. Fax: 829 3688.
Eva Air, 32 Ngo Duc Ke, Dist 1. Tel: 822 4488. Fax: 822 3567.
KLM Royal Dutch Airlines, 244 Pasteur. Tel: 823 1990. Fax: 823 1989.
Royal Cambodge Airlines, 343 Le Van Si. Tel: 844 0126. Fax: 842 1578.
China Southern, 52B Pham Hong Thai, Dist 1. Tel: 829 1172. Fax: 829 6800.
Lufthansa, 132 Dong Khoi. Tel: 829 8529. Fax: 829 8537.
Qantas, Saigon Centre, 5th Fl, Unit 6, 65 Le Loi, Dist 1. Tel: 821 4660. Fax: 821 4669.

Government Offices

HANOI

Office for Foreign Registration (Immigration Police), 63 Tran Hung Dao. Open Monday–Saturday between 8–11am and 1–5pm.
Department of Foreign Affairs for Quang Nam Da Nang Province, 136 Ong Ich Khiem, Da Nang. Tel: 821092.

HO CHI MINH CITY

Service of Foreign Affairs, 6 Thai Van Lung. Tel: 822 4127.
Office of Foreign Registration, 161-163 Nguyen Du.
Customs, 125 Ham Nghi. Tel: 829 0095, 829 0096.
The Vietnamese Information Agency (V.N.A.), 120 Xo Viet Nghe Tinh.
Import – Export, IMEXCO, 8 Nguyen Hue. Tel: 829 7424.
Office for the Control of Cultural Item's Import and Export, 178 Nam Ky Khoi Nghia.

Institute of Franco-Vietnamese Cultural Exchange, 31 Don Dat Street, Ho Chi Minh City. Tel: 822 4577.

Saigon Port, Ho Chi Minh City. Tel: 829 1825.

Tan Son Nhat Airport, Tel: 824 3250, 824 2339.

International Booking Office, 116 Nguyen Hue. Tel: 829 2118, 822 3848.

International Airlines represented at Tan Son Nhat Airport: Air France, Tel: 824 1278; Aeroflot, Tel: 824 3774; Thai International, Tel: 824 6235.

Diplomatic Missions & Consulates

EMBASSIES IN HANOI

Australia, Van Phuc Quarter. Tel: 831 7755. Fax: 831 7711.

Belgium, 48 Nguyen Thai Hoc. Tel: 823 5005. Fax: 845 7165.

Cambodia, 71 Tran Hung Dao. Tel: 825 3788. Fax: 826 5225.

Canada, 31 Hung Vuong. Tel: 823 5500. Fax: 823 5333.

China, 46 Hoang Dieu. Tel: 845 3736. Fax: 823 2826.

Denmark, 19 Dien Bien Phu. Tel: 843 6243. Fax: 823 1999.

France, 57 Tran Hung Dao. Tel: 825 2719. Fax: 826 4236.

Germany, 29 Tran Phu. Tel: 845 3836. Fax: 845 3838.

Indonesia, 50 Ngo Quyen. Tel: 825 3353. Fax: 825 9274.

Japan, 61 Truong Chinh. Tel: 869 2600. Fax: 869 2595.

Laos, 22 Tran Binh Trong. Tel: 825 4576. Fax: 822 8414.

Malaysia, 2-C Van Phuc. Tel: 845 3371. Fax: 823 2166.

Myanmar (Burma), A-3 Van Phuc. Tel: 825 3369. Fax: 845 2404.

New Zealand, 32 Hang Bai. Tel: 824 1481. Fax: 824 1480.

Netherlands, D-1 Van Phuc. Tel: 843 0605. Fax: 843 1013.

Singapore, 41-43 Tran Phu. Tel: 823 3965. Fax: 825 1600.

Sweden, 2 Road 358, Van Phuc. Tel: 845 4824. Fax: 823 2195.

Thailand, 65 Hoang Dieu. Tel: 823 5092. Fax: 823 5088.

United Kingdom, 16 Ly Thuong Kiet. Tel: 825 2510. Fax: 826 5762.

United States, 7 Lang Ha. Tel: 843 1500. Fax: 843 1510.

CONSULATES IN HO CHI MINH CITY

Australia, 5-B Ton Duc Thang, Dist. 1. Tel: 829 6035. Fax: 829 6024.

Belgium, 236 Dien Bien Phu, Dist. 3. Tel: 829 4526.

Cambodia, 41 Phung Khac Hoan, Dist 1. Tel: 829 2751.

Canada, 203 Dong Khoi. Tel: 824 2000. Fax: 829 4528.

China, 39 Nguyen Thi Minh Khai, Dist 1. Tel: 829 2457. Fax: 829 5009.

Denmark, 23 Phung Khac Hoan, Dist 1. Tel: 822 8289. Fax: 822 4888.

France, Nguyen Thi Minh Khai. Tel: 829 7231. Fax: 829 1675.

Germany, 126 Nguyen Dinh Chieu, Dist. 3. Tel: 829 1967. Fax: 823 1919.

Indonesia, 18 Phung Khac Khoan, Dist 3. Tel: 822 3799. Fax: 829 9493.

Japan, 13-17 Nguyen Hue. Tel: 822 5314. Fax: 822 5316.

Malaysia, 53 Nguyen Dinh Chieu, Dist 3. Tel: 829 9023. Fax: 829 9027.

Singapore, 5 Phung Khac Hoan, Dist 1. Tel: 822 5173. Fax: 825 1600.

United Kingdom, 261 Dien Bien Phu, Dist. 3. Tel: 829 8443.

VIETNAMESE OVERSEAS MISSIONS & TRADE REPRESENTATIVES

Albania, Embassy of the SR Vietnam, Tirana.

Algeria, Embassy of the SR Vietnam, 30 Chenoua Hydra.

Australia, Embassy of the SR Vietnam, 6 Timbarra Section, O'Malley, A.C.T. 2606. Tel: 866059. Telex: 62756.

Bulgaria, Embassy of the SR Vietnam, 12 Oborichte Street, Sofia. Cable: VIETHUONG.

Cuba, Oficina Commercial de la RSVN, Calle 16 No. 5 y 7, Miramar, Havana. Cable: VIETTHUONG.

France, Ambassade de la SRVN, 62 rue Boileau, 75016 Paris. Tel: 45245063, 45276255.
Ambassade de la SRVN, Section Commercial, 44 Avenue de Madrid, 92200 Neuilly sur Seine, Paris. Tel: 6248577. Telex: 612922. Cable: COVIETNAMFX

Germany, Botschaft der Sozialistischen, Republik Vietnam, Konstantin Strasse 37, 5300 Bonn, BRD.

Hong Kong. The Representation of the National Export Import Corporations of the SRVN, 17th floor Golden Star Building, 20-24 Lockhart Rd. Tel: 5-283361-3. Telex 63771 VNCOR. Cable: VINACOR.

Hungary, Embassy of the SR Vietnam, 24 Benczur Utca I/1, Budapest VI. Cable: VIETKULKER.

India, Embassy of the SR Vietnam, E 48 Panch Shila Park, New Delhi 110017. Cable: THUONGVU.

Italy, Embassy of the SR Vietnam, Piazza Barberini 12, 00187 Rome. Tel: 4755286, 4754098.

Japan, Embassy of the SR Vietnam, 50-11 Motoyoyogi-cho Shibuya-ku, Tokyo 151. Tel: 4663315. Telex: 32440 Vietnam. Cable: VIETRADE.

Laos, Embassy of the SR Vietnam, Route de That Luang, Vientiane. Tel: 5578, 2707.

Malaysia, 4 Persiaran Stonor, Kuala Lumpur 5040. Tel: (03) 2484036.

Poland, Embassy of the SR Vietnam, U1. Swiedtorkrzyska 36 M-32, Warsaw. Cable: VIETHUSU.

Rumania, Embassy of the SR Vietnam, 28 Hrito Street, Bucarest. Cable: VIETHURU.

Singapore. The Representation of the National Import Export Corporations of the SRVN, 10 Leedon Park. Tel: 4683747. Telex 26936. Cable: VINATRADE.

Sweden, Embassy of the SR Vietnam, Parkvagen 42, S-13141 NACKA. Tel: (08) 7182841. Telex: 15716 COMVIET S. Cable: VIETNAMHANDEL.

Thailand, Embassy of the SR Vietnam, 83/1 Wireless Road, Bangkok. Tel: 252-6950, 251-7201.

United Kingdom, The Embassy of the SR Vietnam, 12-14 Victoria Road, London W8. Tel: 9371912. Telex: 887361.

Practical Tips

Emergencies

Crime

In general, Vietnam is a very safe country to travel in and violent crimes against foreigners are very rare. However, there are dangers. In Ho Chi Minh City, tourists are increasingly becoming the victims of pickpockets, snatch and grab thieves, and hotel burglars. Always leave valuables in a hotel safe, and when you must carry cash, put it in a money belt inside your clothes. When walking or traveling in a cyclo, keep one hand firmly on handbags and cameras.

Daylight travel is pretty safe on Vietnam's highways and trains. There are isolated cases of highway robbery and hijacking, but foreigners are rarely the targets of these attacks. When traveling on buses or trains always stay with your bag. If you intend on taking the train, bring a cable lock to secure your bags to your bed frame when you are sleeping.

The Vietnamese are extremely friendly and generous, but caution must be taken when making casual acquaintances. On Vietnamese buses and trains, foreigners have been poisoned by drugged food and drink offered to them by fellow passengers. Vietnam also has its fare share of con men, who hustle everything from Cambodian gems to "genuine" bones of missing American servicemen. If you are offered American remains or ID tags, simply ignore the offer – more often than not you are being offered a box of animal bones. Trafficking in fake American remains and dog tags is dwindling somewhat. But it is not unheard of for someone to approach a foreigner claiming to know the whereabouts of an American still being held prisoner. These claims should be viewed with skepticism.

Women should take extra precautions when traveling alone as some Vietnamese men can be very aggressive. Their behavior ranges from following you to your hotel room, to being prodded by their friends to physically touch you. If you do stay alone in lower priced rooms, you may want to consider using an extra lock on your door at night.

Women, especially, should be careful late at night. The streets tend to be deserted giving a sense of false confidence to many travelers. In fact this situation is when a cyclo or xe om driver is more likely to hassle a woman. Better to travel in groups, or to arrange transportation ahead of time. A good driver can steer you clear of trouble; paying a little extra to have a driver wait for you is better than having to find a way to get home late at night.

Be careful of sidewalk vendors selling maps, books and souvenirs, or people begging for money, especially in Hanoi and Ho Chi Minh City. They can easily distract you while a friend slips a hand in your pocket, grabs your wallet and is gone before you realize what has happened. Watches are easy prey, too, and even glasses are ripped off by passing motorcyclists.

Medical Services

While Vietnam has ably trained medical care professionals, it lacks adequate equipment, medicine and facilities. The Ministry of Health has designated five hospitals to treat foreigners. However, in an emergency, any hospital is allowed to treat foreigners. Often foreigners report they are directed to the officially designated facilities:

Hanoi:
Bach Mai Hospital, 35 Gia Phong Street. Tel: 852 2089.
Ho Chi Minh City:
Cho Ray Hospital, 201B Nguyen Chi Thanh Street, Dist. 5. Tel: 855 4137.
Thong Nhat Hospital, 1 Ly Thuong Kiet, Tan Binh Dist. Tel: 864 0339.
Da Nang: C Hospital
Hai Phong: Viet Tiep Hospital

Foreign doctors run two out-patient clinics, which is probably the best alternative for medical care. They have a supply of pharmaceuticals. (Medicine of almost every kind can be bought on the street or at pharmacies – *nha thuoc* – but there is a problem of fake drugs being sold.) The two clinics are:
The Swedish Clinic, across from the Swedish Embassy at the entrance of the Van Phuc living quarters on Kim Ma Road. Tel: 825 2464; after-hours emergency. Tel: 821 3555.
Dr Kot Rafi, Van Phuc, Building A-2. Tel: 843 0748.
Both clinics are affiliated with emergency evacuation companies.

There are three medical evacuation companies operating in Vietnam, but to retain their services you must be a member.

AEA International
Ho Chi Minh City, 65 Nguyen Du Street, Dist. 1. Tel: 829 8520. (AEA operates an out-patient clinic here in Ho Chi Minh City.)
Hanoi, 4 Tran Hung Dao. Tel: 821 3555.

International SOS
Ho Chi Minh City, 151 Vo Thi Sau, Dist. 3. Tel: 829 4386.

GESA Assistance: (affiliated with Union of Assurances de Paris)
Hanoi, 25 Lang Ha. Tel: 835 2204.
Ho Chi Minh City, 2 Dong Khoi, Dist. 1. Tel: 823 0169.

TRADITIONAL MEDICINE
Acupuncture, therapeutic massage:
National Institute and Hospital of Traditional Medicine, 29 Nguyen Binh Khiem, Hanoi. Tel: 822 6775.

Business Hours

Offices and public services generally open early from around 7.30am and close for lunch at around noon or 12.30pm, opening again around 1pm until 4.30pm Monday to Saturday. Banks are open from 8am to 3pm Monday to Friday and closed on Saturday afternoons and Sundays. Private shops are open from 8.30am until late in the evening. Shops are generally open seven days a week. Food markets generally close around 5pm.

Media

Newspapers
Outside of Hanoi and Ho Chi Minh City, getting your hands on accurate news in Vietnam can be difficult.

Foreign newspapers, including the *International Herald Tribune*, *Bangkok Post*, *The Nation* (from Bangkok), and *The Asian Wall Street Journal* can be purchased in Hanoi and Ho Chi Minh City. Arrival times are erratic, however. Usually you can buy the same day's paper in Ho Chi Minh City, but often it is a day late in Hanoi. News magazines such as *Newsweek*, *Time*, *The Economist* and the *Far Eastern Economic Review* are also available. French-language newspapers and magazines also are readily available.

There is a newsstand called *Lao Dong* on Nguyen Hue Street in Ho Chi Minh City, across from the Rex Hotel near City Hall. In Hanoi, the Metropole Hotel gift shop sells daily papers, as well as a bookstore on Trang Tien near the corner of Ngo Quyen.

There are some English-language Vietnamese publications, as well. The daily *Vietnam News*, published in Hanoi, contains official news from the Vietnam News Agency (a government-run service), wire stories from Reuters, reprints of stories that have appeared in Vietnamese newspapers, some foreign news and sports scores. News about Vietnam itself tends to be sanitized.

Its primary competitor is published in Ho Chi Minh City. The *Saigon Times Daily* focuses more on Vietnam.

The weekly *Vietnam Investment Review* and the monthly *Vietnam Economic Times* are good sources for business-related activity in Vietnam.

But it should be kept in mind that all of these publications are at least partly owned and managed by the Vietnamese government or its agencies; editors of Vietnamese publications are required to be members of the Communist Party. In other words, don't expect objective news about Vietnam from any of them. That said, the Vietnamese press has begun to get a little more aggressive in its coverage.

In rural areas, it is difficult to find English-language publications.

Radio & Television

The Voice of Vietnam, the official radio station, broadcasts twice a day. Two stations transmit worldwide from Hanoi and Ho Chi Minh City in 11 languages: English, French, Spanish, Russian, Mandarin/Cantonese, Indonesian, Japanese, Khmer, Lao, Thai.

International stations can be received on a shortwave receiver.

Many hotels, even smaller ones, now have satellite dishes that bring in the BBC and CNN. They also show Star TV, which shows a healthy dose of old and new American TV shows, like Baywatch, Santa Barbara and M*A*S*H, and a sports channel that is heavy on cricket, auto racing, golf and rugby. Vietnam TV has nightly broadcasts in English and French.

Postal Services

Post offices are open every day from 7am to 8pm. Every city, town and village has a post office of some sort, and the service is remarkably reliable and fast. Within the country, mail reaches its destination within three days, sometimes faster. There is also an express mail service that promises overnight delivery for about US$9.

Stamps come in small denominations, which means mailing a postcard will leave little room for actually writing a message. However, many post offices now have meter machines so stamps are no longer necessary.

Telegram and telex services are available 24 hours a day in larger cities. Most post offices in major cities also have fax machines where messages can be sent or received, although the cost is quite high, about US$11 for one page to the United States, for example.

CENTRAL POST OFFICES

Hanoi, 75 Dinh Tien Hoang. Tel: 825 3544.
Ho Chi Minh City, 125 Hai Ba Trung, Dist. 1. Tel: 824 3356.
Hue, 8 Hoang Hoa Tham.
Da Nang, 45 Tran Phu.
Can Tho, Hoa Binh Street.
Nha Trang, 2 Tran Phu.
Da Lat, 16 Tran Phu.
Hai Phong, 5 Nguyen Tri Phuong.
Vung Tau, 45 Le Hong Phong.

Telecoms & Fax

International telephone connections are quite clear from Vietnam. However, the costs of calling overseas are among the highest in the world. Direct calls can be placed from hotels, the post office and residences. Reverse charges are not allowed, however. Expect to pay from US$4 to 5 a minute to call the United States, Europe or Australia. Hotels will add a surcharge that can make calls about US$7 a minute. Domestic calling is still haphazard. The circuits between Hanoi and Ho Chi Minh City tend to be quite busy, so calling from one city to another can take many minutes, or even hours.

Fax machines are available in post offices and hotels. Be warned that the cost is quite high. A one-page fax overseas costs about US$11. Hotels will charge even more. Both Hanoi and Ho Chi Minh City have mobile telephone services and paging services.

Country code for Vietnam is 84.

To call within the country, dial 01 followed by the area code followed by the number. Phone numbers are either five or six digits.

Area Codes: Provinces

An Giang	76
Ba Ria-Vung Tau	64
Bac Thai	28
Ben Tre	75
Binh Dinh	56
Binh Thuan	62
Cao Bang	26
Can Tho	71
Dak Lak	50
Dong Nai	61
Dong Thap	67
Gia Lai	59
Ha Bac	24
Ha Giang	19
Ha Tay	34
Ha Tinh	39
Hai Hung	32
Hoa Binh	18
Khanh Hoa	58
Kien Giang	77
Kon Tum	60
Lai Chau	23
Lang Son	25
Lao Cai	20
Lam Dong	63
Long An	72
Minh Hai	78
Nam Ha	35
Nghe An	38
Ninh Binh	30
Ninh Thuan	68
Phu Yen	57
Quang Binh	52
Quang Ngai	55
Quang Ninh	33
Quang Nam-Da Nang	51
Quang Tri	53
Soc Trang	79
Song Be	65
Son La	22
Tay Ninh	66
Thai Binh	36
Thanh Hoa	37
Thua Thien-Hue	54
Tien Giang	73
Tra Vinh	74
Tuyen Quang	27
Vinh Long	70
Vinh Phu	21
Yen Bai	20

Area Codes: Cities

Buon Ma Thuot	50
Da Lat	63
Da Nang	51
Hai Phong	31
Hanoi	4
Ho Chi Minh City	8
Hue	54

My Tho	73
Nha Trang	58
Phan Thiet	62
Vinh	38

Vietnam's tourist industry is being developed along the organised tour line. It is administered by the National Office of Tourism, which carries with it a ministerial rank. Vietnam Tourism is the official representative, responsible for promoting the industry both within the country and abroad. Its network of representative offices throughout the country provides information and services such as transport hire, hotel reservations and at least 17 different organized tours. These range from between 3 to 21 days, with an option of trips into neighboring Laos or Cambodia, at a price fixed more for the foreign wallet than the actual standard of the service. A little patience is needed to overcome the complications that can arise in the absence of sufficient guides and chauffeurs competent in foreign languages.

Vietnam for the most part is open to tourism, yet some areas in the country remain closed to tourists and even to the Vietnamese themselves. "No go" areas include the North's high plateau region, Cao Bang and Lang Son in the North on the Chinese border and Cam Ranh Bay in the Center. However it is not impossible to visit these areas "unofficially", although it's not advisable to tempt fate too far. Any area can suddenly become sensitive these days due to the growing discontent with the present system and if your request to visit an area is completely stonewalled, this may well be the reason.

Getting Around

Orientation

Now that Vietnam has loosened travel restrictions, it is possible to go just about everywhere in the country. However open Vietnam may be, it still can be difficult and time consuming to travel to many places.

National Highway 1, which spans the length of Vietnam from the Chinese border to Cau Mau, is in a state of serious neglect. The 800 km between Hanoi and Hue are torn up so badly that most vehicles can only manage to travel at a kidney jarring rate of 35 km (21 miles) per hour. South of Hue, the road is smooth compared to the northern stretch, but it is still slow and uncomfortable.

At this time there are no tourist class long distance buses in Vietnam. There is a national bus system, including a 48-hour express service from Ho Chi Minh City to Hanoi, but it is not a very safe or comfortable option. Vietnamese bus drivers are notorious for overloading their buses with people, livestock, and produce. If your idea of fun is riding on a bus with your knees pressed against your chest sandwiched between two betel nut chewing grandmothers for 12 hours, then the bus is for you. Fortunately, there are other options.

In Hanoi and Ho Chi Minh City it is possible to hire good Japanese cars and minivans to go on day trips or weeklong excursions. In Ho Chi Minh City you can even hire a convertible Mustang or Citroen to drive the scenic coastal road north to Hue. Hiring a driver and vehicle in Vietnam is good value if your traveling party is large enough to spread out the cost. Ask to go for a test ride before committing to a driver to see if the car is running properly. Expect to pay a minimum of US$40 a day for a comfortable car from a reputable tourist agency.

Sometimes drivers from one part of the country are reluctant to drive into

another. Drivers from Ho Chi Minh City, for example, are hesitant to drive to Hanoi. License plates on cars denote what province the car is from, and drivers fear police will give cars from out of the region trouble. A driver in Ho Chi Minh City might agree to take you as far as Da Nang, for example, and then help you find another driver to take you further north. Car costs can be expensive, but it is always a good idea to negotiate. One-way to keep the costs down is to look for a driver returning to his home base.

For example, someone from Nha Trang might have driven a passenger one way to Ho Chi Minh City and is returning alone. Usually you can negotiate a very cheap fare for such a ride.

A few adventurous souls have managed to see Vietnam with cars and motorcycles that they have unofficially purchased or rented in Hanoi and Ho Chi Minh City. Refurbished American Jeeps can be bought for US$3,000, and a brand new 350cc Czech motorcycle will set you back US$800.

The Vietnamese laws regarding foreigners driving are a little vague. Expatriates are allowed to own vehicles and many have been issued Vietnamese driving licenses. The Vietnamese also recognize international driving permits issued by the Automobile Association. However, more than one foreigner has been arrested for driving without a license. Also beware that there is no road insurance in Vietnam. If you hit someone or have an accident, the Vietnamese will hold you until you have reimbursed the other party – even if it wasn't your fault.

Besides the risks, driving is a great way to see the country and come in contact with the Vietnamese.

Train travel in Vietnam is very slow. The fastest Hanoi – Ho Chi Minh City express train covers 1,730 km (1,073 miles) in 36 hours, so if you need to get somewhere fast you can forget about the train. However, if you want to leisurely soak in the Vietnamese countryside the train has a lot to offer including mountain passes, ocean views, tunnels, French era bridges, and an opportunity to get to know the Vietnamese up close and personal.

Expect to pay at least US$100 for a berth in a four person compartment on the express train from Hanoi to Ho Chi Minh City. There are two express trains every day and berths are reserved fast, so try to make reservations two days in advance. There is a kitchen car on most trains, and waitresses serve food, but it is of questionable quality. A better option is to buy snacks from the many vendors that enter the train at local stops.

There are also local train services on the Hanoi – Ho Chi Minh City line that serve coastal cities. Lines also run from Hanoi West to Pho Lu, East to Hai Phong and North to Lang Son.

Flying is by far the best way to travel if you intend to only visit a few cities in Vietnam. A Vietnam Airlines flight from Hanoi to Ho Chi Minh City costs under US$200, whereas the train for the same distance, if you figure in meals for two days, is roughly the same price. Vietnam Airlines also flies to a few places that are very time consuming to get to by other means, like Phu Quoc Island and Pleiku. The major problem with flying is finding space. Popular flights fill up a few days before departure, so it is imperative to book flights early. It is very common for Vietnam Airlines to bump Vietnamese passengers off domestic flights when foreigners are on the waiting list, as foreign ticket prices are twice the Vietnamese price. You can use credit cards to buy airline tickets in Hanoi and Ho Chi Minh City, but in other cities you may be asked to pay cash.

Scheduled Vietnam Airlines flights from Ho Chi Minh City serve Buon Me Thuot, Da Lat, Da Nang, Hai Phong, Hanoi, Hue, Nha Trang, Phu Quoc, Pleiku, Qui Nhon and Rach Gia.

From Hanoi there are scheduled regular flights to Da Nang, Ho Chi Minh City, Hue, Vinh and Nha Trang.

In the cities the best way to get around is by bicycle or cyclo (trishaw). Bicycles can be rented for as little as US$5 per day from tourist cafes in Hanoi and Ho Chi Minh City. If you plan on staying in one city for a month or two, you may want to consider purchasing a bicycle, as prices are very reasonable. If you have a mechanical problem or a tire puncture, don't worry as there are stands set up practically on every street corner where most repairs will cost a few thousand dong.

No trip to Vietnam is complete without a ride in a cyclo. Vietnam has thousands of waiting cyclo drivers who can be hired by the kilometer or the hour.

Expect to pay at least 3,000 dong for a short ride or 10,000 dong for an hour. It is essential to bargain with cyclo drivers. As a rule, half their first offer and work up. Most cyclo drivers in the South are former ARVN soldiers and speak a little English. Cyclo drivers are indispensable as guides, sources of historical information, and as the procurers of hard to find items.

A faster way to get around town in Hanoi and Ho Chi Minh City is a motorcycle taxi, called a *xe om* (say ome) or Honda *om*, which literally means "hugging taxi" as passengers grab onto the driver's waist. Fares actually are cheaper than on cycles, and of course the ride is quicker. Some of the drivers navigate the roads badly, however, so be careful. If a driver seems unsafe, tell him to stop, get off and pay him. Find another driver. Some women travelers have reported problems with *xe om* drivers getting too friendly; be careful late at night, especially.

There are also automobile taxis in the major cities. They have new cars, with meters and air conditioning and generally are reasonably priced.

Domestic Travel

Hanoi Railway Station, Nam Bo Street (Located at the far Western end of Tran Hung Dao Street), Hanoi. The ticket office is open daily from 7.30–11.30am and 1.30–3.30pm. Buy tickets one day in advance.

Hanoi Bus Station, Kim Lien Street, Hanoi. There are daily express buses at 5am to Buon Me Thuot, Da Nang, Pleiku, Ho Chi Minh City, Kontum, Nha Trang, Quang Ngai and Qui Nhon. Most express buses leave at 5am. Local (non-express buses) leave Kim Lien Station for Sam Son, Thanh Hoa, and Vinh throughout the day.

Saigon Railway Station, 1 Nguyen Thong Street, District 3, (10 km from city center), Ho Chi Minh City. The ticket office is open daily from 7.15–11am and 1–3pm. There are express trains to Hanoi every day.

Ho Chi Minh City Bus stations, southbound buses depart from Mien Tay Station, which is 10 km (6 miles) west of the city in An Lac. You can get a bus to An Lac from the Ben Thanh market bus station. Express and local buses from Mien Tay serve: An Phu, Bac Lieu, Ben Tre, Camau, Can Tho,

Chau Doc, Ha Tien, Long An, Long Phu, Long Xuyen, My Thuan, My Tho, Phung Hiep, Rach Gia, Sa Dec, Tay Ninh, Tra Vinh, Vinh Chau and Vinh Long.

Northbound buses depart from Mien Dong Station, which is 5 km (3 miles) from the center of the city on Highway 13 (the extension of Xo Viet Nghe Tinh St). To get there it is a half hour by cyclo or you can take a bus from Ben Thanh Bus Station. There are express buses every morning at 5am to: Buon Me Thuot, Da Lat, Da Nang, Hai Phong, Hanoi, Hue, Nha Trang, Pleiku, Quang Ngai, Qui Nhon, Vinh and Vung Tau.

Buses to Cambodia leave from the Phnom Penh Garage at 155 Nguyen Hue Boulevard.

Minibuses to Vung Tau leave from 39 Nguyen Hue Boulevard at 7am daily. Buy tickets one day in advance. These buses are miserably overcrowded, so you may want to consider buying an extra seat to give yourself more room.

Nha Trang Bus Station, corner of Hung Vuong and Nguyen Tinh Minh Kai. Express buses leave from the Youth Tourism Express Bus Office, tel: 822010 at 6 Hoang Hoa Tham Street for Buon Me Thuot, Da Lat, Da Nang and Ho Chi Minh City, and from the Express Bus Station, tel: 822397, 822884, at 46 Le Thanh Ton Street. Buses from here serve Buon Me Thuot, Da Lat, Da Nang, Hue, Ho Chi Minh City, Quang Binh, Quang Ngai, Qui Nhon and Vinh.

Nha Trang Railway Station, 19 Thai Nguyen. Ticket Office opens between 7am and 2pm. Northbound trains to Hanoi depart daily at 9.45am–10pm.

Nha Trang Express Bus Station, 46 Le Thanh Ton Street. Open daily between 6am and 4.30pm.

Hue Bus stations. An Cuu Bus Station for southbound buses, An Hoa to northward destinations and Dong Ba for short haul destinations. Contact the bus station at Hung Vuong Street, tel: 823817, for further information.

Hue Railway Station, Le Loi Street. Ticket office opens between 6.30am and 5pm.

Da Lat Bus Station. Beside the old Caltex petrol station. From here a daily express service runs to and from Nha Trang and Ho Chi Minh. Express services also run to Da Nang, Quang Ngai and Qui Nhon two or three times a week. Non-express buses depart for various destinations throughout the country, including Hanoi, Ho Chi Minh City, Phan Rang, Cat Tien, Da Nang, Quang Ngai, but these only leave when they're full.

Da Nang Railway Station. Hai Phong Street – about 1 km from the city center. Bus tickets for express and some non-express services from Da Nang Intercity Bus Station can be purchased from the ticket office at 200 Dien Bien Phu Street which opens from 7–11am and 1–5pm.

Express services run to Buon Me Thuot, Da Lat, Hai Phong, Hongai Hanoi, Ho Chi Minh City, Gia Lai, Lang Son, Nam Dinh and Nha Trang and non-express services to Kontum, Vinh and Sathay.

Other non-express services depart from Da Nang Bus Station to Dong Ha, Hoi An, Hue, Quang Hgai, Qui Nhon, Tra My and various other destinations. **Vung Tau Bus Station,** 52 Nam Khoi Nghia Street. From here non-express services depart for Ho Chi Minh City, Bien Hoa, My Tho, Tay Ninh. Express and minibuses also leave from in front of the Ha Long and Hoa Binh hotels for Ho Chi Minh City.

Where to Stay

Hotels

The Western concept of tourism is something foreign to Vietnam and the country has a very long way to go before it can offer the standard of services and accommodation found in other more developed tourist destinations. Vietnam's hotel infrastructure, particularly in the North and Center, has a long way to go before it reaches international standard. Rooms are often under-equipped, or equipped with fixtures and appliances that don't work and power cuts are frequent. Room rates are quite high, more in line with demand, which often exceeds availability, than the standard of accommodation. Some very good hotels have been built recently in Ho Chi Minh City, Vung Tau, Nha Trang and Da Nang and other existing ho-

tels are being refurbished. The hotels built during the French and American eras in Ho Chi Minh City, Hanoi and Da Nang retain a certain faded charm and well worn comfort.

On the plus side, hotel staffs are friendly, and try to be helpful. Unfortunately, some basic services – such as taking telephone messages – are not up to par. People visiting on business might find such lapses in service frustrating. Charges for international phone calls from hotels tend to be astronomical.

There has been something of a hotel boom in the past years in Ho Chi Minh City and Hanoi. Now it is easy to find accommodations. Although a few years ago demand outstripped supply, today the reverse is true. Often, especially during non-peak times, visitors can bargain for discounts off of the listed price. It is always a good idea to ask. Many newer hotels have offered "soft opening" rates, discounts of up to 40 percent, which they sometimes extend for several months. It is worth asking for that rate. Also, hotels offer better rates for corporate clients, repeat customers and people booked by a travel agent. Thus, all of the rates listed should only be taken as a guide.

Officially, hotels are now required to accept payment only in Vietnamese dong. However, many still accept US dollars. Many larger establishments will now take major credit cards. Often, however, they charge a commission.

Usually, higher-end hotels charge an additional tax of about 10 percent and a service charge of about 5 percent. Often larger hotels include breakfast with the room rate. Sometimes in smaller hotels – called mini-hotels – rooms on higher floors cost less than those on lower floors.

The South

HO CHI MINH CITY (SAIGON)

Bong Sen Hotel, 117-123 Dong Khoi Street. Tel: 84-8 829 1516. Telex: 811273 HOTBS-VT. Fax: 84-8 8298076. 85 air conditioned rooms with prices starting at US$50 for a single and US$65 for a double. Located conveniently in the middle of the central shopping district.

Caravelle Hotel, 19-23 Lam Son Square. Tel: 84-8 829 3704. Telex: 811259 HOTDL-VT. Fax: 84-8 829

9902. Rooms from US$60. The roof of the Caravelle offers a great view of Central Saigon. During the war, cameramen often used the roof of the Caravelle to get unobstructed shots of news events.

Century Saigon Hotel, 68 Nguyen Hue Boulevard. Tel: 84-8 823 1818. Fax: 84-8 822 2958. A comfortable modern hotel located in Saigon's central district. Rooms from US$115.

Continental, 132-134 Dong Khoi. Tel: 84-8 829 9201. Telex: 811344 HOCON-VT. Fax: 84-8 824 1772. If you are a romantic, the Continental is the hotel for you. Located in the center of Saigon, the Continental's bar was a favorite watering hole for journalists during the war and was also Graham Greene's haunt in the 1950s. There are 85 rooms available from US$105 for a single to US$170 for a deluxe double.

Hotel Equatorial, 242 Tran Binh Trong, Dist. 5. Tel: 839 0000. Fax: 839 0011. A new luxury hotel with fine accommodations and services. However, it is located a bit far from the city center. Rooms from US$140.

Majestic Hotel, 1 Dong Khoi. Tel: 829 5512. Fax: 829 5510. The Majestic was recently renovated and now boasts a grand lobby with a piano bar. The rooms have been upgraded and afford nice views of the Saigon River. With the renovation have come higher prices. A standard room (which is quite small) starts at US$135 for one person.

Mondial Hotel, 109 Dong Khoi Street. Tel: 829 6291. Fax: 829 6273. Single rooms from US$50 and doubles starting at US$80.

New World Hotel, 76 Le Loi, Dist. 1. Tel: 822 8888. The largest and fanciest hotel in Ho Chi Minh City, the New World is of a standard of major hotels of Asian cities. Rooms start at US$195.

Norfolk Hotel, 117 Le Thanh Ton, Dist. 1. Tel: 829 5368. Fax: 829 3415. A small boutique hotel catering to business people and journalists. Rooms start at US$85.

Omni Saigon, 251 Nguyen Van Troi, Phu Nhuan District. Tel: 844 9222. Fax: 845 5234. International standard hotel, near Tan Son Nhat Airport. Rooms start at US$180.

Palace Hotel, 56-64 Nguyen Hue Boulevard. Tel: 84-8 829 2860. Fax: 824

4230. Telex: 811208 HOTHN-VT. 130 rooms with prices from US$60 to 140. Restaurant, bars, disco, video, swimming pool, souvenir shop, money changing facilities and laundry.

Pham Ngu Lao. Budget accommodation can be found in abundance in the area surrounding Pham Ngu Lao Street, one kilometer from central Saigon. There are also a lot of tourist cafes in this area where you can hire bicycles, motorcycles and minivans.

Rex Hotel, 141 Nguyen Hue Boulevard. Tel: 84-8 829 2186. Telex: 811201 HOTBT-VT. Fax: 84-8 829 6536. A classic, somewhat eccentric hotel with a popular rooftop garden restaurant. Single rooms range in price from US$69 to 659 for a superior room with city view.

Saigon Prince Hotel, 63 Nguyen Hue, Dist. 1. Tel: 822 2999. Rooms start at US$180 at this luxurious new downtown hotel.

Windsor Hotel, 193 Tran Hung Dao, Dist. 1. Tel: 836 7848. Fax: 836 7889. Large rooms catering to business people on long stays. Restaurant and bakery are among the best in Ho Chi Minh City. A studio room starts at US$85.

VUNG TAU

Royal Hotel (formerly Canadian Hotel), 48 Quang Trung St. Tel: 859852. Fax: (84-64) 859851. Modern hotel with rooms from US$46 to 120.

Grand Hotel, 26 Quang Trung Street. Tel: 856469. Fax: (84-64) 856088. Rooms from US$18 to 48.

Palace Hotel (formerly Hoa Binh Hotel), 11 Nguyen Trai. Tel: 856265, 856411. Fax: (84-64) 856878. 145 rooms, 82 air-conditioned rooms, from US$30, suites US$60. Superb restaurant specializing in seafood.

Nha Nghi 72, Back Beach. Rooms with fan are US$8.

Phuong Dong Hotel, 2 Thuy Van. Tel: 852593. Rooms with air-con from US$30.

Rex Hotel, 1 Duy Tan Street. Tel: 852135. Fax: 859862. Air-con rooms start at US$35.

Sea Breeze Hotel, 11 Nguyen Trai Street. Tel: 856392. Fax: 856856 A comfortable modern hotel with rooms starting at US$40.

Hai Yen Hotel (formerly The International Hotel), 8 Le Loi Street. Tel: 852571. Fax: 852858. 25 rooms from US$20 to 30.

Pacific Hotel, 4 Le Loi Street. Tel: 856740. Fax: 852391. Famous for its Czech restaurant. Rooms from US$25 to 33.

Vietnamese Youth Tourist Centre, 46A Thuy Van. Bungalows start from US$10.

BIEN HOA

Dong Nai Hotel, 57 Highway 15. Tel: 2267.

Vinh An Hotel, 107 Highway 1. Tel: 2377.

The Delta

CAN THO

Quoc Te Hotel (The International), 12 Hai Ba Trung. Tel: 22079. 41 large, air-conditioned, modern and comfortable rooms, US$15–20 for a single and US$25 for doubles with TV and fridge. 3 restaurants, souvenir shop, beauty parlor, dancing, laundry, video room. Located on the Ninh Kieu Pier beside the Hau River.

Hau Giang Hotel, 34 Nam Ky Khoi Nghia. Tel: 35537, 25181, 21851. Doubles US$17–22 and singles US$13–20. A very friendly hotel, excellent food, souvenir shop, dancing, laundry, video room.

Hao Hoa Hotel, 6 Lu Gia Street. Tel: 35407.

Hoang Cung Hotel, 55 Phan Dinh Phung Street. Tel: 35401, 25831. Singles/doubles with air-conditioned and private bath for US$5–7.

Huy Hoang Hotel, 35 Ngo Duc Ke Street. Tel: 35403.

Thuy Thien Hotel, 6 Tran Phu Street. Tel: 35412.

Phuoc Thanh Hotel, 5 Phan Dang Luu Street. Tel: 35406.

MYTHO

Rach Gam Hotel, 33 Trung Trac Street.

Ap Bach Hotel, Tel: 72593.

Lac Hong Hotel, Thang 4 Street. Tel: 72918.

Khach San 43, 43 Ngo Quyen Street. Tel: 72120. Rooms with fan from US$5.

Tien Giang Province Guest House. On the corner of Hung Vuong Boulevard and Rach Gam Street.

RACH GIA

1/5 (First of May) Hotel, 38 Nguyen Hung Son St. Tel: 63414. 18 air-conditioned rooms – when the electrics are working. The plumbing is also very temperamental. Very basic and over-priced accommodation at US$26 for doubles and US$20 for singles. 15 other rooms are even more basic, but so is the price, US$15 for doubles and US$12 for singles. The food however is good.

To Chau Hotel, 4F Le Loi Street (next to cinema), Thi Xa. Tel: 63718. 31 rooms, the first class rooms have air conditioning for US$20.

Binh Minh Hotel. 48 Pham Hong Thai Street. Tel: 63016, 62154. Rooms with fan from US$8.

Thanh Binh Hotel, 11 Ly Truong Street. Tel: 632267, 63053. 9 rooms with fan and bath cost US$6–8.

Nha Kach Uy Ban, 31 Nguyen Hung Son Street. Tel: 63237. Singles with shared bath from US$3.

LONG XUYEN

Thai Binh Hotel, 12 Nguyen Hue, Thi Xa. Tel: 52184. 32 rooms with fans, doubles $6 and air-conditioned rooms US$8. Good restaurant and dance hall.

Long Xuyen Hotel, 17 Nguyen Van Cung Street, Thi Xa. Tel: 52927, 52308. Special rooms have adjoining sitting rooms. Showers and electrics are a bit off and on but the restaurant is excellent. Air-conditioned rooms begin at US$10–12.

Cuu Long Hotel, 35 Long Van Cu, Thi Xa. Tel: 52365, 52865. Rooms are US$8 for a single and US$10 for a double.

CHAU DOC

Chau Doc Hotel, 17 Doc Phu Thu, Thi Xa. Tel: 66484. 30 rooms, double room with fan cost US$6 and air-conditioned cost US$10.

Hang Chau Hotel, Gia Long Street, by the river front. Tel: 66196, 66197. Air-conditioned rooms from US$20.

VINH LONG

Cuu Long Hotel, Duong 1 Thanh 5. Tel: 2494. 20 air-conditioned rooms, restaurants, bar, laundry, souvenir shop and video.

BEN TRE

Dong Khoi Hotel, 16 Hai Ba Trung. Tel: 2240.

HA TIEN

Ha Tien Hotel. On the corner of Ben Tran Hau and Phuong Thanh streets.
Khach San Du Lich, Mac Tien Tich. Tel: 58644. Rooms cost US$10.
To Chau Hotel, To Chau St. US$2 for rooms with shared bath.
Dong Ho Hotel, On the corner of Ben Tran Hau and To Chau Streets. Tel: 52141. Rooms cost US$5.

Central Vietnam

HUE

Century Riverside, 49 Le Loi Street. Tel: 823390. Fax: 823394. Recently remodeled, the Century commands a stunning view of the Perfume River. Breakfast in the restaurant is excellent. Rooms start at US$60.
Huong Giang Hotel (Perfume River), 51 Le Loi Street. Tel: 822122. Fax: 823102. 42 air-conditioned rooms with fridge and telephone, from US$50–230 plus 10 percent service. Terrace restaurant, souvenir shop, post office, telex, Vietnamese massage, tennis, ping pong, billiards, dancing (Saturday evenings), small private jetty, boat trips.
Thuan Hoa Hotel. 7 Nguyen Tri Phuong. Tel: 822553, 822576. Fax: 822470. 78 rooms – 44 air-conditioned, with fridge and telephone. From US$25–75. Restaurant, terrace cafe, small boutique.
Hotel Saigon Morin, 30 Le Loi Street. Tel: 823526. Fax: 825155. Recently totally refurbished. Spacious rooms with high ceilings and hot water start at US$60. The courtyard restaurant is also good.
Dong Phuong Hotel (formerly Nua Thu Hotel), 26 Nguyen Tri Phuong. Tel: 823929. Excellent restaurant. From US$8–US$30.
Thanh Noi Hotel, 3 Dang Dung Street. Tel: 822478. Fax: 827211. Beautifully situated near The Citadel. Rooms from US$15.
San Thuong Tu Hotel, 1 Dinh Tien Hoang Street.
Hang Be Hotel, 173 Huynh Thuc Khang Street. Tel: 823752. Ground floor restaurant.
Thuong Tu Hotel, 5 Dinh Tien Hoang.
Tan My Hotel, Thuan An Beach. Tel: 866033. Souvenir shop, laundry.

Three small villas on Ly Thuong Kiet Street provide some of the most pleasant accommodation in Hue:
Nha Kach, 11 Ly Thuong Kiet Street. US$16–US$20; 16 Ly Thuong Kiet Street. Tel: 823679; and at number 18, Tel: 823889. US$16–20. A grand villa at 5 Le Loi Street, built beside the river, was formerly the residence of the governor of Central Vietnam.

DA NANG

Phuong Dong (the Oriental), 93 Phan Chu Trinh. Tel: 821266, 822854. 36 air-conditioned rooms from US$40–68 plus 10 percent service. Restaurant, bar, telex and IDD services, souvenir and craft shop, laundry.
Da Nang Hotel, 3 Dong Da Street. Tel: 821986. A great value with rooms starting at US$25. Has the fastest laundry facilities in Vietnam.
Marble Mountain Hotel, 5 Dong Da Street. Rooms start from US$25.
Non Nuoc Hotel, 10 Ly Thuong Kiet, Hua Nghi. Tel: 821470, 822137. Air-conditioned rooms from US$20–30. 14 km (9 miles) from Da Nang at the foot of the Marble Mountains, situated on a lovely beach. Advance booking is necessary due to its popularity. Restaurant and bar on the beach.
The Hai Au Hotel, 177 Tran Phu Street. Tel: 822722. Fax; 824165. A modern hotel with air-con rooms starting from US$35.
The Bach Dang Hotel, 50 Bach Dang Street. Tel: 823649. Fax: 821659. Located on the river. Rooms from US$28.

QUI NHON

Dong Phuong Hotel, 39 Mai Xuan Thuong Street. Single rooms from US$8. Probably the most reasonable rates in town.

NHA TRANG

Hai Yen Hotel, 40 Tran Phu. Tel: 22828, 22974. 104 air-conditioned rooms, from US$20–33. Restaurant, bar, disco, souvenir shop, laundry, barber shop. Opposite the beach. Single/double rooms with fan US$7–US$10 per night, air-conditioned rooms are US$15–20 to US$30–40.
Thong Nhat Hotel. 18 Tran Phu Blvd. Than Pho. Tel: 22966. Opposite the beach. 70 rooms from US$7–25.
Thang Loi Hotel, 4 rue Pasteur, Thanh Pho. Tel: 22226, 22241. 70 rooms

from US$5–35. Restaurant, souvenir shop, money changing, laundry.
Bao Dai's Villa. 6 km south of Nha Trang. Tel: 22449, 21124. US$27–35 for a night in spacious room with a view of the sea.

PHAN THIET

Vinh Thuy Hotel, Duong Nguyen Tat Thanh, Thi Xa. Tel: 21294, 22394. 66 rooms, the most expensive hotel, double rooms with air-conditioning cost US$27–34. Very good restaurant and swimming beach.
Phan Thiet Tourist Hotel, 40 Tran Hung Dao, Thi Xa. Tel: 22573. Air-conditioned rooms from US$15.

PHAN RANG

Huu Nghi Hotel, 354 Thong Nhat Street.
Thong Nhat Hotel, 164 Thong Nhat Street, Rooms start at US$8.

DA LAT

Hotel Sofitel, Da Lat Palace, 12 Tran Phu Street. Tel: 25444. Recently renovated, the Sofitel Palace is probably the most sumptuous hotel in all of Vietnam. Originally built in 1922, the renovated hotel maintains a grand colonial style with modern services. The French cuisine in the restaurant is excellent. Most of the rooms are equipped with working fireplaces. The hotel is usually full on weekends, so book early or plan on a weekday stay. Rooms start at US$120. During the slow season, rates are negotiable.
Da Lat Hotel, 7 Tran Phu Street. Tel: 2263. There are 67 rooms from US$20–30.
Minh Tam Hotel, 20A Khe Sanh. Tel: 2447. Villa and rooms from US$25–40. 3 km from the center of the city.
Haison Hotel, 1 Nguyen Thi Minh Khai Street. Very popular with Vietnamese tourists. Rooms are US$10–40.
Hotel Anh Dao, 52-54 Hoa Binh Square. Tel: 2384. Comfortable rooms for US$20–40 including breakfast. Overlooks the market.
Mimosa Hotel, 170 Phan Dinh Phung Street. Tel: 2656. A friendly and affordable hotel. Rooms start at US$5.
Ngoc Lan Hotel, 54 Nguyen Tri Phuong. Tel: 2136. Rooms from US$5–18.
Thanh Binh Hotel. Tel: 2394. Opposite central market. Single rooms start at US$8.

Phu Hoa Hotel. 16 Tang Bat Ho Street. Rooms from US$5–10.

Alternative accommodation can be had in one of Da Lat's many villas which are rented out through Lam Dong Tourism. You can also stay in the Former Governor General's residence or Bao Dai's Summer Palace. It is possible to camp at many public locations in Da Lat, but if you plan on doing so keep in mind that Da Lat can be very chilly in the winter.

The Central Highlands

The Central Highlands have only been open to tourists on a large scale since 1993, so there is limited available accommodation. There are government hotels in Pleiku and Kontum, but they are not very receptive to foreigners and are known to charge outrageous rates for tourists.

BUON ME THUOT

Thang Loi Hotel, 1 Phan Chu Trinh. Tel: 2322. This is the best hotel in town. Rooms start at US$12.
Hong Kong Hotel, 30 Hai Ba Trung. Rooms from US$5.
Hoang Gia Hotel, 2 Le Hong Phong.

The North

HANOI

Hanoi has a short supply of hotel rooms, so it is critical to make bookings for major hotels in advance.
Bodega Cafe & Guesthouse, 57 Trang Tien Street. Tel: 826 7784. This place is always full, but if you can get a room they are a good value at US$15 to 30.
Dan Chu Hotel, 29 Trang Tien Street, Tel: 84-8 825 3323. Fax: 826 6786. It looks a little depressing from the street, but the rooms are quite nice. Rooms from US$65 to 129.
Especen, 79-E Hang Trong. Tel: 826 6856. Fax: 826 9612. 66 rooms at 10 small inns in the Ancient Quarter. US$10–25, double room for two people. Spare, but clean rooms, with private baths.
Flower Hotel, 97 Nguyen Truong To. Tel: 823 7025. US$60, double room for two people. A bit out of the way, the rooms are decorated with rosewood Oriental furniture and are quiet. There are several other mini-hotels located nearby.
Green Bamboo, 42 Nha Chung. Tel: 826 8752. Fax: 826 4949. 7 rooms.

$15, double room for two people. Quiet rooms in the back of a restaurant and tourist company office. A bit on the rugged side, this inn is designed for backpackers.
Hanoi Horison Hotel, 40 Cat Linh Street. Tel: 733 0808. Fax: 733 0888. Brand new 5 star hotel. Rooms from US$190 to 400.
Hoa Binh Hotel, 27 Ly Thuong Street. Tel: 825 3515. Fax: 826 9818. Old, French-style hotel with 102 rooms. From US$20 to 184.
Hotel Sofitel Metropole, 15 Ngo Quyen Street. Tel: 84-4 826 6919. Fax: 84-4 826 6920. The Metropole, or Thong Nhat as it was known before, was renovated in 1992. The Metropole is the center of international business in Hanoi, and its guests are primarily American, French and Asian business people. Rooms start at US$229. Reservations are essential.
New World Hotel, 21 Chau Long. Tel/Fax 829 2815. Situated to the north of the city, near the Truc Bach and West lakes. Rooms from US$15 to 30.
Royal, 20 Hang Tre. Tel: 824 4233. Fax: 824 4234. US$152, double room for two people. A popular disco downstairs; visitors say they aren't bothered by loud music. The rooms are reminiscent of Holiday Inns.
Thuy Tien, 1-C Tong Dan. Tel: 824 4775. Fax: 824 4784. US$80, double room for two people. Newly built with modern facilities on a street nicely located near the center of town and near the Ancient Quarter.

There are several mini-hotels, newly built with TVs and air conditioning, located south of the center of town near Lenin Park, along Bui Thi Xuan, Trieu Viet Vuong, Mai Hac De, Hoa Ma and Nguyen Binh Khiem Streets.

The Ancient Quarter is also filled with many small but adequate mini-hotels. The atmosphere is charming, but with the charm comes some noise.

HAI PHONG

Hong Bang Hotel, 64 Dien Bien Phu Street. Tel: 842229. Fax: 841044. Deluxe double rooms for US$40.
Bach Dang Hotel, 42 Dien Bien Phu Street. Tel: 842444. Rooms are available here from US$18.
The Hoa Binh Hotel. 104 Luong Khanh Thien Street. Tel: 846907. Near railway station. Rooms from US$8.

Duyen Hai Hotel, 5 Nguyen Tri Phuong Street. Tel: 842157. Fax: 841140. Rooms range from US$23 for a single to 35 for a double.
Cat Bi Hotel, 30 Tran Phu Street. Tel: 846837. Rooms are available from US$20 to 40.

HA LONG BAY

Ha Long Hotel, Ha Long Road. Tel: 846320. Fax: 846318. Rooms are available for US$80–160 in this charming colonial hotel.
Son Long Hotel. Bai Chay Street. Tel: 846274. Rooms from US$15 to 30.
Vuon Dao Hotel. Ha Long Road. Bai Chay Beach. Tel: 846455. Fax: 846287. Rooms from US$35 to 70.

THANH HOA

Khach San Thanh Hoa. Located on Highway 1 in the center of town. Rooms from US$5.

SAM SON

There are numerous government hotels along the beach. Expect to pay at least US$10 for a comfortable room. In the summer it can be impossible to find space.

VINH

The Hotel Huu Nghi. Le Loi Street. Rooms are available from US$15.

DONG HOI

The Hoa Binh Hotel. Rooms run between US$15 and US$25.

DONG HA

Nha Khach Dong Ha. Tran Phu Street. Comfortable rooms are US$15.

Eating Out

General

Vietnamese cuisine offers the visitor a wide variety of fine dishes, delicately flavoured with fresh herbs, spices and *nuoc mam* (fish sauce), usually accompanied by *nuoc cham*, a condiment sauce of *nuoc mam*, lime juice, a little grated carrot, chilli, garlic and sugar. Steamed rice (*com*) and soup are eaten at every meal. Different regional specialities lend even more variety to this varied menu. Due to the highly inflated price of meat, seafood and river fish play an important part in the Vietnamese menu, particularly in the South. Pork, chicken, beef, duck and pigeon feature widely on the menu, plus a wide variety of vegetables and tropical fruit. A leftover from the colonial era, French bread is available throughout the country. Sandwiches made with these baguettes, local paté and salad make an excellent snack.

Most localities have their particular noodle soups, which vary in the noodles and meat used and the use of spices and herbs. The most celebrated dish in the North is *pho*, a delicious soup of rice noodles, beef stock, ginger, to which beef, bean sprouts, fresh coriander, basil and mint are added at the very last. In the South an excellent soup, *ho tieu* is enjoyed, this is often made with prawns or crabmeat and pork. Another very popular soup is *bun bo*. Rich and spicy it is eaten with mint, bean sprouts and a twist of lime. The people from Hue make their own special version of this. One of the favorite soups is *canh chua*, made with fish, pineapple, star fruit, okra, and fresh herbs. The famous national dish, *cha gio* is made from crab and pork, mushrooms, prawns, rice vermicelli and bean sprouts, rolled in a thin rice pancake then deep-fried.

These delicious crisp rolls are eaten wrapped in a lettuce leaf with fresh herbs and dipped in an accompanying sauce. *Go cuon*, another national favorite, is made without pork and eaten raw. Look out for *chao tom*, a dish of fried minced crab and pork on sugarcane, served with vermicelli, vegetables and coriander leaves. Another celebrated dish is *cha ca*, fish marinated with *nuoc mam* and saffron then barbecue grilled and served with rice vermicelli, herbs, grilled peanuts and a special sauce. One of Hanoi's oldest streets is named after this delicious speciality. For the more adventurous some speciality restaurants serve turtle, snake, eel, bat and wild game. The fresh seafood particularly lobsters, flower crabs and oysters are excellent. Numerous restaurants specialise in French and Chinese food. An endless variety of Vietnamese dishes await you, ask the locals for recommendations and they will be very happy to initiate you.

Where to Eat

Hanoi and Ho Chi Minh City's large hotel restaurants offer both Vietnamese specialities and Western dishes, particularly French, but be sure to check on the hours and book in advance if you're not a guest. Wherever you are in the country, don't hesitate to frequent the small local eating places serving a variety of Vietnamese dishes at any hour; you will be in for some delicious surprises.

HO CHI MINH CITY

The Rex Hotel Restaurant. The roof top restaurant at the Rex is an international community favorite where you can dine gazing at the Saigon skyline surrounded by tropical bird cages and festive outdoor lighting. The extensive Vietnamese and Chinese menu is supplemented by an equally impressive European menu that includes the best steaks in Vietnam.

Restaurant 99 Pasteur, 99 Pasteur Street. This restaurant serves delicious egg crepes stuffed with shrimp and vegetables. The other house speciality is marinated beef that you grill at your own table. Don't be put off by the fact that the restaurant is in a bus garage – it is probably the best family restaurant in Saigon.

Maxims, 13-17 Dong Khoi Street. Tel: 829 6676. What the food lacks in creativity is more than made up for by Maxim's wild floorshows. Transvestite fan dancers, sword swallowers and a circa 1971 lounge band create a memorable evening.

Givral, 169 Dong Khoi Street. Tel: 824 2750. Givral is an institution in Saigon. The food is reasonably priced Western and Vietnamese fare and it is a great place to have a slow breakfast while watching passerby.

Cafe Phap (Le Bistro). At the corner of Hai Ba Trung Street and Le Thanh Ton Street. For Francophiles and the French community. Cafe Phap offers an inexpensive French country menu featuring flown-in cheese and wine.

Q Bar, City Concert Hall, 7 Lam Son Square. Tel: 829 1299. An intimate bar with surreal decor and music that will make you forget where you are. The Q Bar also boasts the largest selection of alcohol in Southeast Asia and the best guacamole in the Eastern Hemisphere.

Chez Guido Ristorante. Continental Hotel. Tel: 829 9201. Moderately priced Italian dishes and pizza.

Floating Restaurants. At the end of Dong Khoi on the Saigon River. Every evening the boats pick up passengers for a slow two-hour dinner cruise on the Saigon River.

HANOI

There are not that many sit down restaurants in Hanoi, but just about every large hotel has a restaurant where a large variety of Vietnamese and Chinese dishes are served. Hanoi is famous for its delicious *pho*, a thin noodle soup served with mint, lime and bean sprouts.

Le Beaulieu, Sofitel Metropole, 15 Ngo Quyen. Tel: 826 6919. Hanoi's only international class restaurant, but the Vietnamese and European menu is quite unimaginative. Every morning there is a large breakfast buffet featuring freshly baked goods.

Restaurant 202, 202 Pho Hue. A French and Vietnamese menu is served here and the prices are very reasonable.

The Cha Ca La Vong, 14 Cha Ca Street. Tel: 825 3929. The speciality here is fried freshwater fish. The restaurant is very popular with Vietnamese officials and their foreign guests.

Lotus Restaurant. At the intersection of Trang Tien and Ngo Quyen Street. The menu is Vietnamese and Chinese with some Western dishes. The restaurant is on the fourth floor of an art gallery that is well worth a look.

Piano Restaurant. 50 Hang Vai Street. Tel: 823 2423. Vietnamese menu with live music on most nights.

Al Fresco's, 23L Hai Ba Trung. Tel: 826 7782. A variety of steaks, pizzas, pastas and fresh salads.

Seasons of Hanoi, 95B Quan Thanh. Tel: 843 5444. Classic Vietnamese cuisine in a beautiful French-style villa.

HUE

Hoa Mai and Royal Restaurant, Huong Giang Hotel, 51 Le Loi Street. Menu includes sea food, Vietnamese and Western dishes and Hue specialties.

Song Huong Floating Restaurant, 3-2 Le Loi. Tel: 826655. Situated on the Perfume River between the Huong Giang Hotel and the old Clemenceau Bridge.

Lac Thanh Restaurant. Dien Tien Hoang Street. This small restaurant is well known for its *banh khoai,* crepes stuffed with pork, shrimp and sprouts topped with a spicy peanut sauce. For dessert have fresh coffee with a delicious creme caramel.

Lac Thien Restaurant. Dien Tien Hoang Street. Certainly some of the best food in Hue. Try the dried noodles with beef. A lively atmosphere.

Attractions

Museums

Please note that many museums charge extra to bring in a camera or video camera.

HANOI

History Museum (Vien Bao Tang Lich Su), 1 Pham Ngu Lao. Tel: 825 3518. Open Tuesday–Sunday, 8–11.45am and 1.15–4.45pm. Admission: about US$1. Exhibits displayed here cover every era of Vietnam's fascinating and complex history. It houses an excellent archaeological collection dating from the Paleolithic and Neolithic eras, in-

cluding relics from the era of the Hung kings, Neolithic graves, bronze age implements, the beautiful bronze drums of Ngoc Lu and Mieu Mon, Cham relics, stelae, statues, ceramics and an eerie sculpture of the goddess Quan Am with her one thousand eyes and arms. One room features an ornate throne, clothes and artifacts belonging to the thirteen kings of the Nguyen Dynasty.

Army Museum (Vien Bao Tang Quan Doi), 28-A Dien Bien Phu. Tel: 823 4264. Open daily, 8–11.30am and 1.30–4.30pm. Admission: about US$1. From the crumpled metal of a B-52 shot down over Hanoi to a pistol belonging to former South Vietnamese President Nguyen Van Thieu, the Army museum displays a range of war souvenirs from Vietnam's battles against the French and Americans. A grainy black-and-white film shows the final days of the Communist North's assault on South Vietnam in 1975.

Ho Chi Minh Museum (Vien Bao Tang Ho Chi Minh), 3 Ngoc Ha Street. Tel: 846 3746. Open Tuesday–Sunday, 8.30–11.30am and 1.30–4.30pm. Admission is free. Set in a modern concrete structure, the museum tells the story of Ho Chi Minh's rise from a worldwide traveler to revolutionary to leader of modern Vietnam.

Fine Arts Museum (Vien Bao Tang My Thuat), 66 Nguyen Thai Hoc. Open Tuesday–Sunday, 8–11am and 1–4pm. Admission: about US$1.

Revolutionary Museum (Vien Bao Tang Cach Mang), 25 Tong Dan. Tel: 825 4151. Open daily, 8–11.30am and 1.30–4.30pm. Admission: about 50 cents (US). The museum documents the struggles of the Vietnamese people from 2,000 years ago until 1975. Among the exhibits are some of the long wooden stakes used to cripple the Mongol fleet during the battle of Bach Dang in Ha Long Bay and an enormous bronze war drum dating from 2,400BC.

Temple of Literature (Van Mieu), Quoc Tu Giam Street, between Van Mieu and Ton Duc Thang Streets. Tel: 845 2917. Open daily, 7.30am–5.30pm. Admission: about US$1. Tablets engraved with the names of scholars from Vietnam's Confucian era are the highlight of this temple in a pleasant, outdoor park setting. Musicians perform hourly in a recently renovated area.

Ho Chi Minh Mausoleum (Lang Chu Tich Ho Chi Minh), Ba Dinh Square, near Hung Vuong Street. Tel: 845 5124. Open daily except Monday and Friday, 8.30–11.30am. Closed from September to December. Admission is free.

Geology Museum (Vien Bao Tang Dia Chat), 6 Pham Ngu Lao. Tel: 826 6802.

HO CHI MINH CITY

Reunification Palace (Hoi Truong Thong Nhat), Nam Ky Khoi Nghia Street at Le Duan; the entrance for visitors is at 106 Nguyen Du. Tel: 829 0629. Open daily, 8–10am and 1–5pm. Admission: about US$5. Here you can visit the official residence of the former president of what was South Vietnam. Sit in a chair with huge elephant tusks where President Thieu greeted visitors. Stand on the rooftop helipad. Visit the underground bunkers with its war planning rooms and a small theater where archival films are shown. See the former president's dining room.

War Remnants Museum (Bao Tang Chung Tich Chien Tranh), 28 Vo Van Tan. Tel: 829 0325. Open daily, 7.30–11.45am and 1.30–4.45pm. Admission: 7,000 Vietnamese dong (less than US$1). A museum of propaganda presenting a somber look at the effects of the Vietnam War. Visitors cannot help but leave feeling unsettled and depressed. Photos (and more) of victims of Agent Orange, the chemical defoliant used by the US, a guillotine used by French colonialists, tiger cages from the prison island of Con Dau: it's all graphically displayed.

Fine Arts Museum (Bao Tang My Thuat), 97-A Duc Chinh St, Dist. 1. Tel: 821 0001. Open Tuesday–Saturday, 8–11.30am and 2–4.30pm. Admission is free. Revolutionary-era paintings, lacquer and sculpture as well as ancient Cham, Khmer and Thai artifacts.

Revolutionary Museum (Bao Tang Cach Mang), 65 Ly Tu Trong. Tel: 829 9741. Open daily except Monday, 7.30–11.30am and 1.30–4.30pm. Admission: about US$1. Photographs, maps and souvenirs from the French and American wars, housed in the former Gia Long Palace.

History Museum (Bao Tang Lich Su). Located just inside the entrance gate to the zoo, Nguyen Binh Khiem Street. Tel: 829 8146. Open daily, 8–11.30am and 1.30–4.30pm. Admission: about US$1.

Military Museum (officially called the Museum of Ho Chi Minh's Campaign, Bao Tang Chien Dich Ho Chi Minh), 2-T Le Duan. Tel: 822 4824. Open daily, 8–10.30am and 1–4pm. Admission: about US$1.

Ho Chi Minh Museum. Across the Khanh Hoi bridge at 1 Nguyen Tat Thanh St, Dist. 4. Tel: 829 1060. Open daily except Monday and Friday mornings, 7.30–11.30am and 1.30–4.30pm. Admission: 8,000 Vietnamese dong (less than US$1). Called the Dragon House, this was used as a customs house and is where Ho Chi Minh allegedly stayed before he departed from Vietnam to embark on his global travels. His life as it relates to Vietnam's long struggle for independence is described here with photographs and maps. From outside the museum there is a good view of Ho Chi Minh City's vibrant downtown and of the Saigon River.

HUE

Imperial Museum (Vien Bao Tang Hue), 11 Le Loi St. Tel: 822489. Open daily except Sunday, 7.30–11.30am and 2–4.30pm. Admission: about US$1.

Military Museum (Vien Bao Tang Quan Su), 6 Le Loi St. Tel: 822152. Open daily except Sunday, 7.30–11.30am and 2–4.30pm. Admission: US$1.

DA NANG

Cham Museum (Vien Vo Cham, or Bao Tang Dieu Khac Cham), 2 Tieu La. Tel: 821951. Open daily, 7am–5.30pm. Admission: about US$2.

Cu Chi Tunnels

Some foreigners call the tunnels Cong World, a theme park built in and around the tunnels that helped the communists win the war.

As much as Vietnam says it wants to forget about the war, it is at the same time busily sprucing up war battlefields.

About 75 km (45 mi) northwest of Ho Chi Minh City, the Cu Chi Tunnels provide vivid testament to the tenacity and ingenuity that helped Vietnam win the war against a superpower like the United States. Communist soldiers fighting French colonialists originally dug the first of the tunnels in the 1940s. The system was expanded in the early 1960s; eventually, the tunnels with their many tributaries ran for over 240 km (150 mi). Built on three levels, soldiers and sometimes villagers lived in the tunnels. There are cooking rooms, ventilated through small holes and tunnels that masked the source of the smoke. There were booby traps, such as floors that gave way causing intruders to fall into a pit with sharpened bamboo stakes. There were escape routes, including tunnels that ended at a river, where guerrillas would swim to safety.

The subterranean garrison gave the communists a toehold within 20 miles of Saigon. Some of the tunnels even ran underneath the headquarters of the US Army's 25th Division.

Today, only some of the tunnels are open to visitors. They have been enlarged – eight inches higher and eight inches wider – to accommodate taller and bulkier frames of western tourists. Small lights have been strung along the floor to help visitors find their way, but guides will switch them off to give a sense of what the darkened existence was like for soldiers. Visitors can even eat a staple of the Cu Chi Tunnel diet, tapioca.

Some guides working at Cu Chi are veterans of the war who lived in the tunnels. The bombing of the area, they say, was constant, and by the late 1960s, US carpet-bombing had finally destroyed much of the network.

But the effectiveness of the tunnels – allowing VC guerrillas to virtually appear out of nowhere – is evident.

Strangely, the sound of gunfire still fills the air at Cu Chi. Tourists can fire AK-47s or M-16s, at $1 a clip, at a shooting range with paper targets of tigers and crocodiles. At the Wartime Souvenir Shop, some odd trinkets are for sale: toy tanks made out of bullet casings, GI dog tags (probably fake) and green pith helmets.

Just outside the grounds, the government is building a mammoth pagoda to honor war victims, as another draw for tourists.

Festivals

Festivities last three days (officially), preceded, particularly in Ho Chi Minh City and Hanoi by a week-long flower market.

Traditional & Religious Festivals

Many traditional and religious festivals take place in Vietnam, particularly in the North in and around Hanoi during Tet. Dates, unless otherwise stated, fall in the first lunar month.

Dong Ky Festival, a firecracker competition festival, held on the 15th in Dong Ky village, Tien Son District. One of the largest and most spectacular festivals.

Mai Dong Festival, which takes place from the 4th to 6th at the Mai Dong Temple in Hai Ba Trung District, Hanoi, is held in honor of Le Cham, the Trung Sisters' brave female general who fought against the Chinese in the first century.

Dong Da Festival, held on the 5th, in Hanoi's Dong Da District, commemorates King Trung Quang's victory at Dong Da and those who died in this battle against the Tsing in 1789.

An Duong Vuong Festival, occurs between the 6th and 16th, in the temple of the same name in Co Loa village near Hanoi. Held in memory of King Thuc An Duong Vuong, one of the founders of ancient Vietnam who built the Co Loa Citadel.

Le Phung Hieu Festival, on the 7th, at the temple of the same name in Hoang Hoa district, Thanh Hoa Province.

Lim Festival, held on the 13th in the Lim village pagoda, Ha Bac Province. Features singing and a wide range of cultural and artistic activities.

Ha Loi Festival, on the 15th at Ha Loi Temple in the Me Linh suburb of Hanoi. Commemorates the Trung Sisters.

Den Va Temple Festival, dedicated to

Tan Vien, God of the Mountain, held in the Bat Bat suburb of Hanoi on the 15th.

Ram Thang Gieng, the most important Buddhist festival, takes place on the 15th.

Van Village Festival, celebrated in Hanoi's Viet Yen District from the 17th to the 20th.

Khu Lac and Di Nau Festival, occurs on the 7th and 26th in Tam Thanh District, Vinh Phu Province.

Lac Long Quan Festival, from the 1st to 6th days of the third lunar month, at Binh Minh village, Ha Tay Province. Dedicated to Lac Long Quan, the quasi-legendary ancestor of the Vietnamese people. Features traditional music, elders dressed in traditional silk robes, fireworks displays and a stunning display of young ladies carrying altars laden with fruit and flowers through Binh Minh's narrow streets.

Huong Tich Festival, held throughout the Spring in the spectacular Huong Son mountains West of Hanoi in Ha Tay Province, can be visited at the same time as Lac Long Quan Festival.

The Buffalo Immolation Festival, held during Spring in the Tay Nguyen Highlands.

Thay Pagoda Festival, held on the 7th day of the 3rd lunar month in Quoc Hai, Ha Tay Province, is dedicated to To Dao Hanh, a revered Buddhist monk and teacher. An excellent opportunity to see the traditional water puppet theater in an historical and idyllic setting. Also features rowing contests and mountain climbing.

12th March, the Den Festival takes place at the site of the ancient capital of Hoa Lu in Ha Nam Ninh Province. It commemorates King Dinh Bo Linh and General Le who fought against the Sung invaders.

16th March, De Tham Festival in Hanoi's Yen The district.

8th April, the Dau Pagoda festival in Thuan Thanh.

Easter, celebrated more in the South.

12th April, the anniversary of Vietnam's first King, Hung Vuong.

15th May, Buddha's birth, enlightenment and death, celebrated in pagodas, temples and private homes throughout the country.

July/August, on the first day of the 7th lunar month offerings of food and gifts are made in homes and temples for the wandering souls of the dead.

September/October, the Mid-Autumn Festival on the day of the full moon in the 8th lunar month. Celebrated with sticky rice mooncakes filled with lotus seeds, salted duck egg yolks, peanuts and melon seeds. Brightly colored lanterns depicting all manner of things – dragons, boats, butterflies – are carried by children in evening processions.

The Kiep Bac Temple Festival, held in Hai Hung Province on the 20th day of the 8th lunar month commemorates the national hero Tran Hung Dao who wiped out the invading Mongol forces in the 13th century.

25th December, Christmas.

Shopping

What to Buy

Traditional Vietnamese handicrafts offer a wide variety of wares to choose from. These include lacquerware, mother-of-pearl inlay, ceramics, pottery, precious wood, tortoise shell, embroidery, silk paintings, bamboo and wickerware, baskets, wool carpets, sculpture, wood, marble and bone carvings, jewelry, jade, engraving, silk and brocade. You may like to add a *non la*, the famous Vietnamese conical hat and an *ao dai*, the traditional costume worn by the Vietnamese fairer sex, to your wardrobe. Green pith helmets, worn by soldiers during the war and by cyclo drivers and laborers today, are sold, as well as the old-fashioned "Uncle Ho" sandals made from used tire treads. In Ho Chi Minh City, a popular item are helicopters, airplanes and cyclos made out of Coca-Cola and Tiger beer cans.

Heavy taxation has discouraged the sale of antiquities, which has become almost clandestine and very limited in the North and strictly controlled in the South. Only after enquiring of the proprietor will you discover all that may be available, as the best pieces are never displayed. Antique shops in the center of Ho Chi Minh City and the old town of Hanoi sell Vietnamese wood or Laotian bronze Buddhas, old porcelain, objects in silver and ivory, small jade statuettes and objects used by the various cults. Prices are in US dollars and subject to bargaining. However, bear in mind that it is forbidden to export certain objects and in principle clearance must be obtained before you take antiquities out of the country.

Russian vodka, caviar and even French champagne may be found at very reasonable prices.

Clothing is comparatively cheap and local tailors can very quickly produce well made garments to the design of your choice.

Where to Buy
HO CHI MINH CITY

Cultrimex (state run), 94 Dong Khoi. Tel: 829 2574, 829 2896. Handicrafts, paintings, lacquer work, reproductions of antiquities. Closed Sundays.

Artexport (state run), 159 Dong Khoi. Objets d'art and antiquities.

Hoang Oanh, 45 Dong Khoi. Antiquities and objets d'art.

"47" 47 Dong Khoi. Antiquities and objets d'art.

Sodasy, 115 Le Than Ton. Tel: 829 7752. Produces Natural shell and ivory articles.

Cuu Long, 177 Dong Khoi. Ao dai and fabrics.

Lac Long, 143 Le Than Ton. Leather and skin goods.

Fahasa Bookshop, 1st Floor, 40 Nguyen Hue. Tel: 822 5796. Books in English, French, Vietnamese and Russian.

Ben Thanh Market, at the intersection of Ham Nghi, Le Loi, Tran Hung Dao and Le Thanh Ton Streets, is the city's central market, where fruits, vegetables, rice and meats are sold, as well as electronics, clothes, household goods, and flowers. There are also some small food stalls selling soup and rice dishes.

Le Thanh Ton Street. Several shops sell embroidery and silk clothes in Western styles. A shop across from the Norfolk Hotel sells modern glass, ceramics, linens and wood items, all made in Vietnam. Near the New World Hotel a shop sells glass, ethnic fabrics and ceramics of good quality.

Dong Khoi Street. Ho Chi Minh City's fashionable address, with swank shops selling perfume, cosmetics, watches, jewelry and clothes.

Le Cong Kieu. Near the Fine Arts Museum, shops here sell antiques. This area might be called Ho Chi Minh City's flea market. Nearby on Yersin Street is Dan Sinh Market, also known as the American Market, with electronics, tailor shops and a few old war relics: fake GI dog tags, gas masks and Army jackets.

HANOI

Souvenirs of Vietnam, 30A Ly Thuong Kiet. Vietnamese handicrafts

Cultrimex Gallery, 22B Ha Ba Trung. Silk paintings, paintings, antique reproductions.

Xunhasaba. 32 Hai Ba Trung. Ministry of Culture sponsored society for the sale and export of books, periodicals, reproductions of objets d'art and handicrafts. Foreign language publications are also available.

Souvenir Shop, 89 Dinh Thien Hoa.

Rong Dat, 105 Hang Gai. Embroidery.

Han Art, 43 Trang Tien Street. Tel: 824 0038. Ceramics, lacquerware.

Hanoi Gallery, 61 Trang Tien Street.

International Bookshop, 61 Trang Tien Street. Tel: 824 8914.

Book Sach, 57 Trang Tien. Foreign language publications.

Vietnamese Bookshop, On the corner of 19 Ngo Quyen and 40 Trang Tien. Foreign language publications.

Hanoi Foreign Trade Company, 56 Trang Tien Street.

Souvenir Shop, 89 Dinh Thien Hoang.

Hanoi has two principal markets, Dong Xuan Market in the heart of old Hanoi and Hom Market on the corner of 81 Pho Hue and Tran Xuan Soan. You will find Hanoi's main commercial area on Trang Tien Street and the southern area around Hoan Kiem Lake. For antique hunters, if you start at Hang Dao Street and walk through the old town of Hanoi to Le Duan Street and above Lenin Park you will discover numerous small antique shops selling some lovely pieces, particularly in Kim Lien Street, and at numbers 66 to 74 Rue de la soie and 8 Cha Ca Street.

Markets. These sell all manner of goods, including fresh fruits and vegetables, meat and eggs, as well as packaged goods. Some sell electronics, household goods and clothing.

Cho Hang Da, at the corner of Dau Duong Thanh and Hang Dieu. Tel: 825 7104.

Cho Hoa Binh, at the corner of Tran Nhan Tang and Pho Hue. Tel: 826 2191.

Cho Hom, at the corner of Tran Xuan Son and Pho Hue. Tel: 825 6172.

Cho Long Bien, near the Long Bien Bridge. Tel: 825 8708.

Cho Mo, at the corner of Truong Dinh and Minh Khai. Tel: 863 3023.

Cho Hang Be, 2 Da Ngu. Tel: 825 7032.

Cho Cua Nam, on Cua Nam. Tel: 824 6352.

Cho 19-12 (or Cho Ma), 41 Hai Ba Trung. Tel: 826 2910.

Silk and embroidery: There are a number of shops on Hang Gia Street in the Ancient Quarter.

Musical instruments: Wooden percussion instruments, stringed instruments and bamboo xylophones are sold in several shops in the Ancient Quarter on Hang Non Street.

Antiques: Several shops on Le Duan Street, near Lenin Park, sell antiques.

Jewelry and watches: There are Russian watches, with pictures of Gorbachev, on Hang Dao in the Ancient Quarter.

Souvenirs: There are many shops near Hoan Kiem Lake, on Hang Khay Street, selling lacquerware, conical hats, jewelry. Items should be inspected closely for quality.

Language

General

Vietnamese, the national language, is spoken by practically all the population. Variations in dialect, accent and pronunciation exist between the North, South and Center and among the ethnic minorities who have their own dialects. The Vietnamese language has its origins in the Austro-Asiatic languages and has been influenced by the Sino-Tibetan Thai language. Through the centuries of Chinese occupation the Vietnamese adopted the Han characters. In the 13th century they developed their own written language – Nom. In the 18th century, on the initiative of a French Jesuit priest, Alexandre de Rhodes, missionaries translated the language into its Romanized form, Quoc Ngu, which was first used by the Catholic church and the colonial regime's administration. Gradually its use spread, replacing the old written form by the 19th century. Variations of spelling, particularly noticeable in place names, is common and there appears to be no hard and fast standardization of spelling. The languages of Vietnam's ethnic minority groups are drawn from the many Southeast Asian linguistic groups of Austro-asiatic, Austronesian or Malayo-polynesian, Tibetan-Burman, Kadai and Mia-Yao.

Vietnamese Pronunciation

Vietnamese is not an easy language to pronounce. The syllable is the language's base unit. Most syllables have their own particular meaning and each syllable can be pronounced in six different tones to convey six meanings. They bear no relationship to one another, either. In the Romanized written form these tones are expressed by five diacritical accents and one atonic, where the syllable has no accent. For example the syllable "bo" can mean a children's toilet, father, lover, to chop, impolite or a government ministry. Obviously that leaves much room for confusion for any novice and anyone on the receiving end of a beginner's efforts. (You might accidentally call someone's father his lover, for example, or worse yet, his toilet.)

French is still spoken by many of the older, educated generation in Vietnam. English is spoken by more and more young people, and a fair amount of middle-aged people, particularly in the South.

Greetings

The basic hello – *chao*, is always followed by another word that varies depending on the age and sex of whom you address.

for an old lady/*Chao ba*
for a young lady/*Chao co*
for an older lady/*Chao chi*
for an old man/*Chao ong*
for a young man/*Chao anh*
for an older man/*Chao bac*
for a young person/*Chao em*

goodbye/*Tam biet*
See you again/*Hen gap lai*
I am sorry/*Xin loi*
please/*Xin moi*
thank you/*cam on*
yes/*da*
no/*khong*
My name is .../*Toi ten la ...*
What's your name?/*Ten ong la gi?*
  (pronounced zee)
How are you?/*Bac co khoe khong?*
Fine thank you/*Cam on binh thuong*
I/*toi*
a little/*it*
how much?/*bao nhieu?*
today/*hom nay*
tomorrow/*ngay mai*

Asking For Directions

O dau? – where?, comes at the end of the sentence directly after the noun. For example if you want to ask for the Post Office – *Buu dien, Buu dien o dau?*

hotel/*khach san*
bank/*ngan hang*
hospital/*benh vien*
bookshop/*hieu sach*
taxi station/*ben xe tac xi*
bus station/*ben xe*
train station/*ga xe lua*
airport/*san bay*

I am thirsty/very thirsty/*Toi khat/lam*
I am hungry/*Toi doi*
I am sick/*Toi om*
I have stomachache/*Toi bi da day*
I have diarrhea/*Toi bi di ngoai*
I have a fever/*Toi bi sot*
I have toothache/*Toi bi dau rang*

Further Reading

General

There are bookstores with English-language books, newspapers and magazines, including English translations of Vietnamese literature and history, in Hanoi and Ho Chi Minh City.

In Hanoi, there are several bookstores on Trang Tien between Ba Trieu and Phan Chu Trinh. There is a government bookshop with English language publications and maps at 46 Tran Hung Dao.

In Ho Chi Minh City, there are several bookstores on Nguyen Hue and Le Loi Streets, in the city center.

It is also possible to buy, for a very cheap price, photocopies of classics such as *The Quiet American* and *The Sorrow of War*. Street vendors selling maps and postcards often sell books, as well.

Non-Fiction

A Bright Shining Lie – Neil Sheehan. Vintage Books, New York, 1988.
The Birth of Vietnam – Keith Weller Taylor. University of California Press, Berkeley 1983.
In the Mist of War – An American's Mission to Southeast Asia – Major General Edward Geary Landsdale. Harper & Row, New York, 1972.
Vietnam Since the Fall of Saigon – William J. Duiker. Ohio University, 1989.
Understanding Vietnam – Neil L. Jamieson. University of California Press, 1993.
Following Ho Chi Minh – Bui Tin, C. Hurst, 1995. (Bui Tin was an editor of the Communist Party daily newspaper who is now a dissident living in France.)
We the Vietnamese – edited by Francois Sully. Praeger Publishers, 1971.

Tradition on Trial 1920–1945 – David G. Marr. University of California Press Berkeley, 1981.
Vietnamese Anti-colonialism 1885–1925 – David G. Marr. University of California Press, Berkeley. L.A. & London, 1971.
Fire in the Lake – Francis Fitzgerald. Vintage Books, New York, 1972.
Why Vietnam? – Archimedes L. Patti. University of California Press, Berkeley, L.A. & London, 1980.
Vietnam: A History – Stanley Karnow. Viking Press, New York, 1983.
River Journeys – William Shawcross. Describes the author's Mekong River trip made in 1983.

Vietnamese Authors

The Tale of Kieu – Nguyen Du. English translations sold in Vietnam bookstores.
The Sorrow of War – Bao Ninh. Pantheon (US English-language edition), 1995. (Bao Ninh is a North Vietnam war veteran who writes one of the first realistic portraits of the Vietnam War from a northern soldier's perspective.)
Paradise of the Blind – Duong Thu Huong.
Novel Without a Name – Duong Thu Huong. Morrow (US English-language edition), 1995. (Duong Thu Huong has been imprisoned for her writings that included veiled criticisms of the government; she is a veteran of the war from Hanoi.)

Other Insight Guides

Pocket Guide: Vietnam
Vietnam's eternal neighbor to the north, China is a world unto its own. This book takes travelers from the heights of the Himalaya to the alleys of Beijing. Magazine-style essays dig into the depths of the Chinese culture.

Index

A
B
C
D
E
F
G
H

J
a
b

d
e
f
g
h
i
j
k
l

The Insight Approach

The book you are holding is part of the world's largest range of guidebooks. Its purpose is to help you have the most valuable travel experience possible, and we try to achieve this by providing not only information about countries, regions and cities but also genuine insight into their history, culture, institutions and people.

Since the first Insight Guide – to Bali – was published in 1970, the series has been dedicated to the proposition that, with insight into a country's people and culture, visitors can both enhance their own experience and be accepted more easily by their hosts. Now, in a world where ethnic hostilities and nationalist conflicts are all too common, such attempts to increase understanding between peoples are more important than ever.

Insight Guides:
Essentials for understanding

Because a nation's past holds the key to its present, each Insight Guide kicks off with lively history chapters. These are followed by magazine-style essays on culture and daily life. This essential background information gives readers the necessary context for using the main Places section, with its comprehensive run-down on things worth seeing and doing. Finally, a listings section contains all the information you'll need on travel, hotels, restaurants and opening times.

As far as possible, we rely on local writers and specialists to ensure that the information is authoritative. The pictures, for which Insight Guides have become so celebrated, are just as important. Our photojournalistic approach aims not only to illustrate a destination but also to communicate visually and directly to readers life as it is lived by the locals.

Compact Guides
The "great little guides"

As invaluable as such background information is, it isn't always fun to carry an Insight Guide through a crowded souk or up a church tower. Could we, readers asked, distil the key reference material into a slim volume for on-the-spot use?

Our response was to design Compact Guides as an entirely new series, with original text carefully cross-referenced to detailed maps and more than 200 photographs. In essence, they're miniature encyclopedias, concise and comprehensive, displaying reliable and up-to-date information in an accessible way.

Pocket Guides:
A local host in book form

However wide-ranging the information in a book, human beings still value the personal touch. Our editors are often asked the same questions. Where do *you* go to eat? What do *you* think is the best beach? What would you recommend if I have only three days? We invited our local correspondents to act as "substitute hosts" by revealing their preferred walks and trips, listing the restaurants they go to and structuring a visit into a series of timed itineraries.

The result is our Pocket Guides, complete with full-size fold-out maps. These 100-plus titles help readers plan a trip precisely, particularly if their time is short.

Exploring with Insight:
A valuable travel experience

In conjunction with co-publishers all over the world, we print in up to 10 languages, from German to Chinese, from Danish to Russian. But our aim remains simple: to enhance your travel experience by combining our expertise in guidebook publishing with the on-the-spot knowledge of our correspondents.

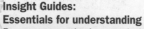